T0319782

Crisis or Recovery in Japan

Crisis or Recovery in Japan

State and Industrial Economy

Edited by

David Bailey

Professor of Economic Policy and International Business, Birmingham Business School, University of Birmingham, UK

Dan Coffey

Senior Lecturer in Economics, Leeds University Business School, UK

Philip Tomlinson

Lecturer in Business Economics, School of Management, University of Bath, UK

Edward Elgar
Cheltenham, UK • Northampton, MA, USA

Published by
Edward Elgar Publishing Limited
Glensanda House
Montpellier Parade
Cheltenham
Glos GL50 1UA
UK

Edward Elgar Publishing, Inc.
William Pratt House
9 Dewey Court
Northampton
Massachusetts 01060
USA

A catalogue record for this book
is available from the British Library

Library of Congress Cataloguing in Publication Data

Crisis or recovery in Japan : state and industrial economy / edited by David Bailey, Dan Coffey, Phil Tomlinson.
    p. cm.
   Includes bibliographical references and index.
1. Japan–Economic policy–1989- 2. Industrial policy–Japan. 3. Globalization–Economic aspects–Japan. I. Bailey, David, 1966- II. Coffey, Dan, 1966- III. Tomlinson, Phil, 1969-
   HC462.95.C75 2007
   330.952–dc22

                                      2007000727

ISBN: 978 1 84542 095 6

Printed and bound in Great Britain by MPG Books Ltd, Bodmin, Cornwall

Contents

Contributors

David Bailey is Professor of Economic Policy and International Business at the Institute for Economic Development Policy at the University of Birmingham, and a member of DARE (Democratic Communities in Academic Research on Economic Development). His research interests include economic development policy, with particular regard to foreign direct investment and the role of the transnational corporation, the economics of transition, and European integration and enlargement. He has undertaken extensive work on structural change in the Japanese economy. He is widely published, and is co-author of several books including (with George Harte and Roger Sugden) *Making Transnationals Accountable: A Significant Step for Britain* (Routledge, 1994).

David Coates is Worrell Professor of Anglo-American studies in the Department of Political Science at Wake Forest University. He was previously Professor of Government and Director of the International Centre for labour studies at the University of Manchester. He has published widely on a range of economic and political issues and is the author of a large number of books, including *Models of Capitalism: Growth and Stability in the Modern Era* (Polity Press, 2000) and (as editor) *Varieties of Capitalism: Varieties of Approaches* (Palgrave Macmillan, 2005). His current research interests include 'third way politics' and the responses of organized labour to global production and trade, as well as comparative political economy including Japan.

Dan Coffey is Senior Lecturer in Economics at Leeds University Business School, where he was until recently Director for all economics-related MA programmes. His research interests span organization and operations in manufacturing industries, political economy and industrial sociology. His recent projects include a book on production myths and the world car industry, published as *The Myth of Japanese Efficiency: the World Car Industry in a Globalizing Age* (Edward Elgar, 2006). He publishes in a wide range of journals and is the co-editor (with Carole Thornley) of *Industrial and Labour Market Policy and Performance: Issues and Perspectives* (Routledge, 2003). He is active in associations which include the European Union Network for Industrial Policy (EUNIP).

Keith Cowling is Emeritus Professor of Economics at the University of Warwick. His main research interests are in industrial organization, economic democracy, development and industrial policy and exploring the deficiencies of monopoly capitalism. He has played significant roles as an industrial policy adviser and published extensively in the fields of industrial economics and policy. He is the author of a number of books, including *Monopoly Capitalism* (The Macmillan Press Ltd, 1982) and (with Roger Sugden) *Beyond Capitalism: Towards a New World Economic Order* (Pinter Press, 1994). Recent research includes innovative work on the causes of 'hollowing out' in Japan. He is a member of DARE (Democratic Communities in Academic Research on Economic Development) and a founding member of the European Union Network for Industrial Policy (EUNIP).

Donald W. Katzner is Thompson Professor in the Department of Economics at the University of Massachusetts, Amherst. In a distinguished career he has pursued research in a number of areas, with work on microeconomics and general equilibriun theory and a series of contributions to the study of problems involving non-measurable variables, the firm in organization theory, and the analysis of historical time and non-probabilistic uncertainty. As well as a range of papers he is author of a number of books, including *Analysis without Measurement* (Cambridge University Press, 1983), *The Walrasian Vision of the Microeconomy* (University of Michigan Press, 1989), *Time, Ignorance, and Uncertainty in Economic Models* (University of Michigan Press, 1998) and *Unmeasured Information and the Methodology of Social Scientific Inquiry* (Kluwer, 2001). In addition he has worked on the general impact of culture on economic behaviour with a particular focus on Japan and the Japanese economy as a special illustrative case.

Hiroyuki Odagiri is Professor of Economics in the Graduate School of Hitotsubashi University, Tokyo. His major research interests are in industrial organization with a particular focus on the economics of the firm and innovation, which he has extensively explored in the context of the competitiveness of Japanese firms and the Japanese economy. He is widely published in books and journals, and is the author of *Growth through Competition, Competition through Growth* (Oxford University Press, 1992) and (with Akira Goto) *Technology and Industrial Development in Japan* (Oxford University Press, 1997). His opinions have been sought by bodies which include the World Bank Institute and the Japanese Government, and he is currently Director of Research at the National Institute of Science and Technology Policy in Japan.

Terutomo Ozawa is Professor of Economics at Colorado State University. His current research focuses on the theory of international production with particular regard to the relationships between foreign direct investment, economic development and competitiveness, and on the applicability of Japanese developmental paradigms to other regional contexts. He is extensively published in a wide range of journals and is the author of a large number of books, which include *Institutions, Industrial Upgrading and Economic Performance in Japan: The 'Flying Geese' Paradigm of Catch-Up Growth* (Edward Elgar, 2005). His other research interests include flexible versus mass production methods and the impact on international trade and investment patterns.

Ulrike Schaede is an Assistant Professor at the Graduate School of International Relations and Pacific Studies at the University of California, San Diego. She has held visiting teaching positions at the Haas School of Business at the University of California Berkeley and Hitotsubashi University, Tokyo. She has been a visiting scholar at the research institutes of the Bank of Japan as well as Japan's Ministry of Finance and the Ministry of International Trade and Industry. Her current research interests include trade associations and government–business relationships in Japan and Japan's financial organization, and the role of the Ministry of Finance in Japan. She has published in leading academic journals, and is the author of *Japan's Managed Globalization: Adapting to the 21st Century* (M. E. Sharpe, 2000).

Roger Sugden is Professor of Commerce at the Institute for Economic Development Policy at the University of Birmingham, and a member of DARE (Democratic Communities in Academic Research on Economic Development). His research interests include economic governance, development and democracy, with a particular focus on transnational corporations, small firms and industrial clusters. He is widely published and recent publications include (with Christos Pitelis and James Wilson) the edited book *Clusters and Globalization: The Development of Economics* (Edward Elgar, 2006). He has played leading roles in international research and learning projects, and is a founding member of the European Union Network for Industrial Policy (EUNIP).

Carole Thornley is Senior Lecturer in the School of Economic and Management Studies at the University of Keele, where she is also Director of Postgraduate Research for the Institute for Public Policy and Management. She is an expert on employment systems and structures, industrial organization and business strategy, and has previously worked for major global manufacturing multinationals in Belgium. She is widely published in books and journals which include the *British Journal of Industrial Relations*, the *Industrial Relations Journal*, and *Work, Employment and Society*, and has worked on numerous commissioned projects. She is an experienced adviser to trade unions and has submitted evidence to many official inquiries and reviews. She is co-editor (with Dan Coffey) of *Industrial and Labour Market Policy and Performance* (Routledge, 2003).

Philip R. Tomlinson is Lecturer in Business Economics in the School of Management at the University of Bath, and a member of DARE (Democratic Communities in Academic Research on Economic Development). His research interests are in industrial economics and political economy, with a particular focus on globalization, economic governance, development and industrial policy. He has published singly and jointly in a number of books and leading journals which include the *Economic Journal, The International Review of Applied Economics* and *The Manchester School*. His recent research includes collaborative work on the effects of globalization and the 'hollowing out' of the Japanese economy that has drawn international media attention. He is a member of the European Union Network for Industrial Policy, (EUNIP).

Richard A. Werner is Professor of International Banking at the University of Southampton. His research interests are in financial markets and banking institutions, with a particular emphasis on the impact of Japanese financial institutions upon the macro economy. He has published extensively in a number of leading international journals and is the author of *Central Banking and Structural Changes in Japan and Europe* (Soshisha Press, 2003) as well as the widely acclaimed study *New Paradigm in Macroeconomics: Solving the Riddle of Japanese Macroeconomic Performance* (Palgrave Macmillan, 2005). He has extensive experience in working for research institutes and the financial sector in Tokyo, where he was chief economist at Jardine Fleming Securities (Asia) Ltd.

1. Introduction: the attributes of the crisis

David Bailey, Dan Coffey and Philip R. Tomlinson

I INTRODUCTION

The collapse of the so-called 'bubble economy' in Japan in the first part of the 1990s saw a sharp drop in the rate of annual GDP growth between 1991 and 1992 followed by several years of stagnation, several years of recovery, and then a precipitous dip into recession – 'the worst since the Great Depression' (Gilpin, 2000: 278) – between 1997 and 1998; this was followed by a further period of stagnation marked alternately by hopes of an imminent and definitive revival and the fear of calamity. At the time of writing the Bank of Japan has just raised interest rates from a floor value of zero, based on a historically modest period of expansion in the national economy and the mildest of inflationary price rises. Whether this turns out to signal a definitive break from a difficult period as measured against main macroeconomic indicators, or another false dawn, remains to be seen. But however events subsequently unfold, Western perceptions of the efficacy of the Japanese economic machine have been indelibly marked: if the extent of Japanese exceptionalism and the causal forces supporting the Japanese 'economic miracle' was a hot topic for debate in the 1980s, by the close of the century – and notwithstanding the momentous and undisputable achievements of Japan in the field of economic development – debate had swung heavily to consider instead the extent of the Japanese malaise and the institutional factors sustaining it: 'Japanese, American and other experts', in the words of one eminent Western commentator on international affairs, now saw 'dire economic problems', and the need not only to take measures to stimulate the economy but also to institute wholesale economic reforms (ibid.: 279–82).

This book contributes to the ongoing debate by bringing together a series of contributions which consider the Japanese economic malaise and its impact on perceptions of Japan as an economic role model for others to emulate from a variety of perspectives, while pushing to the foreground of debate some issues that have perhaps hitherto lurked in the background. As befits its subject matter the contributors in question include leading economists and political scientists working in Japan, North America and Europe, providing a set of contributions that are both interdisciplinary in scope and international in origin, offering both new reflections and original research findings.

II THE ATTRIBUTES OF THE CRISIS

It is possible to think of Japan as having undergone a crisis in a twofold sense. First, we might consider the crisis in the Japanese economy as such: which essential issues arise from the fact of a prolonged period of recession and threat of recession with respect to our understanding of Japan's economy and economic institutions? In this regard the book commences with commentaries which offer different perspectives on this problem. These consider in turn how the behaviour of economic actors and institutions in Japan might be informed by culturally embedded and specific features which vitiate the simple application of an orthodox Western (Walrasian) economic model to the analysis of the Japanese case; how an empirically led appraisal of the role of money and banking in the Japanese economy might explain both the asset price inflation of the 1980s and the subsequent long period of underperformance in the 1990s and beyond characterized by a persistent shortfall between actual and potential national output; and the power of giant corporations in Japan to pursue strategies which fail from a societal viewpoint. Second, we might consider too how, as the difficulties of Japan have unfolded, the status and respect accorded Japan as a world economic role model has declined. In this regard the book addresses not only the immediate question of Japan's economic travails at the level of the way the Japanese economy actually works and what policy inferences follow, but also the longer-term issue of Japan's status and reputation as a model for emulation.

One broad set of issues that is often overlooked is the particular crisis faced by Japanese industry and the problem of 'hollowing out' experienced by Japan's industrial base since the early 1990s, and the middle-section of the book is devoted to questions of state policy towards Japanese industry, and the impact of globalization on Japan's national economy. Issues here include the manifestation of the crisis in Japan's industrial regions and clusters, the future role of government regulation and the architecture of reform. These issues are again relevant not only to a complete understanding of important structural aspects of the crisis and attendant policy responses but also to the severe jolt taken in a wider international arena to the repute of Japanese economic organization. Arrangements in the industrial sphere have long been prominent in what today is often referred to in pithy terms as the 'competitiveness debate' – witness, for example, the interest shown by non-Japanese commentators in Japan's famous *keiretsu* networks, or the extensive debate on the attributes of Japanese firms as a 'source of competitive strength' (subtitle of a suitably illustrative volume compiled on this subject by Aoki and Dore (1994)). Again, the Japanese crisis is a twofold crisis, both aspects of which are explored in this book.

The studies in this book therefore comprise perspectives on (a) Japan's economic and industrial crisis, (b) the role of globalization in the crisis, (c) Japanese state industrial policy and industrial prospects, and (d) the status of Japan as a role model. The divisions must not of course be drawn too hard or fast. To understand the economic and industrial crisis of Japan is to ask overlapping questions. Issues relevant to the economic and industrial crisis in Japan – whether the explanation lies in the particular form of culturally induced responses to economic stimuli, the policies of Japanese banks and governing bodies, or the conduct of giant Japanese corporations in the context of globalization – are clearly relevant to what lessons are to be learned from Japan as a model of economic and industrial development. Reflection on the 'standard' or 'classical' model of the Japanese economy in the post-World War II era, on the role of administrative guidance and of an orchestrated state 'catch-up' policy, on social solidarity and on the impact of globalization and the opening up of the Japanese economy, is just as obviously relevant to the debate on international competitiveness.

The contributors to this book are almost by necessity drawn from a range of academic disciplines: in this book the reader will find essays written not only by economists but also by political scientists and specialists in international economic relations. Moreover, and as befits the keen international interest both in the historically impressive successes of Japan on the world stage in modern times and its current uncertainties, the contributions are multinational as well as interdisciplinary.

III CHAPTER CONTENTS AND PROGRESSION

The individual chapters comprising this book, subject of course to our warning against overly simple lines of demarcation, divide broadly into three categories with respect to their place within the thematic structure of the collection as a whole. The development of themes and issues is best understood via a brief overview of content.

Chapter 2, by Donald W. Katzner ('The workings of the Japanese economy') considers the problems posed by Japan's recent travails from the viewpoint of what is non-applicable in the dominant Western model of market capitalism. The economic concerns of participating economic agents are culturally specific: whereas the vision of Western capitalism enshrined in the perfectly competitive (Walrasian) ideal posits self-interest as a motivating principle for economic actors, in Japan individuals are better described as valuing their personal contributions to the economy and society above incomes received. To understand a Japanese economy in terms that reflect Japanese cultural norms and values and hence the motives and concerns of Japanese citizens would imply a model written from a Japanese perspective: imported Western economic models are in this regard both superficial and ill-adapted to Japanese circumstances. Katzner explains why the culturally specific assumptions informing the perfectly competitive ideal of Western economics are vitiated in the Japanese case. The chapter explores in this context the particular content of Japanese institutional arrangements with respect to the industrial structure, the labour market, the distribution system and the role of the state; and it sets out the reasons why Western notions of efficient resource allocation are inappropriate in the Japanese case and policy recommendations good for the US (say) may be dangerous for Japan.

Chapter 3, by Richard A. Werner ('The cause of Japan's recession and the lessons for the world') sets out a careful review of the macroeconomic performance of Japan over the past 20 or so years combined with an original analysis of the causes of the long period of economic underperformance that set in with the 1991/1992 recession. The approach of structural reformers to Japan's economic malaise, which sees supply-side measures like deregulation, liberalization and privatization as being crucial to sustained macroeconomic recovery, is rejected on grounds of both empirics and theory. In this latter regard, Werner criticizes the structural reformers for confusing constraints on the potential output of an economy (on the supply side) with problems on the demand side which cause actual output to fall short of potential. After rehearsing the abundant evidence that the 1990s saw a declining trend in the utilization of productive capabilities, the chapter progresses to consider monetary explanations of the crisis: following a careful review of the main approaches taken by monetary economists to the failure of successive reductions in interest rates (both short- and long-run) to stimulate the Japanese domestic economy, supported by an assessment of the evidence for and against, Werner sets out the terms of an innovative analysis rooted in his own distinctive contributions towards an alternative approach to money and transactions. Identifying the creation of bank credit as the relevant constraint on the Japanese economy, the chapter concludes with an assessment of which policy measures could have been effective, political factors weighing against their adoption, and short- and long-term prospects for Japan.

Chapter 4, by Keith Cowling and Philip R. Tomlinson ('Transnational monopoly capitalism, the J-mode firm and industrial 'hollowing out' in Japan') adopts a stance towards the Japanese economic crisis of the 1990s based on the monopoly features of industrial capitalism. They argue that the root cause of these problems lies in the concentration of economic power in the upper echelons of corporate Japan and the subsequent globalizing activities of the country's large transnational firms. Cowling and Tomlinson argue that these firms have pursued their own global strategic interests, often at the expense of other stakeholders in Japan such as small firms and workers: the subsequent 'hollowing out' of Japan's industrial base represents in this sense a particular kind of strategic failure, in which corporate interests diverge from wider public interests. This analysis is developed first via an assessment of the characteristics of the Japanese firm, and a critique of the Aoki 'J-mode' model which seeks to establish these firms as being significantly different entities from their Western counterparts. After considering how economic power was concentrated within corporate Japan as a by-product of Japanese post-World War II industrial policy, Cowling and Tomlinson then explore the empirical realities of the consequences of corporate control of the Japanese economy for small firms, workers and Japan's industrial regions and macro economy.

These opening chapters set out some major themes. There are obvious differences of emphasis: the importance of culture as well as economy for Katzner; the workings of the Japanese monetary economy for Werner; the almost dialectical development of the Japanese corporation working first in accordance with and then against the wider interests of Japanese economic development. The next chapters explore transformations.

Chapter 5, by Ulrike Schaede ('Globalization and the Japanese subcontractor system'), considers the challenges of globalization to Japan's subcontractor system and the Japanese *keiretsu*. Using recent data, Schaede charts the movement in the 1990s of Japan's larger industrial suppliers in following their main contractors to produce overseas, a movement coinciding with new global cost pressures in manufacture which have had a significant impact upon Japan's domestic subcontractor system: the consequences of this for smaller Japanese subcontractors, and the notable decline in the membership of Japan's *keiretsu* networks along with the dismemberment of many cooperative supplier groups that have long been a distinctive feature of Japan's industrial structure, are explored. Carefully acknowledging that these changes may have both a positive and a negative impact upon Japan's domestic industry, Schaede considers the emergence of a new subcontracting system in which Japanese corporations look towards the global outsourcing of supplies involving fewer but larger suppliers and with supply-chain relations managed on an 'arm's length' basis, and with a greater emphasis upon competitive bidding than has been experienced in the traditional *keiretsu* model. The chapter concludes with an assessment of the requirements for survival, both of Japanese suppliers and for Japanese industries, in the new global environment.

Chapter 6, by Terutomo Ozawa ('Institutionally driven growth and stagnation – and struggle for reform') broaches the Japanese experience from the perspective of the interactions between the inner matrix of domestic institutional set-ups and the outer matrix of evolving global institutions and norms. Ozawa considers the past workings of Japan's *dirigiste* catchup regime, how institutional obsolescence set in, and how its economy has struggled to renovate its domestic set of institutions and practices: the bold thesis advanced is that the 'Japanese disease' (perceived to be a case of severe institutional sclerosis) is a necessary and cathartic event for Japan if it is to escape the trap of institutional obsolescence which has been the inevitable cost attached to the way in which Japan's economic catch-up strategy was organized and executed. In an analysis rooted in a rich understanding of geopolitical contexts in which a diminished American tolerance for Japanese catch-up after the end of the Cold War combined with Japanese economic success to drastically alter Japan's global and political economic environs, the chapter considers how Japan's part-aversion to foreign investment in Japanese industry is paradoxically morphing into an 'eagerness' to seek help from foreign firms. Ozawa asks whether the victory of Prime Minister Junichiro Koizumu signals that Japan is approaching a likely tipping point for critical institutional alteration.

Chapter 7, by David Bailey and Roger Sugden ('*Kūdōka*, restructuring and possibilities for industrial policy in Japan') looks to the causes and extent of Japan's '*kūdōka*' – the process of hollowing out or de-industrialization – during the 1990s and early 2000s. The transformations under consideration here are twofold, encompassing both underlying structural reasons for this process and steps needed to redress these structural problems at the level of policy. In explaining Japan's *kūdōka*, Bailey and Sugden find much of relevance in a 'government failure' approach, whereby the export success of certain sectors combined with import protection in others to produce a trade imbalance, continual yen appreciation and a rising cost base, spurring outward foreign direct investment by Japanese firms and a hollowing out of Japan's domestic industrial base. However, they argue that this analysis is an incomplete one unless due consideration is also given to the central role of Japanese transnational corporations in driving the hollowing out process, as a necessary link in understanding exactly how and why Japanese government policy failed. A policy framework to counter the attendant strategic failure is set out involving a mix of careful deregulation alongside a 'new' industrial policy that addresses economic governance issues, aimed at diffusing strategic decision making in the Japanese economy and at reinvigorating Japan's declining clusters of small firms.

Chapter 8, by Hiroyuki Odagiri ('The national innovation system: a key to Japan's future growth') considers the relationships between Japan's national innovation system and the changing nature of business within the country. Following a review of the evolution of innovation in Japan since 1945, and the shifting policy emphasis from imported technology in the post-World War II 'catch up' period to the home-grown science-based innovation of more recent decades, Odagiri discusses the importance of the changing research and development (R&D) boundaries of the firm for future business competitiveness. Drawing upon recent specific examples from Japan's biotechnology sector, the case is made for firms to rethink boundaries and to consider greater interorganizational collaborations in R&D activities, as for example via strategic alliances with other firms or a wider use of outsourcing. Within this changing environment Odagiri also sees a positive role for the public sector, whether through direct government support for small firm start-ups or through the university sector. An optimistic appraisal is given as to whether recent changes in Japanese business practices (including moves towards greater labour mobility and more flexible inter-firm relations) will have a positive effect upon the rate of scientific innovations both in the specific example of the biotechnology sector and in the more general case of the Japanese economy at large.

The remaining two chapters broach the question of Japan's economic difficulties from the viewpoint of how this has affected Western debate on the Japanese model, from the viewpoint both of the Japanese 'national' economy and of the Japanese corporation.

Chapter 9, by David Coates ('The rise and fall of Japan as a model of "progressive capitalism"') considers Japan in its sometime role as the elected model for a more progressive form of capitalism. Focusing on literature written in the West on Japan in order to address non-Japanese themes, Coates considers how the visible and sustained successes of the post-World War II Japanese economy combined with an increased perception amongst Western commentators of the distinctiveness of Japanese institutions and modes of economic organization to generate a gradually burgeoning literature which identified Japan both as an economic role model and as an alternative to liberal market orthodoxies. In an erudite account, Coates shows how early Western texts on the Japanese growth story in the post-war era moved from accounts written 'within the centre of existing economic orthodoxy', and with explanations rooted in 'ordinary economic causes', to an emerging body of writing in the 1970s and 1980s driven by commentators with a broader purview (industrial sociologists, cultural historians, industrial relations specialists and management scholars) concerned to identify factors which rendered Japan qualitatively distinct *vis-à-vis* the West. Coinciding with the rise of neoliberalism in the US and UK in the 1980s, Japan was cast as a more collectivist alternative and an example of a successful capitalism run along non-neoliberal lines. The chapter explores the subsequent impact on this perception both of the prolonged period of difficulty experienced by the Japan economy in the 1990s and beyond, and of growing criticisms of the 'dark side' of the Japanese miracle.

Chapter 10, by Dan Coffey and Carole Thornley ('"Can Japan compete?" reconsidered') considers the issue of changing perceptions about Japan and Japanese corporations as economic challengers in the world economy from the viewpoint of the developing nuances of the international 'competitiveness' debate. Observing that strength in manufacture is frequently adopted as one benchmark of the relative competitiveness of industrialized economies, Coffey and Thornley consider how the economic difficulties which beset Japan in the 1990s are reflected in the treatment accorded its leading manufacturing firms in the best manufacturing practices literature. The phrase 'lean production' is often used today as a summary term by which to encapsulate a series of contributions to best manufacturing practice believed to originate in Japan. Drawing a careful distinction between the interests of private firms and the economic success of nations, and following a critical review of some exemplary contributions to the US competitiveness debate, the chapter considers both the reception given in the US to the idea of lean production, and the subsequent use of this notion in criticisms both of Japan's competitiveness as a nation and of Japan's corporations as strategists. In a provocative twist, Coffey and Thornley argue that, while the evidence to support the idea of lean production as a positively effective and novel set of manufacturing practices has always been nugatory, viewed as a fiction it is a construct which has the potential to shed much light on aspects of the changing course of global economic rivalries.

REFERENCES

Aoki, M. and R. Dore (eds) (1994), *The Japanese Firm: Sources of Competitive Strength*, Oxford: Oxford University Press.
Gilpin, R. (2000), *The Challenge of Global Capitalism: The World Economy in the 21st Century*, Princeton and Oxford: Princeton University Press.

2. The workings of the Japanese economy[1]

Donald W. Katzner

In explaining the way a particular economy works, economists are guided, in part, by those personal economic matters considered to be important by the people who participate in it. These concerns, of course, may vary from society to society or culture to culture. Thus, for example, the typical American cares about such things as his economic status and welfare, his job security and the extent to which he is financially rewarded for his contributions to productive activity. By contrast, the personal economic concerns of a Japanese individual, which are, against their own criteria, as keenly felt as those of the American citizen, differ in numerous and significant respects. Economic status, although not having the same meaning in Japan as the US, is important, but only in relation to the social status that it confers. Economic well-being beyond that due to a given position in the social hierarchy is nice, but it is neither urgent nor expected. Job security matters, but in light of the loyalty between employer and employee (often expressed as an unwritten, life-time employment contract), most individuals have some measure of it. And the rewards bestowed by the economy are evaluated by the individual more in terms of the contribution he is able to make through his work to his company, to social harmony and to society in general than with respect to income received.[2] In all cases, explanations of economic activity, including both the models constructed to expound them and the visions that lie behind them, have to recognize these kinds of concerns if they are to be relevant to the real behaviour that is being explained. And to the extent that such concerns modify across societies or cultures, the explanations, models and visions to which they relate must, of necessity, reflect the relevant differences.

In America, the economic concerns of the individual, framed with respect to American cultural norms and values, may be thought about and influence economic explanation in reference to a particular vision of Western capitalism. That vision, henceforth referred to as *the* vision of Western capitalism, expresses what may be called the (perfectly) competitive ideal. In this vision, frequently articulated by the so-called model of

Walrasian or general equilibrium, consumers and firms are motivated in their economic behaviour by self-interest, and markets function freely and openly to determine, entirely through price competition, the prices of goods and services, and the quantities of them that are produced, bought and sold. As a consequence, and continuing to confine attention to the competitive ideal, the prices that arise as outcomes of the economic process simultaneously reflect, in the case of produced goods, the values to society of the last units transacted and the opportunities forgone for those last units to be produced. Prices also serve more generally as signals that guide producers in the production of outputs and the hiring of inputs. Of course, it is quite clear that, in the operation of the actual American economy, divergences of varying degrees from the competitive ideal are observed, and with that, varying degrees of producers' control over market selling prices arise. To the extent that such non-ideal competition among firms obtains and is accompanied by less than perfect competition in factor markets, the finely balanced marginal equivalences and optimization outcomes of the competitive ideal will not, in fact, be realized.

Regardless, and in contrast to the perfectly competitive or Walrasian vision of the workings of the American economy, that is, the vision of Western capitalism as it applies to the American situation, there is no well-developed and generally accepted vision of the workings of the Japanese economy that explicitly addresses, from a uniquely Japanese perspective, the concerns of the Japanese citizen described above. To the extent that a vision of the objectives, structure and functioning of that economy exists, it is substantially an imported vision, superficial and ill-suited to Japanese circumstances, of the way a Western capitalist economy, like that of the US, operates. The latter vision, moreover, makes only a limited attempt to accommodate the unique features of Japanese economic and cultural life. Perhaps this is due to (i) the absence of an urgent necessity to justify and explain ideologically or otherwise the workings of a uniquely Japanese system; and (ii) the reality that many Japanese economists have been trained in Western traditions. But, in any case, the fact remains that, although it is possible to speak of certain unique aspects of Japanese economic intercourse, there is, as yet, no comprehensive vision of the way in which that uniqueness coheres into a unified and interrelated economic system.

The purpose of this chapter is to explain why, and in what respects, the Japanese economy does not fit the imported mould derived from Western capitalism in general and the US economy in particular. Although, as is well known, the American economy does not exactly conform to that structure either (that is, the vision purporting to explain the workings of the US economy provides an ideal picture that only approximates American economic reality), the Japanese economy differs from it to a far more significant degree. Indeed, the difference is so great that the use of the vision of the workings of the US economy to shed light on the workings of the Japanese economy must be called into serious question.

Subsequent argument fits into a growing debate in the economics literature on the extent to which cultural divergence between the US and Japan is sufficiently strong and significant to warrant fundamentally different approaches to explaining economic behaviour in the two societies. On the one hand, Fallows (1994), Greif (1994), Johnson (1982), Katzner (1999, 2001, 2002) and Prestowitz (1988), to cite but a few, suggest or imply that it is; on the other, the so-called Chicago School as exemplified by Becker (1976, esp. p. 14), although not explicitly taking a position with respect to Japan, and writers like Koike (1984), would not agree. The present chapter falls clearly into the former camp. It begins (section I) by describing the reasons why some of the basic culturally determined assumptions underlying the competitive ideal and the Walrasian model are irrelevant and inappropriate in explanations of the way in which the Japanese economy works. It then shows (section II) how certain Japanese institutional arrangements (which could also be thought, in part, to be culturally derived), namely industrial structure, the labour market, the distribution system and government participation in the private sector, drive the Japanese economy still farther, as compared with the US, from the competitive ideal. Finally (in section III), it suggests that neither Western notions of efficiency expressed with respect to Pareto optimality and minimum unit cost, nor policy recommendations suitable for the US economy, need be apropos in Japan or even meaningful in the Japanese context.

I MOTIVATIONS AND MARKETS

The Japanese economy, like the US economy, is made up of consumers, firms and markets. Consumers purchase goods and services with income earned from the sale of labour to firms and from interest from past savings. The latter are mostly held in accounts at private banks and the Post Office – not so much in the form of stocks and bonds. Firms hire inputs to produce outputs and obtain funds for expansion from both private banks and the government. Clearly the government is an important player here, and its role and impact on the economy is much more complex and extensive than that of the government in America. For, in addition to affecting the allocation of resources through purchases, transfer payments, the imposition of taxes and monetary policy, the Japanese government, as has just been indicated, runs institutions that collect individual savings and lends funds to private firms. Parallel to the US, the decisions of consumers and firms to buy and sell, supplemented, in the case of Japan, by government decisions to be discussed in greater detail below, provide the impetus for economic behaviour.

Now it is important to recognize, as has been argued elsewhere (Katzner, 1999, 2002), that in any given society the making of private economic decisions is based, to a considerable extent, on cultural norms and values. In America, the important norms and values are the sanctity of the individual, self-reliance, success, freedom and justice, and these lead Americans, in part, to the pursuit of their individual self-interest. Moreover, one frequently employed method of measuring economic success in America (an important part of the value 'success' listed above) is defined in terms of the material objects with which the individual is able to surround himself. As a rule, the bigger the house, the more opulent the furniture, the more expensive the car, the greater the evidence of success. This suggests that, the larger an individual's income, the more he will consume. It is also often thought that, the greater the consumption, the greater the well being (for example, Bellah et al., 1985, chs 2,3).

But in Japan, the fundamental norms and values are different. They include service and loyalty to the collective, be it family, company, or society; the fulfilment of obligations to family, superiors and others from whom favours have been received; the preservation of honour; the maintenance of harmony within groups and with nature; hard work; and frugality (Bellah, 1957; Benedict, 1946, chs 5–8; Nakane, 1970, ch. 2).[3] This list neither includes nor appears to result in the emergence of self-interest on the part of individuals. It may be supposed, then, that self-interest, as it appears in the West, is not a significant element of Japanese culture and that it cannot, therefore, be an important motivating force behind Japanese economic behaviour. The same can be said of the push to consume as a means of increasing well being and of exhibiting the success that has been achieved. The absence of self-interest and the drive towards material consumption are two of the more significant features of the Japanese economic landscape that distinguish it from that of the US.

What, then, propels individual consumer decision making in Japan and leads to the purchases of goods and services, the supply of labour and the act of saving? Although there is no generally accepted, Japanese-oriented answer to this question, several possibilities can be speculatively suggested. Whereas, in general, Americans (such as a cashier or an executive) work to further their interests and enhance their social statuses through the increased income generated by advancement in a career, the Japanese (here one might also cite a cashier or an executive) work to fulfil their obligations to themselves and those around them, and to serve the community. In addition, decisions to supply various kinds of labour may have roots in the social status that different types of employment bequeath (more will be said of the latter below). The purchase of goods and services may be determined largely by the kinds and quantities of them that are deemed appropriate to a person's location in the social hierarchy. The place of purchase may relate to the presence of an already established long-term relationship with, and loyalty to, a particular supplier. And finally, the need to save may, to a considerable extent (though not entirely), be derived directly from the cultural norm of frugality mentioned above. Regardless, prices along with the amount of income the individual has to spend still define the available opportunities among which the individual must choose.

It is worth digressing for a moment to suggest the complexity of the sources of these motivations. This can be done by exploring in some detail the need to save apart from the cultural norm of frugality. Culturally and emotionally the Japanese tend to be more withdrawn than Americans. This is so for at least two reasons. First, the search for harmony with society and nature by individuals in Japan is primarily an inward-looking quest. By that it is meant that the complex tangle of historical, religious and philosophical influences prevalent in Japan have created in the Japanese mind a disposition to adjust individual behaviour in such a manner as to harmonize with the interests of relevant groups and society, and with the physical environment. Second, except for intimate family, the people with whom Japanese persons work closely, and small numbers of friends (and the latter two categories often overlap considerably), the Japanese are wary of interacting with other Japanese (Benedict, 1946, ch. 8). On the one hand, they do not want to increase the heavy burden of obligations that they and others already carry. On the other, they go to great lengths to avoid taking actions and making mistakes in relation to others that would bring possible dishonour both to themselves and to the others involved. Monetary saving, too, is an act of withdrawal. It conforms to, and is consistent with, these other actions that lead to withdrawal. It is impetuses like these that combine with the general value of frugality in generating the motivation to save in Japan.

In the American economy, firms are owned by individuals who are driven by self-interest to seek the highest return on their investments consistent with the level of risk they are willing to bear. This translates into the pursuit of profit maximization on the part of firms, with all of its implications for firm decisions in relation to the production of outputs, the hiring of inputs and the borrowing of funds for continued operations and expansion. But in Japan, where firms are, by and large, primarily owned by institutional investors and other firms, and not by individuals, and where motivations other than self-interest are fundamental, the operation of firms in such a manner as to maximize profits is not a major concern. Thus, as a rule, firms do not necessarily mix inputs in production so as to minimize the production cost of each volume of output. They would not necessarily hire each kind of input up to the point at which the value to the firm of the last unit employed equals its cost (price, wage or salary). And they would not necessarily produce a quantity of output such that the additional cost of producing the last unit of output is the same as its selling price. Rather, firms would tend to make production, input and borrowing decisions in confluence with the Japanese cultural norms and values listed above. Those decisions are made, that is, on the basis of how they best serve the community in general and the social interests of the firm and its employees. The firm's decisions might also reflect an obligation to maintain appropriate relations with other firms with which it might be in some way affiliated, including the banks to whom it is indebted and from whom it might borrow funds in the future.

It is clear that, Japanese cultural norms and values being what they are, the freedom from legal and institutional constraints required by Americans in the conduct of their economic activity is not needed or prized in Japan. Nor does the absence of equal opportunity of all persons in the making of choices violate the Japanese sense of justice as it does for an American. Moreover, the informational requirements of Japanese consumers and firms necessary to conduct their economic affairs are somewhat different from those of American consumers and firms, and the role that that information plays in the making of decisions is different. In Japan, of course, firms need to know the technical matters relating to the production of outputs from inputs and, as pointed out above with respect to consumers, both consumers and firms need to know prices to understand what opportunities exist. But, unlike the situation that prevails in the US, the relationship between prices and what consumers want is murky in Japan because the dictates of a person's social status may be more important for determining economic purchases than personal preferences. Indeed, the pull between what a person might want and what they think they ought to have might lead to inconsistencies and instabilities in those purchases. Thus, in contrast to their role in the US economy, the functioning of Japanese prices as signals to firms indicating what they should produce is called into question. But even if Japanese prices could be used as signals to direct production and hiring decisions, it is unlikely that Japanese firms would always employ them for that purpose. That is because Japanese firms sometimes make investment decisions on the basis (Nakane, 1970, p. 90) of 'keeping up with the competition' or 'doing what the competition does' in order to maintain their social status. (This is consistent with the overall goal described above of serving the social interests of the firm and its employees.) Also they do not always rely on price information in relation to personnel decisions. Thus, for example, out of loyalty to them, employees are not necessarily fired when, at the margin, their value to the firm falls below their cost.

As in America, the prices of goods and services are established in markets. But the competitive pressures of buyers forcing prices to rise when there are shortages and of sellers pushing prices down in the face of surpluses are not as strong. For, even in retail markets, the producers of commodities retain considerable control over the prices at which their outputs are sold. And this is abetted by the loyalties of buyers to particular sellers even if it means paying higher prices for the same or similar products. There is intense competition among firms in Japan, but it does not always appear as price competition. Apart from price, Japanese firms may compete energetically with respect to the quality of the products they produce, the variety of products they make available and the service in relation to those products they provide. And the most meaningful consequence of competition is the determination of the firm's niche in the social hierarchy of firms – not profits (although that may be a secondary result). A high social rank is prized by both the firm and its employees. Indeed, the employee's own social rank is determined by the rank he holds in the firm along with the rank the firm holds in the social order. It is social status, not monetary success or material surroundings, that is of primary importance to the Japanese. With respect to the individual, the economic status that provides and accompanies social status, meaning by that the economic qualities of the job that is held, including the income and consumption opportunities that go with it, is of considerably less significance (ibid., pp. 88–93).

In any case, the Japanese economy clearly answers fundamental economic questions (what will be produced, what inputs will be used in that production and who will get what is produced) in a manner that diverges from answers provided by the US economy. In particular, it is neither necessary nor necessarily desirable in Japan that everyone be able to buy and sell exactly what he wants at prevailing market prices or that, in the production and allocation of commodities across the economy, the benefits of each good are balanced against the value of other opportunities that might have been procured from the same resources. It follows that, although the introduction of impediments to the free movement of prices in the US is thought to have serious consequences, additional blocking of the 'free movement of prices' in Japan is of little concern since there is much less free movement of prices to begin with.

It is implicit in the above discussion that the ideal (competitive) economic system in terms of which the actual US economy may be analysed and understood, and with respect to which its performance is measured, does not apply in Japan. The actual Japanese economy is so far from that ideal in so many ways that the employment of the ideal as a basis for evaluating the Japanese economy and understanding how it works is not very useful. This, of course, does not mean that scattered small bits and pieces of the ideal system might not be appropriate for explaining certain isolated fragments of Japanese economic life. For example, various versions of non-ideal competitive forms (for example, monopolistic competition, oligopoly and monopoly) that arise in practice in the US economy, and that contain some, but not all, of the characteristics of the ideal form, may have considerable resonance to actual Japanese economic experience. Those kinds of departures from the ideal competitive system, to the extent that they appear in Japan, are no different from those in the US. Rather than exploring them in greater detail, however, it will be more worthwhile to consider different deviations from the competitive ideal that do not appear in the American economy but which, at the same time, are significant features of the Japanese economic landscape. For it is deviations of this sort that tend to move the Japanese economy still further (relative to the US position) from the competitive ideal than it already is. The specific deviations in relation to Japan discussed below arise with respect to industrial structure, the labour market, the distribution system and the role of the government in economic affairs.

II INSTITUTIONAL ARRANGEMENTS

Industrial Structure

Consider the Japanese industrial structure first. Two important features of it are the focus of subsequent attention: the organization of firms into enterprise groups (called *keiretsu*), and the distinction between 'large' firms on the one hand, and 'medium-size' and 'small' firms on the other (for example, Ito, 1992, ch. 7). There is substantial overlap between these categories in that one firm can belong to more than one enterprise group, and the same enterprise group can contain large firms as well as mid-size and small ones.

An enterprise group is a collection of firms that are linked together through a network of mutually beneficial economic relationships. There are both horizontal and vertical enterprise groups. The horizontal groups are made up of companies in different major industries. The six largest groups combined employ about 5 per cent of the Japanese labour force and earn about 15 per cent of the Japanese economy's sales and profits. A typical list of industries represented in them might include banking, insurance, construction, textiles, chemicals, mining, steel, electronics, automobiles and so on. Each group also contains at least one trading company that specializes in only exporting and importing. The same six horizontal groups share three common characteristics. First, there is a collection of core group members that functions as a strategic decision-making unit for the entire group. The latter unit varies in importance from one enterprise group to another. Second, members of an enterprise group, including the banks, usually own shares of stock issued by other members. These shares tend not to be sold, and the amount of group shares held by group members can climb above 25 per cent of total group shares issued. Such within-group stock ownership is often very effective in preventing outsiders from gaining unwanted control of individual group members. Third, enterprise group members tend to raise significant quantities of the total funds that they borrow for business purposes from the banks and insurance companies in their respective groups. The percentage of borrowed funds in the group taken out from within-group banks and insurance companies can also be as high as 25 per cent. (As with all firms, to the extent that a member's use of borrowed funds, or debt capital, introduces a high debt-to-equity ratio in its financing structure or, that is, a high degree of financial leverage, a further element of risk is borne by its equity ownership.) The remaining horizontal enterprise groups are much smaller than the six under discussion here.

The vertical enterprise groups are also smaller than the six largest horizontal groups and tend to be made up of a manufacturer together with its suppliers and distributors. As suggested above, a company that is a member of a horizontal enterprise group can also be in the core of an independent, vertical enterprise group.

The advantage of membership in an enterprise group is that the member firms are obliged to render mutual assistance in many aspects of their operations. This is especially true during difficult economic periods. When sales are slow, manufacturers will help supplier affiliates by not reducing orders as much and as quickly as they might otherwise. (Non-affiliate suppliers would lose a greater proportion of, or even all, orders, and lose them earlier.) Likewise, when shortages arise, suppliers would fill orders for manufacturing affiliates first. Banks and insurance companies would tend to save funds for, and be more generous in their loans to, members of the enterprise groups to which they belong. And so on. Thus the interdependencies among members of enterprise groups tends to moderate the variability of their economic performances. But, since showing favouritism in this way often results in reduced revenues or increased costs, members in enterprise groups tend to have smaller profits and grow at slower rates than they otherwise would. This, of course, is not a significant issue in Japan because of the culturally derived lack of emphasis on the pursuit of individual self-interest and profit maximization.

Turning to the size distinction among Japanese firms, the large corporations differ qualitatively in both organization and operation from the small and medium-size companies. And this difference goes beyond what one would expect from the above discussion of enterprise groups and what one might observe with respect to size disparities in the US. In Japan, large firms tend to hire male employees upon graduation from school and to keep them until their retirement. They rarely hire persons in mid-career and typically pay higher wages than those paid by the smaller firms. Although there are exceptions, employment in medium-size and small firms is less permanent and more often temporary and seasonal, and wages are usually lower. Some medium-size and small firms supply parts to large corporations and might have some enterprise-group affiliation with them. Others are in the service sector (for example, retail shops and restaurants) and are family-owned and operated.

To the extent that these differences between large firms and medium-size and small firms exist, one of their consequences is a parallel division of the Japanese labour force into workers with 'lifetime' employment in large companies at relatively high wages, and workers with less permanent employment in medium-size and small companies at relatively low wages. Taking into account the obligations among members of enterprise groups described above, it is still generally true that, when an economic slow-down occurs, large companies order less from their suppliers, though orders from suppliers outside their enterprise groups tend to be reduced more and affected first. In any case, with orders decreased, the suppliers lay off some of their temporary workers. Thus, in hard times, the work force of the small and medium-size firms acts as a buffer protecting the jobs of the workers in the large corporations. The employees in those large corporations may be reassigned from, say, white- to blue-collar positions, but the pressure to terminate them is less than it would be if the large corporations produced their own supplies, and the threat to the lifetime employment system is thereby lessened.

One more point, although a slight digression, deserves brief mention here. Boards of directors of American corporations generally include individuals appointed from communities outside of the firms they are directing. Even though those boards may be controlled by their chief executives, their purpose is, largely, to represent stockholders' interests. This has tended to mean that corporate activity has focused more on the enhancement of short-term earnings, and that significant portions of corporate profits have been returned to stockholders as dividends (although it remains true that substantial retention of earnings is a principal source of financing expansion, and short-run profits are sometimes sacrificed for long-run gains). It is primarily through boards of directors, then, that the

American pursuit of self-interest is translated into profit maximization in US corporations. By contrast, the members of boards of directors of Japanese corporations are usually drawn from inside their corporate entities and, if they are members, from inside their enterprise groups. As a result, these boards frequently represent interests other than those of the non-group stockholders and thus, in particular, Japanese corporations typically are managed more for their employees than for such stockholders. Dividends are relatively small and the outlook is decidedly longer run. In contrast to the appearance of American cultural values and norms such as self-interest in the running of US corporations, this is a reflection of the Japanese values of loyalty and service to the community, firm and employee, and of Japan's cultural indifference to self-interest and the maximization of profits.

The Labour Market

Additional departures from the competitive ideal that are unique to Japanese experience also arise with respect to the labour market in Japan (for example, Abegglen and Stalk, 1985, pp. 198–208; Ito, 1992, ch. 8). Beginning with the lifetime employment system which has been briefly mentioned earlier, roughly 25 per cent of the Japanese labour force (mostly males employed by the large corporations) have an unwritten lifetime contract with their employer. According to that contract, the company is to provide employment until retirement and the employee is to be totally loyal to the company. The latter means, in part, that the employee will do virtually any job he is asked to do. Employees are hired directly from school (as previously indicated) and, over the years, are rotated in and out of many different company jobs. Each starts at the bottom of the corporate hierarchy and progresses through higher and higher levels. If a particular skill is needed that is not available in the company, new people are not brought in. Rather, the appropriate portion of people already working for the company are either sent to school or otherwise trained. Upon retirement, an employee will often be found a position in one of the company's subsidiaries or affiliates for a few more years. Even in smaller firms that do not provide 'formal' lifetime employment and where workers are considered 'temporary,' employees frequently exhibit the same kind of obligation and loyalty to the company. And the employers, equally obliged and loyal in return, are often very reluctant to let them go, sometimes to the point of threatening the firm with, and even resulting in, bankruptcy.

Generally speaking, Japanese employees work longer hours than US employees (Horioka, 1998, p. 6). Those covered by the lifetime employment system typically leave home early on Monday to Friday mornings and do not return until 10:00 or 11:00 at night. Working Saturday mornings in addition is not uncommon. Sometimes work is combined with social activity at restaurants and bars during evening hours. Employees under lifetime contract often take only half of their paid vacations, mainly for family events like weddings and funerals. It is not that Americans do not work hard, but, as a rule, they do not put in as many hours as the Japanese, and when they do work hard, they do so for different reasons. While the American pursuit of self-interest and material consumption frequently results in hard work, the Japanese work hard because, without any intervening motivations like self-interest, hard work is one of their chief cultural values.

In large Japanese companies, especially those providing lifetime employment, there is a strong and pervasive feeling that everyone is part of the company 'family'. Close emotional ties develop between supervisor and subordinate, between those who usually work together and between within-company friends. Along with the long hours of work are the sharing of highly personal thoughts and experiences, socializing at bars and restaurants, company-sponsored social events and company support at such private affairs as weddings and funerals. It is not surprising that in large companies the dividing line between employees' private lives and work lives tends to blur.

Unlike US firms, there are relatively few distinctions between white- and blue-collar workers in Japan. The gap in salaries is small and both belong to the same union and eat in the same cafeteria. Employees who are considered incompetent or who are no longer useful to the large companies are not given much responsibility. Also they are not fired. Sometimes they are assigned a desk next to a window with a nice view and nothing to do. Such employees are called 'window watchers' because they only sit and look out of the window. However, the shame of being reduced to a window watcher is considerable. Many will quit the company within a few years of becoming one.

Japanese companies of all sizes typically consider women workers as either temporary until marriage or after-having-had-and-raised-children returnees. In neither case are they given lifetime employment contracts, and they usually work as secretaries, sales persons and production-line labourers.[4] Women who are looking for more permanent employment with opportunities to advance and develop a career will frequently seek out jobs in foreign companies with offices in Japan. Such companies make no lifetime employment guarantees and tend to lie outside the social hierarchy described above, thereby leaving their employees without social rank. That would create major problems for Japanese men who, as a result, try to avoid jobs in foreign companies. But these 'failures' are of little consequence for

Japanese women who are unable to procure a lifetime employment contract anywhere anyway, and who do not need a social rank from their employment since, upon marriage, their social ranks become those of their husbands. Indeed, it is precisely because foreign companies are not constrained by the same cultural rules that restrict the operation of Japanese companies in general that they are able to offer opportunities to women that are not available elsewhere.

Although there are exceptions, promotions in Japanese firms normally turn on seniority. Salaries and wages depend on seniority and need. The typical Japanese employee (including executives) receives, in a normal year, approximately one-third of his pay in the form of semi-annual bonuses. The smaller bonus comes in June or July; the larger one in December. The amount of the bonus hangs on the profitability of the firm during the year. It tends to be larger for the employees of the larger firms and for people with more seniority. Under adverse economic conditions, when it becomes necessary to cut costs, bonuses can be reduced or eliminated. This is a second mechanism, in addition to the buffer provided by the temporary employees of mid-size and small firms, that helps to lower the pressure to break lifetime employment contracts when the economy enters recession.

It should also be noted that the salaries of executives of American firms are often far larger than those of comparable executives in Japanese companies, especially when all forms of compensation are taken into account. For example, the average compensation of the chief executive officers of 30 major corporations in the US were recently found to be 212 times that of the average American worker while, in Japan, the comparable number was 16 (Oshima, 1998, p. 198). This discrepancy in US firms, though difficult to explain from a Japanese perspective, where the pursuit of self-interest and material consumption are decidedly less important in the general scheme of things, is easily understood in the context of American cultural norms and values. For, according to the standard vision of the way in which the US economy works, individuals are paid according to their worth to the firm in relation to what the market will bear. Any interference with the operation of markets is, as a rule, not tolerated because it obstructs the preservation of equal opportunity for all and, consequently, offends the American sense of justice, and also because it destroys the unfettered ability of individuals to pursue their own self-interest as best they can.

Another significant way in which the Japanese labour market diverges from that of the US is in reference to labour unions. Unions exist in Japan because, in spite of the obligations and loyalties between employer and employee, collective bargaining that engages labour and management is still a practical and effective way of reaching agreement on compensation, working conditions and other matters of mutual concern. In contrast to

America, national unions in Japan are usually based on industry type (such as metals) rather than on specific skills (for example, truck drivers). There are similarities too. National unions band together in large organizations like America's AFL-CIO. Labour–management negotiations take place at both national and local levels, but, in Japan, local agreements can vary widely across firms within an industry, often depending on the overall performance of the firm in question. Negotiated contracts are typically for a single year. Generally, negotiations begin in February and end in May. (Of course, in the US, contracts are usually for more than one year. Negotiations can start at any time, depending on the expiration date of the old contract, and frequently last longer than three or four months.)

But the main difference between US and Japanese unions occurs with respect to the constitution of the local unions. A single local union in Japan consists, as a rule, of most of the employees of a single firm (that is, all those of the rank of subsection head and below) and no one else. It includes both white- and blue-collar workers: lower-level executives, secretaries, managers, sales personnel, production-line workers, and so on. Perhaps because of the tendency of the Japanese to view their large corporations as families of employees, perhaps because of the loyalties between employer and employee, and perhaps because the latter derives his social status from being employed by his employer, local unions are more reluctant than their US counterparts to engage in activities that might damage the firm. It is a common perception within the local unions that hurting the firm hurts themselves. Hence negotiations are not usually as adversarial, or at least not in the same way, as in the US.

The Distribution System

The Japanese system for distributing produced goods to consumers through wholesalers and retailers has a number of distinctive features, some of which push the Japanese economy even further from the competitive ideal (for example, see Ito, 1992, ch. 13). Observe, first, that Japan has many more retailers per capita than the US. This may be due, in part, to government regulations that limit the size, number and operation of large retail establishments.[5] But it also has something to do with the fact that, since they have very limited storage space at home, the Japanese tend to shop much more frequently than Americans. With roads choked by automobiles and not much parking space available, small neighbourhood stores to which one might walk are a great convenience. Even the use of buses and trains to travel to shopping areas has its drawbacks since it is more time-consuming than a walk to a neighbourhood store, and a person can still carry only so much home. In any case, retail establishments tend to be small; on average, each is operated by only four persons, and over half function with only one or two. Many are family owned and operated businesses.

Japanese wholesalers are a little larger, but, with so many retailers, large numbers and many layers of wholesalers are needed. To illustrate, suppose, for the sake of argument, that one wholesaler can distribute goods to five retailers. If there are more than 25 retailers, more than five wholesalers are needed, and a wholesaler on a level above the first five wholesalers is required to distribute goods to them. As the number of retailers grows, the number of levels of wholesalers grows along with the number of wholesalers themselves. Thus the Japanese distribution system as a whole involves relatively more individuals than that in the US and is relatively more cumbersome.

In addition to the larger proportion of resources devoted to distribution in Japan, many manufacturers have developed their own wholesaling and retailing systems to distribute their products to consumers. The wholesalers and retailers in these private systems carry only limited brands of goods as prescribed by the manufacturer. One variant of this arrangement is that large retail stores are frequently staffed by persons on loan from the manufacturers. These people sell and otherwise promote their own manufacturer's products at the retail level. Although private distribution systems with characteristics similar to these exist in the US (for example, in the American automobile industry and in supermarkets), they are much more common in Japan. But, regardless of whether manufacturers have their own distribution system, it is generally the case that retail prices are maintained by implicit agreements between them and the retailers who handle their goods. Wholesalers are often the conduits for these agreements and matters relating to them. The agreements themselves necessarily include provisions for income for wholesalers at all wholesaler levels, and this suggests, due to the relatively large number of wholesaler levels in Japan, that the prices of these products may differ still further from those obtained under conditions of the competitive ideal referred to earlier. Moreover, retailers are permitted to return unsold merchandise even if those items were actually purchased from the manufacturers. All of this points towards rather close relationships between manufacturers, wholesalers and retailers. Indeed, those relationships are essential to the Japanese distribution system. They foster long-term connections and deep obligations and loyalties that manufacturers enhance with personal socializing, reliable delivery records and the provision of consistent quality and after-sale service. Such obligations and loyalties, recall, are important in Japan from a cultural standpoint. As has been mentioned earlier, consumers also like to establish long-term relationships with retailers, and will often continue to buy from those retailers even if prices are lower elsewhere.

Do the characteristics of the Japanese distribution system described above effectively close off consumer markets in Japan to foreign competition? The answer is both yes and no. On the one hand, the obstacles standing in the way of any newcomer, and especially of foreigners with little understanding of Japan, trying to break into that system are clear. Part of the problem arises from government regulations that, although previously alluded to, have not been considered in detail here. But attempting to enter a system in which strong long-term relationships and loyalties have already been established is even more formidable. On the other hand, a number of American companies (for example, Motorola and Microsoft) have been quite successful. Regulations can be, and have been, reduced and eliminated through negotiation, but it is more important to have a product that the Japanese consumer wants and is willing to buy, and that the time and effort needed to establish a distribution arrangement with the appropriate relationships among the individuals involved be expended.

Government Participation

All governments engage in activities that have impacts on the economies in relation to which they function. They impose taxes and spend the funds taxes raise. They create armies. They build and enhance roads, ports and dams. They regulate, police and prosecute. Government in the US and Japan is no exception. In the US, one of the goals of government that emerges directly from the American cultural values and norms described earlier is to interfere as little as possible in private economic operations, and maintain and enhance the free and competitive functioning of markets. But in Japan, where cultural values and norms favour the collective above the individual, it is seen as the obligation of government to play an active part in private economic development. This means, among other things, that government activities will often lead the Japanese economy farther from the competitive ideal.

To be specific, the Japanese government energetically helps industries and companies that have what it considers to be bright futures (see, for example, Johnson, 1982; Ito, 1992, ch. 7). Until they are thought to be able to stand on their own, it protects them from foreign competition with tariffs and quotas on competing goods imported from abroad. (This is also one source of the regulations mentioned above with respect to the Japanese distribution system.) The government further provides these companies with preferential (that is, low-cost) loans and access to other resources, such as foreign exchange, that they might require. During adverse economic times it helps industries it favours to reorganize to reduce competition within and among them and to lower costs and excess capacity. It has also subsidized firms in financial difficulty so that they do not have to release employees. (This has the effect of providing one more mechanism for the preservation of the lifetime employment system.) Even declining industries like mining and aluminium have been helped in order to slow their demise. All of this would be intolerable in the US, and some of it patently illegal. And, by not permitting markets to operate independently, it forces the outcomes of economic activity to be more distant from those that would be delivered by the competitive ideal.

The Japanese government has had considerable success in pursuing these policies. It was, to a large extent, responsible, after the devastation of World War II, for rebuilding the Japanese economy into the world's second largest economic machine. But when it chooses the wrong projects to support (as in the case of the Japanese approach to high definitional TV), or makes other errors (as when it ignored the role of Japan's banks in the speculative bubble in Japanese land prices in the late 1980s), the costs to Japan can be very high.

III THE RELEVANCE OF WESTERN EFFICIENCY AND ECONOMIC POLICY

The contrasts between the US and Japanese economies that emerge from the descriptive presentation of the last section are rather striking. They become even more pronounced when certain specific characteristics of the American economic environment are brought clearly into view. First, as previously indicated, in the US the formation of enterprise groups is severely limited by anti-trust laws and the accompanying bureaucratic regulation. The activities of such groups would often be perceived as improperly, and sometimes illegally, reducing competition and restraining trade. Second, the qualitative distinction between large firms and medium-size and small firms in Japan is inapplicable in America. Of course size makes a difference in the US, but not in the same kinds of ways. Third, although Americans can and do spend their entire careers in a single firm, there is no lifetime employment system in US companies with an unwritten commitment between employer and employee. Fourth, as a rule, American workers are not rotated from job to job within firms. Rather than learning how to do many things, as their Japanese counterparts do, they tend to become highly specialized in particular areas. Fifth, a US employee who has acquired marketable skills in one firm will often leave (and is often expected to leave) to improve his status and salary. Loyalty to the firm that taught him his skills, to the extent that it might exist, does not override the pursuit of his self-interest. Sixth, American women are able (and often encouraged) to have significant careers in firms of all sizes. Seventh, bonuses in the US are usually limited to a company's top executives. Eighth, there are significant economic and social differences between white- and blue-collar workers in America. Ninth, the American distribution system is more open and easier for foreigners to break into than that in Japan. In particular, the close relationships, obligations and loyalties between manufacturers, wholesalers and retailers in Japan generally do not exist in the US, and some activities that those relationships, obligations and loyalties might produce are prevented by law. Tenth, and lastly, it should be emphasized that government in America, as has already been pointed out, is focused more on staying out of private economic affairs than on helping to manage them. Indeed, the responsibility of the American government is seen to be centred primarily on the creation of an environment that facilitates the successful pursuit of independent economic activity.

In addition to these contrasts, previous argument has also suggested that the workings of the Japanese economy cannot really be understood in terms of the Western capitalist vision, as that was described at the outset, that is often invoked in thinking about the US economy. The reasons for this may be summarized as follows. The motivations that direct the economic behaviour of consumers and firms in Japan are different from the self-interest that propels action in the Western capitalist vision. Price competition in Japanese markets is not the most important form of competition among Japanese firms, and it is insufficient to ensure that the prices established in those markets convey the information necessary to result in an outcome consistent with that of the vision of Western capitalism. Enterprise groups, the qualitative differences between large firms and medium-size and small firms, the lifetime employment system, the determination of pay and promotion on the basis of seniority, the large and multilayered distribution system with its close ties among manufacturers, wholesalers and retailers, and the active participation of government in guiding the private allocation of resources in directions towards which markets do not necessarily point, all introduce factors and forces that are not present in the Western capitalist vision and that are sufficiently significant to require that they be addressed in explaining the workings of the Japanese economy. The Western capitalist vision is therefore not relevant as a standard for understanding and making judgements about that economy. It is true, of course, as was acknowledged at the beginning, that the very stringent conditions of the competitive ideal are not completely fulfilled in the US economy either. But previous discussion has shown that the actual economic circumstances in Japan are much further from the conditions of the competitive ideal than those in the US. Another way of saying this is that market failure or divergence from the competitive ideal, as defined in the context of the vision of Western capitalism, is so endemic in Japan that it renders that vision useless as a basis for thinking about the Japanese economy.

It follows that notions of efficiency characterized with respect to the Western capitalist vision have no applicability with respect to Japan. There are two such efficiency concepts that are worthy of mention here. On the one hand, the outcomes of the ideal competitive system produce what people want at minimum input cost. This is equivalent to saying that, in any one of those outcomes, it is not possible through reallocation of resources to make one person feel better off without making someone else feel worse off. On the other hand, the outcomes of the ideal system lead to production everywhere at minimum unit cost. By either of these standards, the outcome of Japanese economic activity must necessarily appear, except coincidentally, to be inefficient. This is because many of the conditions that lead to efficiency in the Western capitalist vision are not satisfied in Japan, and many of the conditions that actually do prevail in Japan would, in that same vision, prevent efficiency from being achieved. But, even so, there can be little doubt that the Japanese economy has achieved considerable success. It has already been pointed out that that economy rose from the ashes of World War II to become the second most powerful in the world. And it is both interesting and ironic that, in spite of the inefficiencies that are, and have been, present by the standards of the vision of Western capitalism, during the 1980s many in America and the West regarded the Japanese economy as the most efficient on earth.

To provide specific illustrations of how the inefficiencies that arise according to American or Western standards are 'overcome' by the Japanese economy, consider the fact that, by criteria derived from the vision of Western capitalism, Japanese companies, especially during recessionary times, would, owing partly to lifetime employment contracts and loyalties between employer and employee, appear to have too many employees. This possibility, to the extent that it occurs during recessions, is mitigated in Japan, as previously suggested, through government subsidies, through the bonus system and by the willingness of companies to accept less than maximum profit.[6] With respect to the last mitigating effect, too many employees in the Western scheme of things would mean smaller profits. With respect to the second, if profits become too small, or the company were threatened by losses, one Japanese solution could be to reduce, if not eliminate, bonuses.

An offsetting effect to the general overhiring of workers arises from the long hours of effort that, as previously indicated, are contributed by a Japanese person to his company. Many of these hours are overtime hours for which the employee is not compensated. Indeed, it has been estimated by Higa and Lupardus (1998, p. 92) that, in 1994, the typical Japanese male employee was paid for only 82 per cent of the hours he actually worked. The willingness of individuals to give these extra hours to their employer could be attributed to the Japanese cultural value of hard work, to a sense of loyalty and obligation to their employers, or to both. But, in any case, the underpaying of employees, or the unpaid overtime put in by them clearly counterbalances, at least to some extent, the overhiring of labour by Japanese companies. Another counterbalancing effect is, of course, the readiness mentioned above of companies to be content with less than maximum profit.

A further example relates to the possibly excessive (again, when compared to the US) quantities of resources used by Japan to distribute goods to consumers. Such practices would tend to increase costs and lower profits which, as in the previous examples, would not be considered to be a problem by the Japanese. (The need, in Japan, for large numbers of retailers and the wholesalers who support them has already been indicated.) Moreover, application of the vision of Western capitalism suggests that, if it were possible to reduce the resources devoted to distribution (perhaps by removing the regulations that restrict the development of large-scale retail outlets), those saved resources could be used to produce more goods and services for everyone. But the Japanese do not necessarily desire, and are not even necessarily concerned about, such increases in material consumption. It is the harmonious functioning of, and the benefits they perceive accruing to, the collective or society at large that are most important to them. Regardless, the 'inefficiencies' of the distribution system are overcome in some measure by higher prices charged for consumer goods produced and sold in Japan and, once again, the willingness of Japanese companies to accept less than maximum profit.

Finally, it should be noted that policy prescriptions that might be relevant in America to mitigate the effects of such economic ills as unemployment and inflation, need not necessarily work in Japan. Since these prescriptions tend to spring from the vision of Western capitalism with respect to which the American economy is understood, their best chances of having the effects desired are in the US (or any other Western) economy. But it has been argued here that the Japanese economy does not work in the same way as the American economy. Therefore implementing the same policies to achieve the same purposes in Japan is quite problematic. In order to judge the efficacy of American policy prescriptions applied to the Japanese situation, it would be necessary to have a vision of the workings of the Japanese economy. Without that, there is no way of knowing whether a cut in taxes in Japan, say, might stimulate spending, or raising interest rates there might lower investment. Clearly, the application of American policy prescriptions to resolve Japanese economic problems under those conditions is like shooting in the dark without a clear perception of the target.

NOTES

1. Thanks are due to Charles Yuji Horioka and Douglas Vickers for their help and guidance with this chapter.
2. Of course, these statements of what is considered to be important by Americans and Japanese are generalizations that need not apply to the same degree (if at all) in every situation. They are still useful, however, in that they are relevant in many contexts and, as such, provide one way of understanding contrasts between the US and Japan.
3. Like the statement of American and Japanese economic concerns at the outset, these norms and values (as well as those previously attributed to Americans) are generalizations that are not uniformly applicable to all Japanese (or, respectively, all Americans). But they are sufficiently significant to be useful in understanding, in an approximate way, motivations behind economic behaviour in Japan (and, respectively, in America). Recall note 2.
4. Since 1985, it has been illegal in Japan to discriminate against women in employment, and small numbers of women have been hired by large firms on the same terms as elite-track males with permanent employment status.
5. These regulations were relaxed somewhat in 1992 to make it easier for large-scale retail concerns to open.
6. The argument in relation to the latter two is more fully developed in Katzner (2001).

REFERENCES

Abeggien, J.C. and G. Stalk, Jr (1985), *Kaisha, The Japanese Corporation*, Tokyo: Tuttle.
Becker, G.S. (1976), *The Economic Approach to Human Behavior*, Chicago: University of Chicago Press.
Bellah, R.N. (1957), *Tokugawa Religion*, Glencoe: Free Press.
Bellah, R.N., R. Madsen, W.M. Sullivan, A. Swidler and S.M. Tipton (1985), *Habits of the Heart: Individualism and Committment in American Life*, Berkeley: University of California Press.
Benedict, R. (1946), *The Chrysanthemum and the Sword*, Boston: Houghton Mifflin.
Fallows, J. (1994), *Looking at the Sun*, New York: Pantheon.
Greif, A. (1994), 'Cultural beliefs and the organization of society: a historical and theoretical reflection on collectivist and individualist societies', *Journal of Political Economy*, **102**, 912–50.
Higa, T. and K. Lupardus (1998), 'Why don't workers claim all their overtime?', in J. Mak, S. Sunder, S. Abe and K. Igawa (eds), *Japan: Why it Works, Why It Doesn't – Economics in Everyday Life*, Honolulu: University of Hawaii Press, pp. 91–7.
Horioka, C.Y. (1998), 'Do the Japanese live better than Americans?', in J. Mak, S. Sunder, S. Abe and K. Igawa (eds), *Japan: Why It Works, Why It Doesn't – Economics in Everyday Life*, Honolulu: University of Hawaii Press, pp. 3–10.
Ito, T. (1992), *The Japanese Economy*, Cambridge: MIT Press.

Johnson, C. (1982), *MITI and the Japanese Miracle*, Stanford: Stanford University Press.

Katzner, D.W. (1999), 'Western economics and the economy of Japan', *Journal of Post Keynesian Economics*, **21**, 503–21.

Katzner, D.W. (2001), 'Explaining the Japanese economic miracle', *Japan and the World Economy*, **13**, 303–19.

Katzner, D.W. (2002), '"What are the questions?"', *Journal of Post Keynesian Economics*, **25**, 51–68.

Koike, K. (1984), 'Skill formation systems in the US and Japan: a comparative study', in M. Aoki (ed.), *The Economic Analysis of the Japanese Firm*, Amsterdam: North-Holland, pp. 47–75.

Nakane, C. (1970), *Japanese Society*, Berkeley: University of California Press.

Oshima, H.T. (1998), 'Is Japan an egalitarian society?', in J. Mak, S. Sunder, S. Abe and K. Igawa (eds), *Japan: Why It Works, Why It Doesn't – Economics in Everyday Life*, Honolulu: University of Hawaii Press, pp. 195–204.

Prestowitz, C.V., Jr. (1988), *Trading Places*, New York: Basic Books.

3. The cause of Japan's recession and the lessons for the world

Richard A. Werner

I INTRODUCTION

On 14 July 2006, the Bank of Japan raised the call rate for the first time in six years. It also raised the official discount rate (ODR) for the first time in 15 years. This decision was made under the leadership of central bank governor Toshihiko Fukui, who at the time remained under intense public pressure to resign. The reason for Mr Fukui's sharp drop in public support is a revelation concerning his private investments: while Japanese individual investors, who keep the majority of their assets in bank deposits, have received near-zero return on these savings since the near-zero interest rate policy began in 1998, Mr Fukui almost doubled his investments in the fund run by controversial shareholder activist Mr Murakami. This former MITI official turned ardent structural reformer, who has since been arrested on insider trading charges, had started his fund in 1998, and Fukui was one of the small circle of day-one investors. In many ways, these pieces of information turn out to be close to the heart of the key events in Japan over the past 20 years.

This chapter reviews the recent economic performance of the Japanese economy, on the back of which the Bank of Japan decided to raise short-term interest rates. It then attempts to make an assessment of the medium-to-long-term outlook for Japan. An important question is whether Japan's economy has finally emerged from the long period of economic underperformance. To answer it, however, it is necessary to gain an understanding of what has caused Japan's unusually long period of economic difficulties which began in the early 1990s. That, in turn, requires a brief flashback to the era of the late 1980s, which is commonly known as the 'bubble period', when asset prices rose significantly. It was the bursting of this bubble that ushered in the long recession. Therefore an understanding of the causes of the bubble is also necessary. Insights into the entire chain of causation behind the macroeconomic events in Japan over the past two decades will allow us to draw some conclusions and identify the major lessons, both for Japan and for other countries, that can be drawn from events in Japan.

After a brief review of the latest economic data on Japan, this chapter then asks a series of questions and attempts to answer them using the latest relevant research findings. The main question is: why has Japan been in such a long recession? This is broken up into more detailed questions: what has been the role of structural reform in stimulating the economy? Why has interest rate policy been ineffective during the 1990s? Has the Bank of Japan done all it could during the 1990s to stimulate the economy? What caused the bubble of the 1980s in the first place? What lessons can be learned for the status and role of central banks? What are the lessons concerning methodology in economic research and economic theory?

It is found that the Japanese experience, while being highly costly for the people in Japan and beyond, has at least had the salutary effect of teaching us an unusually large number of lessons, ranging from general implications that include a re-evaluation of the major economic theories and research methodologies as well as specific policy lessons, such as the effectiveness of structural reform policies, how to render fiscal policy effective, and the implications for the independence and optimal role of central banks. It also turns out that Toshihiko Fukui has been intimately linked to key decisions during the entire 20-year period that has affected Japan and the world so profoundly, so that a review at this time of the end of zero interest rates, and even the possibility of a premature resignation of Fukui seems timely.

II   RECENT ECONOMIC PERFORMANCE

In fiscal year 2005, which is the year ending on 31 March 2006, the Japanese economy grew by 3.0 per cent in real terms and 1.7 per cent in nominal terms. This was the third consecutive year of positive annual nominal GDP growth and the fourth of positive real GDP growth. Since the long period of economic underperformance began in Japan around fiscal year 1991, there had been a significant recovery in fiscal year 1996, which lasted little more than a year, and again in 2000, which also lasted only about a year (see Figure 3.1). The downturn in fiscal year 2001 was particularly severe, with nominal GDP shrinking by 2.4 per cent and real GDP falling by 0.8 per cent. Since then, however, growth has been steadily recovering, and this recovery has culminated in the strong results of fiscal year 2005.

YoY (%)

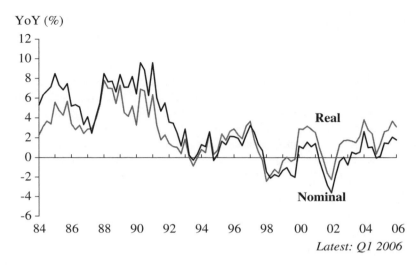

Latest: Q1 2006

Source: Profit Research Center Ltd., Tokyo.

Figure 3.1   Nominal and real GDP

What has been particularly encouraging is the recovery of nominal GDP growth. Since the high inflation era of the 1970s, there has been a global emphasis on calculating economic variables in 'real' terms, including real GDP. This procedure is not without problems. The fundamental issue is that transactions actually take place in nominal terms, so that 'real' variables are a purely theoretical concept, arrived at by adjusting nominal prices for inflation expectations. However, the latter are not measurable. Moreover, even if current inflation is used, it is far from clear precisely which measures of inflation should be employed. Furthermore, during deflation, it is possible that with shrinking nominal GDP, real GDP may be rising purely owing to deflation. In those circumstances, witnessed in Japan repeatedly in the past decade, it is little consolation for businesses to be told that the economy is growing in 'real' terms, when aggregate sales are shrinking and corporate balance sheets are deteriorating. The empirical reality of accounting principles – which are entirely in nominal terms – does not allow companies to benefit from the theoretical concept of 'real growth', when losses mount and insolvency looms because of shrinking nominal growth. Fortunately for Japan, nominal growth now seems to have recovered as well, and there is a good chance that the long period of stagnation and deflation may have ended. To make a serious assessment of this question, however, requires an understanding of the causes of Japan's past travails. For this purpose, a number of other questions need to be answered.

III   WHAT HAS BEEN THE ROLE OF STRUCTURAL REFORM IN STIMULATING THE ECONOMY?

After a number of significant fiscal stimulation packages during the 1990s had failed to end Japan's long economic stagnation, and after interest rate policy (to be discussed below) had also disappointed, the discussion of theorists and policy makers shifted significantly. Fiscal and monetary policy are demand-stimulation policies, and their apparent failure led many to conclude that instead supply-side policies were the solution to Japan's problems. The recommended policies were deregulation, liberalization and privatization, since such structural reform was said to increase the growth potential (the 'supply side') of the economy.

What is the theoretical and empirical support for this structural reform argument? Theoretically, it is true by definition that an economy's maximum potential output is the function of the quantity of factor inputs and their productivity. In Japan's case, it has been frequently argued that the quantity of factor inputs has structurally become constrained (owing, for example, to the demographic problem of an ageing society, which restricts the labour force, or a lack of incentives for entrepreneurs to invent new technologies). At the same time it has been pointed out that the post-war Japanese-style economic structure has been based less on free market forces than on various forms of non-market mechanisms, and these restrictions on markets have constrained total factor productivity. Thus, the argument goes, structural reforms are needed to boost both the quantity of factor inputs (for instance by giving more incentives to entrepreneurs to be creative and inventive, through greater rewards for dominant shareholders and fewer administrative restrictions on their activities) and the productivity of their use (by shifting the economic structure more decisively towards free markets through programmes of deregulation, liberalization and privatization).

This argument has become well-rehearsed, by economists and journalists and in publications by central banks. How accurate is it? There are two fatal flaws, one concerning the theoretical argument, and the other concerning the empirical evidence. Put simply, the theory is faulty, and the empirical evidence has disproven it.

The reader may wish to reread the statement describing the argument, in an attempt to spot the fallacy. Like a magician's sleight of hand, a logical non-sequitur was slipped into the argument which has apparently been able to mislead a large number of intelligent observers and experts. As the argument concerns the supply side of the economy, it is based on the assumption that the problem of weak economic performance has been due to a lack of supply (that is, low productivity or lack of factor inputs) and not lack of demand. Since the supply side concerns the maximum potential output, it can only be relevant if actual output is equal to potential (and thus there is no deficiency in demand). Thus this theory denies the possibility that lack of demand may exist and explain the weak economic performance.

The more formal statement of the structural reform argument, in the form of neoclassical growth theory or the neoclassical fundamental theorem of welfare economics, states explicitly that it assumes perfect information, zero transaction costs, complete and competitive markets, and so on, on the basis of which it can argue that markets are in equilibrium and actual output equals potential output. Thus the fundamental assumptions needed in order for actual output to be equal to potential are so extreme that we know they never held in Japan, or any other country for that matter. Therefore, it is not clear why the structural reform theory can be thought to be relevant at all to the world we live in, let alone Japan's situation in the past decade and a half.

The second flaw with the structural reform argument is that there is no empirical evidence in its support. There are a number of testable hypotheses with which we can evaluate the empirical evidence in favour of the structural reform argument. One possibility is to research whether productivity has been weak enough to explain the disappointing economic growth. Careful studies of productivity growth, such as that by Jorgenson and Motohashi (2003) found that Japan's total factor productivity growth accelerated in the second half of the 1990s and was stronger during this time period than during the phase of significant economic expansion from 1975 to 1990.[1] Meanwhile, studies that proclaimed to have found empirical evidence for faltering productivity growth turned out to have been fundamentally flawed.[2]

Another way to test the neoclassical productivity argument is by making use of neoclassical trade theory, which argues that the trade balance is a measure of total productivity. Figure 3.2 shows the annual moving sum of the Japanese monthly trade surplus. As can be seen, it reached a peak of more than ¥14 trn in 1987. However, twice during the 1990s a similar peak was reached, namely in 1993 and 1998/9. Indeed, despite the significant economic slump of the 1990s, Japanese exports remained strong, Japan continued to increase its foreign exchange reserves and there was no evidence of a decline in productivity. The result is all the more meaningful, as during the 1990s the yen, as measured by nominal exchange rates, was on average significantly stronger than during the 1980s. We conclude that, by this measure, no evidence is found for a significant decline in Japanese productivity during the 1990s, when compared with the 1980s.

Another example of the ways the structural reform theory can be tested is to examine empirically one of its central tenets, namely that structural

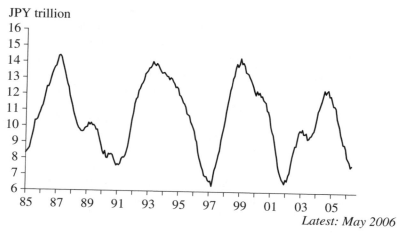

JPY trillion

Latest: May 2006

Source: Profit Research Center Ltd., Tokyo.

Figure 3.2   Trade surplus (annual moving sum)

reform towards freer markets, such as through deregulation, liberalization and privatization, will improve economic performance (by raising productivity). In Japan's case we can, for instance, use a measure for structural reform towards a greater role for market mechanisms, and compare this with GDP growth. While this is less known to most observers, since the early 1970s the Japanese economy has undergone a gradual shift away from the non-market based structure of the 1960s, and towards the textbook ideal of free markets. One representative measure of this structural shift is the number of cartels (measured by the number of exemptions to the anti-monopoly law). The neoclassical efficiency argument says that more cartels should be associated with weaker economic performance, and fewer cartels with stronger economic performance. What is the empirical evidence?

As is readily visible from Figure 3.3, the empirical evidence rejects this hypothesis soundly. When the number of cartels was increased in the 1960s, this seemed to have no negative effect on growth. Since Japan has deregulated and liberalized an increasing number of markets, privatized its industries and reduced the number of cartels, economic performance has not improved. To the contrary, it seems to have deteriorated. When the number of cartels hit zero in the late 1990s, so did growth. Instead of the negative correlation hypothesized by the structural reform argument, there seems to be a positive correlation between cartels and growth.

There is another simple but effective test of the structural reform argument. As it is based on the assumption that the economy is held back by a

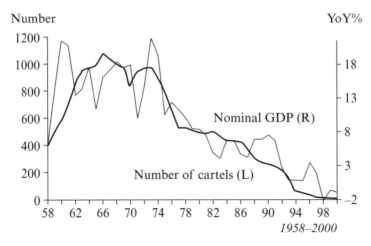

Source: Werner (2005).

Figure 3.3   *The correlation between cartels and growth*

lack of supply, with demand as large as supply, any evidence that demand is lagging behind, that is, which is not at the full employment level and that therefore resources are underutilized, would result in a sound rejection of the structural reform theory. Such evidence is abundant. During the 1990s, unemployment rose to a post-war record high, peaking only in 2002 and 2003. By 2003, the manufacturing capacity utilization, as measured by METI's operating rate, had remained on a long-term declining trend, far below the peaks seen at the end of the 1980s (see Figure 3.4).

There is further evidence that physical capital was not fully utilized. A total of 202 109 companies became insolvent in the period from January 1990 to March 2003. Bankruptcies usually involve scrapping of stock and inputs, writing down of assets, lost capital, staff lay-offs and discontinuity in the use of facilities. They also are usually observed when demand is weak, not when demand is at its maximum and the economy is held back by a lack of supply.

There is much further evidence against the supply-side structural reform argument, such as the behaviour of prices in Japan since the early 1990s. Japanese consumer price inflation, as measured by the domestic CPI, exhibited a significant decline, which in 1999 turned into outright deflation. The only G7 country in the past century to do so, Japan has recorded eight consecutive years of deflation, yet, the structural reform argument, which requires full utilization of all factors of production, is more likely to coincide with inflationary pressures, due to supply bottlenecks.

Crisis or recovery in Japan

Source: Werner (2005).

Figure 3.4   Manufacturing sector operating rate (seasonally adjusted)

This evidence cannot be reconciled with the idea that a lack of factor inputs (land, labour, capital or technology) held back the economy: there is overwhelming evidence that labour and capital stock were underutilized. Land remains unchanged. This leaves us with the possibility that a sudden decline in technological progress was the cause of Japan's recession. This is, however, also rejected, by the evidence, reviewed above, that Japanese productivity did not falter during the recession period. A more direct test can be conducted by reviewing whether the number of patent registrations declined during the 1990s or early 2000s period. Figure 3.5 shows the number of new patent and trademark registrations in Japan. As can be seen, they rose significantly during the 1990s, peaking at an unusually high level in 1996, and ending the decade at a significantly higher number than at its beginning.

In conclusion, it can be said that the structural reform theory is not supported by any empirical evidence. The facts reject it clearly and without reservations. Its claim that resources are fully utilized and the economy is held back by a lack of supply is not tenable. This conclusion may explain why attempts at structural reform during the 1990s, such as the far-reaching reform implemented during the Hashimoto government, which included significant administrative reform, the 'Big Bang' deregulation of the financial sector and accelerated liberalization of regulations in over 1000 areas, did not have any positive effect on economic growth. Such reforms,

Number (million)

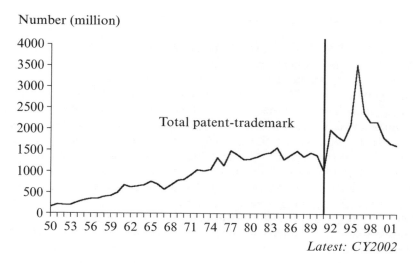

Source: Werner (2005).

Figure 3.5 New patent and trademark registrations in Japan

although again proclaimed to be crucial for an economic recovery by the Koizumi government, affect the supply side of the economy, yet Japan's recession has apparently been due to a lack of demand. Supply-side reforms do not stimulate demand, and indeed may have an adverse effect on demand, as they tend to increase competition, bankruptcies and deflationary pressures. These findings solve the question of whether supply-side or demand-side policies have been needed to create a recovery in Japan. However, they raise new questions, namely how it is possible that so many decision makers (including prime ministers Hashimoto and Koizumi), experts (academic economists and especially the large number of central bankers and central bank economists) and commentators (financial journalists in particular) have been uncritically regurgitating the unsubstantiated assertion that Japan 'needs structural reform' to stimulate the economy. This is an issue to which we will return.

IV WHY HAS INTEREST RATE POLICY BEEN INEFFECTIVE DURING THE 1990S?

Since from the above it is clear that a lack of demand has been the cause of Japan's long period of economic weakness, it is of interest next to examine the effectiveness of the standard policies to stimulate demand. Elsewhere, a more detailed examination of the role of fiscal policy is presented (Werner, 2005, 2006), which showed that monetary policy has been the main cause of Japan's travails. We therefore begin with an examination of the effectiveness of interest rate policy.

The Bank of Japan acted on numerous occasions during the 1990s to reduce interest rates. This was based on the conventional understanding of mainstream economic theory that lower interest rates stimulate the economy (while higher interest rates act to dampen growth). In Japan's case, the official discount rate (ODR) was reduced from 6.0 per cent in 1991 to a low of 0.1 per cent as recently as mid-2006. The call rate was reduced from 8.1 per cent in 1991 to a low of 0.001 per cent as recently as 2005. Long-term interest rates (ten-year benchmark JGBs) also were on a declining trend during the 1990s, falling from 6.7 per cent in 1991 to 0.5 per cent in early 2003. Further, real interest rates also fell significantly during the 1990s. Despite these extraordinary interest rate reductions, the much-anticipated positive effect on the economy remained elusive for over a decade. This has puzzled economists.

The most influential attempt at explaining this phenomenon was made by Paul Krugman, who argued that Japan's situation resembled a Keynesian liquidity trap (Krugman, 1998). Unlike Keynes, who defined a liquidity trap as a situation where long-term interest rates have fallen so low that they cannot fall any lower, Krugman defined it as a situation where nominal short-term interest rates could not be lowered by the central bank any further, because they had already reached zero. Many observers believe that the liquidity trap hypothesis has explained the failure of interest rate policy. This, however, is not the case. To the contrary, the liquidity trap hypothesis is merely a tautology, which says that, when nominal interest rates have fallen to their lowest level, they cannot fall any lower. More damaging to the liquidity trap argument, however, is the fact that it entirely fails to address the question at hand, namely why interest rate *reductions* have not stimulated the economy. Throughout the 1990s, interest rates fell significantly. The liquidity trap argument, however, is merely about the point when interest rates have stopped falling – which they did only in the early 2000s. It does not say anything about the observation period of over a decade when interest rates *fell*.

The first attempt at explaining why interest rate reductions did not stimulate the economy was offered by the so-called 'credit view' approach, which emphasized bank lending. There are three versions of it, namely the 'lending view', the 'credit rationing argument' and the 'balance sheet channel'. The lending view, as proposed for instance by Bernanke (1993), Gertler and Gilchrist (1993) and Kashyap and Stein (1993), argues that monetary policy is transmitted to the economy not only through the interest rate channel, but also through the bank lending channel, and hence is more effective than commonly understood. However, empirical support for this claim, at best, has not been strong. Thus the leading proponents of the lending view have conceded: 'Clearly, the Bernanke and Blinder (1988) model is a poorer description of reality than it used to be, at least in the United States' (Bernanke and Gertler, 1995, p. 41).[3] 'In summary, because of financial deregulation and innovation, the importance of the traditional bank lending channel has most likely diminished over time' (ibid., p. 42). In Japan's case, things are even clearer: while the lending channel argument expects monetary policy to be more effective than usual, working through the additional channel of bank lending, this was not useful to explain events in Japan, since here was a country where monetary policy was far less effective than had been expected.

The credit rationing approach seemed to offer a more useful explanation. It argues that bank lending is not a perfect substitute for other forms of funding, especially for small firms. There seems much empirical evidence in support of this thesis, also in other countries, such as the US. Since Japanese financial markets are often considered 'less efficient' than US financial markets, by this logic it would be reasonable to expect Japanese small firms to suffer even more from credit rationing, especially when there are reasons why banks might have become more risk-averse and less able to bear the risk premium implied with lending to small and medium-sized enterprises. Thus the credit rationing argument, advanced early on in a non-traditional version, and initially dismissed, found more proponents as the Japanese recession refused to go away. However, there is also a fundamental flaw to this argument in its traditional form: while the lending view makes a macro-economic case (which does not work in the case of Japan), the traditional credit rationing hypothesis concerns purely microeconomic issues. Even if bank lending to some types of borrowers was rationed, this would not establish why or how the overall economy should be negatively affected in a systematic way, especially since funding from non-bank sources or foreign bank sources did seem to increase in Japan during the 1990s. Critics such as Meltzer (1995) pointed out that lending must decline by more than other fund raising in capital markets has increased, and it must be explained why foreign lenders and other non-bank lenders failed to compensate for increased credit rationing by banks. No such explanations have been presented. To the contrary, in the case of other countries it was found that a reduction in bank lending is met by an increase in the extension of trade credit and other forms of direct financing (see Calomiris et al., 1995; Mateut, et al., 2003). In the case of Japan, Werner (2005), using flow of funds data, showed that 'there is little evidence that other sources of funding have not been able to make up for any potential decline in either bank lending or lending from financial institutions. The evidence in support of the lending view, or in support of the argument that credit rationing hampered growth, must therefore be considered insufficient and not in line with the theoretical requirements of the respective theories'. There were other problems with the credit rationing argument; Krugman (1998), for instance, dismisses it by pointing out that banks with non-performing loans should have an incentive to increase lending (to help their borrowers), instead of cutting lending to them.

The demise of the credit rationing argument became apparent in the early 2000s, when many commentators that may earlier have favoured it had not only quietly dropped it, but were now arguing quite the opposite: in line with Krugman's moral hazard argument, they now claimed that, instead of lending too little, the problem in Japan was that Japanese banks were lending too much. Kashyap (2002), for instance, criticized Japanese banks for lending 'excessively'. Such excessive lending has had a negative impact on the economy, because 'suppressing the normal process of creative destruction leaves all banks with fewer good borrowers to lend to. Absent good borrowers, the banks have an even greater incentive to roll over loans to deadbeat borrowers', which, in turn, has been a 'covert unemployment compensation programme' (p. 54). In line with this argument that there has been excessive lending, Kashyap recommends closing down some Japanese banks, namely those owned by the government. The IMF (2002) also recommended that Japan decrease the number of commercial banks and public financial institutions through closures. As such views had become dominant since about 2002, it is probably fair to say that the credit rationing argument had been dismissed. However, at the same time there seems little evidence for the claims made by Kashyap and the IMF that Japan suffered from too much lending: as will be seen below, bank lending is positively correlated with economic activity. During much of the 1990s, bank lending growth slowed and in the second half of the 1990s even turned negative, with negative consequences for economic growth. Such facts cannot be reconciled easily with Kashyap's assertions that Japan suffered from 'excessive' bank lending.

Partly owing to the difficulties of the above two versions of the 'credit view' approach, a third version was developed. It incorporates aspects of the lending and credit rationing approaches and attempts to explain why a lack of bank lending to small firms might have a disproportionately large effect on the economy. This version is commonly summarized under the 'balance sheet' approach label. Representative papers are those by Gertler and Gilchrist (1993), Bernanke and Gertler (1995) and Kiyotaki and Moore (1997). According to this theory, interest rates affect borrowers' balance sheets, hence the external finance premium of firms and therefore both demand for and supply of funding for firms. The balance sheet channel is said to work even if the central bank cannot influence bank lending. However, it is necessary for interest rates to affect corporate balance sheets, so that lower interest rates will improve the balance sheet position of potential borrowers. With more than a decade of interest rate reductions having failed to make a significant positive effect on corporate balance sheets, this approach also suffers from virtually insurmountable empirical obstacles in the case of Japan. The many necessary assumptions made in Kiyotaki and Moore's (1997) model also did not seem to apply to Japan's case and an attempt at providing empirical support for the balance sheet channel with Japanese data was not successful.[4]

As a result it must be concluded that the mainstream literature could not provide a consistent and convincing explanation for interest rate policy failing to stimulate the economy. However, an alternative explanation had been suggested early in the 1990s, which proved robust throughout the following 15 years. Werner (1992) suggested revisiting the fundamental link between the monetary side of the economy and the tangible, 'real' side. There is a significant body of empirical evidence that there is a close link between economic growth and the financial sector.[5] This link is explicitly represented in the 'quantity equation', also sometimes known as the 'equation of exchange' (or, in a monetarist context and with further assumptions, referred to as the 'quantity theory'). In its non-logarithmic, static form, it is commonly represented as follows:

$$MV = PY \qquad (3.1)$$

It is assumed by all macroeconomic theories that the velocity V is constant, so that a stable relationship exists between the supply of money M and nominal GDP (PY). Although Milton Friedman has compared this relationship in its reliability to the constants in the physical sciences (Friedman, 1956), it has proved far less reliable and, especially since the 1980s, appears to have broken down entirely, reflected in several dozen articles about the 'velocity decline', the 'breakdown in the money demand function' or the 'mystery of the missing money' (for a survey, see Goodhart, 1989; Goldfeld and Sichel, 1990; Boughton, 1991).

Mainstream approaches have failed to explain this 'puzzle' or 'anomaly' in the case of the major economies where it had been identified. Far from being an exception, Japan's experience of unexplained economic performance turns out to be just one further – albeit major – nail in the coffin of the traditional macroeconomic theories. It would be appealing if an explanation of events in Japan could also account for the breakdown of the traditional equation of exchange in most other economies.

Werner (1992, and subsequent work) suggested such an explanation. Originally, the equation of exchange was formulated with reference to transactions taking place during a certain time period, and the money actually used during these transactions. In words, it says that:

> *the amount of money changing hands to pay for transactions during a given time period must be equal to the nominal value of these transactions.*

Fisher (1911), citing Newcomb (1885), aggregated this as

$$MV = PQ \qquad (3.2)$$

where Q stands for the quantity of transactions.[6] Thus PQ refers to the total value of all transactions in the economy. Since, however, statistics on transactions were not published at the time (and even today are hardly ever published by those who have access to them, namely the central banks and banking clearing systems), economists proceeded to use national income, GNP or GDP as a proxy for PQ, the value of transactions.[7] This approximation became so entrenched that today monetary economics textbooks mistake it as an 'identity' that is true by definition. Handa (2000), for instance, says that equation (3.1), $MV = PY$,

> is an identity since it is derived solely from identities. It is valid under any set of circumstances whatever since it can be reduced to the statement: in a given period by a given group of people, expenditures equal expenditures, with only a difference in the computational method between them.

Yet equation (3.1) is only accurate when $Q = Y$ and thus all transactions are recorded in the GDP accounts (or, considering growth rates, when Q and Y grow at the same rate). It is recognized, though not widely known, that financial and real estate transactions are not reflected in GDP statistics. Thus, when the amount of money which is used for real estate transactions rises, this may result in higher real estate prices, but not necessarily greater consumer price inflation or nominal GDP growth. In line with this we note that, in many countries with asset price 'bubbles', economists puzzled over an apparent 'velocity decline'.

If one wants to analyse the link between the monetary sector and nominal GDP it therefore becomes necessary to separate the money that is used for financial and real estate transactions. How can this be done? Traditionally (and at least since Phillips, 1920, and Keynes, 1930), money 'M' had been defined as private sector assets, ranging from M0 to M4. These so-called 'money supply' aggregates actually measure private sector savings. Apart from the analytical problem that it is virtually impossible to be sure which types of private sector savings to include and which to exclude (hence the proliferation of M aggregates in empirical work and monetary policy in the past), savings also cannot be divided by the type of transactions they are used for, because they are not used for transactions at all. Indeed, this is a fundamental fallacy in the implementation of the quantity equation hitherto: although the equation of exchange refers to transactions, economists have defined the money used for transactions as deposit aggregates. Instead of using measures of money in circulation, they measured money out of circulation. Instead of measuring the actual money supply, economists have focused on a subset of the savings supply.

It is therefore necessary to identify how money that is actually used for transactions can be measured. To approach this question, it is initially useful to consider growth rates of equation (3.2):

$$\Delta(MV) = \Delta(PQ) \qquad (3.3)$$

Equation (3.3) says that an increase in the value of all transactions (PQ) requires that more money be used to pay for these transactions.

Before proceeding, a brief comment on methodology is necessary. In the sciences, the inductive or empirical methodology is widespread, whereby empirical facts are gathered, collated and evaluated in order to identify patterns, from which causal relationships are postulated that are congruent with the data. The resulting hypotheses and theories are then tested again and modified or refined accordingly. In mainstream economics, the deductive methodology has become more widespread in the past decades, whereby axioms and first principles are posed, then augmented with a number of auxiliary assumptions so that hypotheses or theories can be formulated. There is less emphasis on empirical reality, and consequently the process of progressing knowledge using the deductive methodology would appear to be slower and more wasteful, involving more cul-de-sacs and fewer systematic advances. The suggestion was therefore made to use the methodology common in the natural sciences and to base the formulation of economic theories firmly on empirical and inductive grounds (see Werner, 2005).

To analyse how it is possible for more money to be circulated, the inductive approach requires a thorough investigation of the payment mechanism common in modern economies. It is found that the majority of transactions (approximately 95 per cent or more) are not in the form of cash, but take place via the banking system, where they are settled purely as entries into accounts. An economy that settles its transactions to such an extent via bank book entries is called a 'credit economy', as identified by authors such as Wicksell (1907). How can the net amount of aggregate money that is used for transactions increase in such a credit economy as we are examining in equation (3.3)? In such an economy – and all our modern economies are of this type – the net amount of transactions can only increase if there has been an increase in credit. How, therefore, is credit increased (or decreased) in such a credit economy? The two types of players that can engage in the universally acceptable increase or decrease of credit (credit creation or credit destruction) are the central bank and the commercial banks. The latter usually account for about 90 per cent of credit creation. Credit creation by commercial banks involves the creation of new purchasing power that previously did not exist ('out of nothing') and its allocation to particular members of the economy, giving them a new claim on finite resources.

Owing to their narrow reliance on the deductive methodology that is so frowned upon in the natural sciences, modern mainstream textbooks and indeed refereed journal articles on macroeconomics and banking have succeeded in becoming ignorant of the facts of credit creation. Most economists today are therefore blissfully unaware that one individual bank can create new purchasing power. In a common textbook example, whereby banks have to meet a reserve requirement of 1 per cent, it is believed that a new deposit of $100 at a bank will result in a new reserve with the central bank of $1, and new bank lending of $99. However, in actual fact a healthy bank would instead use the $100 that has been deposited in its entirety as a reserve with the central bank, and then proceed to 'lend' $9900 by pretending that the borrowers have deposited this amount in their accounts with the bank, and crediting them accordingly. The $9900 in new loan extension is simply credited to the borrower as an entry in their deposit account, so that the bank's balance sheet shows an increase in both assets and liabilities by $9900. In doing so, the bank meets the reserve requirement, as deposits (including the reserve) increased by $10 000 and the reserve amounts to 1 per cent ($100). Unlike other industries, bankers are in this process not hindered by the laws of physics, which decree that something cannot be created from nothing. Since transactions are settled through the banking system, this newly created money can then be used and transferred, while banks will rebalance their books between them via the inter-bank market (see Werner, 2005).

Given the momentous implications of the simple facts of credit creation, and since history is the source of the empirical facts that the inductive researcher requires to build theories in economics, it would be desirable to review the historical development of today's banking and central banking systems, including Japan's, in greater detail. The facts are fascinating, as banking and bank credit creation are approximately five thousand years old and originated in Babylon. The development of the Japanese credit creation system is of particular interest, as important insights into the credit creation process gained in Germany were introduced early in Japan and successfully capitalized on for its economic development. Such an investigation is beyond the scope of this chapter, however, and the reader is referred elsewhere (Werner, 1993, 2003, 2006).

For our purposes, we conclude that credit creation, denoted as ΔC, is a more accurate measure of what was previously referred to as ΔM.[8] Unlike deposit aggregates, credit creation measures purchasing power that is actually used for transactions, as the original equation of exchange demands.

$$\Delta(CV) = \Delta(PQ) \tag{3.4}$$

Equation (3.4) says that an increase in the value of transactions is only possible if credit creation has increased. We can now proceed to distinguish between transactions which are part of GDP, and those which are not. Thus we divide the data into that credit (called C_R) used for 'real transactions' that are part of GDP ($P_R Q_R = P_R Y$) and that credit (called C_F) used for non-GDP ('financial') transactions ($P_F Q_F$).[9] In growth terms:

$$V\Delta C_R = \Delta(P_R Y) \tag{3.5}$$
$$V\Delta C_F = \Delta(P_F Q_F) \tag{3.6}$$

With this simple framework, it becomes straightforward to solve the puzzles that have surrounded the Japanese economy. According to equation (3.6), when banks create credit for financial and real estate transactions, as they did in the 1980s, asset prices have to rise. When banks reduce such credit creation, asset prices fall. As banks lent too much for speculative purposes, and as they reduced lending suddenly from 1989 onwards, the credit for financial (and hence speculative) purposes formerly granted turned into bad debts. This paralysed banks so that they became more risk-averse and reduced their overall lending. What the mainstream 'credit view' approaches above have neglected was the special role of banks as creators of the purchasing power in the economy. Thus increased rationing of credit by banks had to have a direct and negative impact on the economy, according to equation (3.5): if banks lend less for transactions that are part of nominal GDP (consumer loans, loans for plant and equipment investment and so on), then nominal GDP cannot grow as much as before. Since banks were sharply reducing their lending, the economy had to fall into a protracted recession. Increased loans from foreign financial institutions or non-banks, as well as increased funding from domestic or international capital markets could not possibly make up for the lack of bank credit creation, because the former do not create credit, and hence do not increase economic growth.

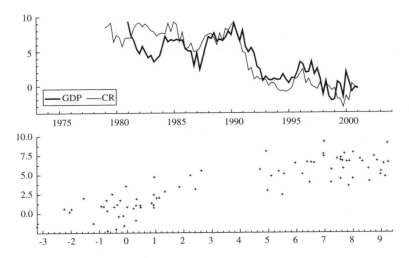

Figure 3.6   Credit creation used for 'real transactions' and nominal GDP growth

The relationship of equation (3.5) was empirically tested and strongly supported by the facts. A general-to-specific research methodology was adopted which started out with a much larger model that included all the traditional explanatory variables (including interest rates and 'money supply' deposit aggregates). When this was reduced to the parsimonious form, only the credit variable remained, as equation (3.5) suggested (see Werner, 1997, 2005). The finding was robust, also in ex ante forecasting, and over different time periods, and remained without obvious statistical problems. Tests for Granger 'causality' (Engle and Granger, 1987) between $\Delta nGDP$ and ΔC_R found a unidirectional 'causation' from credit creation in the 'real circulation' to nominal GDP growth. The original (not fitted) data are shown in Figure 3.6, where the correlation can be easily identified.

Under these circumstances, neither traditional fiscal policies nor interest rate policies will work: Fiscal policy is a transfer policy that does not normally affect credit creation. Hence it is growth-neutral. Even record fiscal expenditure packages were doomed to failure (as had been warned well in advance; see for instance, Werner, 1992, 1996d), because of the mechanics of funding such fiscal spending: the government issued government bonds to pay for the increased spending. The bonds withdrew money from the economy when, for instance, life insurance companies bought them. This same money was then injected in the form of fiscal spending. But if the total amount of purchasing power did not increase, as equation (3.5) shows, there could not be nominal GDP growth.

Interest rate reductions also were doomed to failure (as warned early on by Werner, 1992, 1994b). As can be seen, equations (3.5) and (3.6) do not include interest rates as variable. In other words, it is possible for growth to accelerate or decelerate irrespective of interest rate policy. It is not driven by the price of money (interest rates) but by its quantity (credit creation). This explains the puzzle of the failure of interest rate reductions to stimulate the economy. In actual fact, it is a common phenomenon witnessed in many other countries. Within an inductive methodology this finding is not surprising: the assertion that interest rates are a key causal factor of economic growth, and are inversely related to it, could only become widespread thanks to the deductive methodology, where such claims are simply assumed to be true. However, such axiomatic reasoning, especially when consistently contradicted by the facts, has little merit. An inductive methodology would not assume perfect information, and hence would not dream of postulating equilibrium. However, prices are only the dominant adjustment mechanism (and this applies to the price of money as well) in a theoretical dream world of perfect information where they equilibrate demand and supply. In the world we live in, information imperfections are common and hence there is no equilibrium. Therefore markets are rationed, and rationed markets are determined by quantities, according to the 'short-side principle': whichever of demand or supply is smaller will be the transacted quantity. In the case of money this quickly leads to the conclusion: since the demand for money is virtually unlimited (because of its particular usefulness, as well as institutional factors such as the limited liability of directors and hence asymmetric incentive structures), the short side is its supply. Thus the quantity of money supplied must be the overarching budget constraint on economic activity, as we also know from equation (3.3). Since this money is created through credit, and if we want to focus on nominal GDP, we know that credit creation used for GDP transactions is the limiting factor of economic growth (equation 3.5).

This, then, explains why Japan has been mired in such a long recession: bank credit creation has failed to recover for over a decade. It had slumped originally owing to the increased risk aversion of banks, which was triggered by bad debts. These, in turn, were triggered by the excessive bank lending of the 1980s.

These findings raise further questions. First, did the Bank of Japan do all it could during the 1990s to stimulate the economy? Quite apparently, it failed to mitigate the problem of falling bank credit creation during the 1990s. However, there have been a number of tested and tried policies that could have been adopted successfully under such circumstances of declining bank credit creation, and these policies could have been adopted at any time during the dozen or so years after 1990. These include, as was pointed out at the time (Werner, 1994b, 1995a, 1995b, 1995c, 1995d, 1996a, 1996b, 1996c, 1997) the following two policies.

First, the Bank of Japan could have restored the balance sheets of banks swiftly and at zero costs to society, and hence increased their appetite to lend, by taking all the non-performing loans onto its own balance sheet. Soon after the end of World War II, the Bank of Japan successfully engaged in a similar policy in order to restore the health of the banking system when it suffered far larger bad debt problems. In actual fact, during the 1990s, the Bank of Japan rejected suggestions by the government that it do more about helping the banking system.

Second, the Bank of Japan could have compensated for the lack of bank credit creation by increasing its own credit creation sufficiently (for instance by expanding bill rediscounting or CP and bond purchase operations). In actual fact, the Bank of Japan failed to adopt such a policy and even reduced its credit creation significantly on several important occasions during the 1990s. It also sterilized all government-ordered foreign exchange intervention and publicly rejected calls by the government that it stimulate credit creation. The so-called policy of 'quantitative easing', adopted in 2001 and ending in 2006, was merely a public-relations exercise, as it did not commit the central bank to any serious expansion in net credit creation (instead, it distracted attention by focusing on the irrelevant bank reserves with the central bank – funds that constitute money out of circulation).

There are a number of policies that the government could have adopted itself, such as ceasing the issuance of government bonds and instead funding the public sector borrowing requirement exclusively through borrowing from the commercial banks. Or it could have issued government paper money, which would also have monetized fiscal spending without the burden of interest payments (such a policy was adopted by President Kennedy in 1963, though it died with him later that year). Alternatively, the government could have altered the 1998 Bank of Japan Law to render the recalcitrant central bank less independent and more accountable. However, there is evidence that the government and its leaders failed to understand the economic rationale, and hence necessity, behind such proposals. Meanwhile, the failure of the Bank of Japan to adopt helpful policies cannot easily be explained by ignorance: such policies had either already been adopted by the Bank of Japan before, or were very much within the framework of monetary policy implementation that the central bank had been following since about 1942 (see Werner, 2003).

The conclusion must be that the Bank of Japan has failed its duty and mandate (which until 1998 bound it to support government policy; it was declared government policy to stimulate a lasting economic recovery) and is responsible for the prolongation of the recession of the 1990s and early 2000s. Responsibility for the prolonged recession of the 1990s and beyond thus lies with the highest-ranking decision makers that had risen from inside the Bank of Japan, namely Yasushi Mieno, governor from 1989 to 1994, and Toshihiko Fukui, deputy governor from 1994 to 1998 (and since then the *éminence grise* influencing the quantity of credit policy of the Bank of Japan; see Werner, 2003). During the 1990s and beyond, both gentlemen have said or implied in public that it has not been their policy goal to stimulate an economic recovery, but instead they had been more interested in triggering structural change. Bank of Japan officials have also acknowledged publicly that the recession has been useful in forcing such structural change (for quotations, see Werner, 2003).

There is a second question, however. Since ultimately the cause of the banking crisis of the 1990s and hence sharp recession was the bubble of the 1980s, it is necessary to consider the question of what caused the bubble in the first place. In a narrow sense we have already found the answer: equation (3.6) shows that increased credit creation used for real estate transactions will raise real estate prices. An empirical test of equation (3.6) also found it supported by the facts: real estate lending since the 1970s has been the robust and unidirectional explanatory variable of real estate price movements in Japan (Werner, 1997, 2005). The more interesting question is, therefore, why did banks lend so excessively during the 1980s?

Many observers, enthralled by the axiomatic mainstream models which assert interest rates as key explanatory variables, have argued that low interest rates were the cause of the excessive lending in the 1980s, as nominal short-term interest rates fell to 2.5 per cent in 1987 and stayed at such an 'excessively low' level for more than two years. However, in the late 1990s, interest rates had fallen far lower, and ultimately reached a level two thousand times lower than in the 1980s – yet there was no evidence of another 'bubble' economy or excessive lending in the 1990s. Again, an inductive research methodology is more likely to yield objective and accurate answers. Thus a researcher set out in the early 1990s to engage in extensive field work, involving primary interviews, in order to identify the main determinants of Japanese bank lending (Werner, 2002, 2005). The finding was that, throughout the 1980s and until at least the early 1990s, the Bank of Japan engaged in so-called informal 'guidance' of bank lending, whereby it would first determine an overall economy-wide credit creation target, then divide this into loan growth quotas for the different types of banks, and then inform the individual banks of their quarterly loan quota, which could be either positive or negative, higher or lower than previously, and which had to be fulfilled. These credit controls also involved the qualitative 'guidance' towards or away from particular industrial sectors, such as lending to the real estate sector or consumer loans. Any overshooting or undershooting

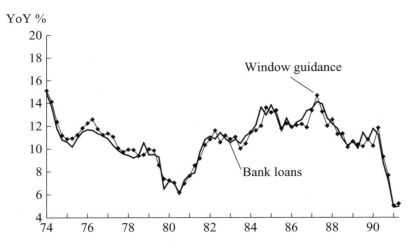

Source: Bank of Japan; Nomura Research Institute.

Figure 3.7   *Bank of Japan window guidance and actual bank lending three months later*

was punished and close to full compliance was achieved. While the Bank of Japan had claimed in various publications that such credit controls (usually called 'window guidance' in Japan's case) had become disused since 1982, the empirical research established beyond any doubt that they continued. The loan growth quotas were raised during the late 1980s, and lending especially to the real estate sector was strongly encouraged by the Bank of Japan. Figure 3.7 shows the loan growth quota imposed by the Bank of Japan and announced to the various constituent banks before the beginning of the respective quarter. Second, it shows the actual bank lending for that quarter, measured after the end of that quarter. As can be seen, and as econometric tests have confirmed, the 'window guidance' credit controls worked extremely efficiently in manipulating bank lending as the central bank wished. In econometric tests it was also shown that all other potential monetary policy variables, such as the official discount rate, the call rate or High Powered Money, cannot add any further explanatory power and in a model reduction from a broader general model to the parsimonious form can be dropped, leaving window guidance as the sole explanatory variable.

Bank of Japan quantitative credit policy as implemented in its 'window guidance' was not influenced by political pressure from the Ministry of Finance or international agreements such as the Plaza Agreement of September 1985. To the contrary, Bank of Japan staff, when interviewed, felt that the 'window guidance' was the ideal policy tool to prevent the stimulation of excessive bank lending and hence a financial bubble, when and if there is political pressure to lower interest rates excessively. Indeed, during much of the 1960s, it could be argued that interest rates were kept at artificially low rates, yet the Bank of Japan stayed in control of bank lending through its successful implementation of 'window guidance' credit controls. In rationed markets (which applies to all markets, since no market is characterized by perfect information) it is not surprising that price signals are superseded by quantities.

One of the interview subjects reported in 1992:

> The Bank of Japan has promoted loan expansion in the bubble period . . . My own opinion is: when one reduced the interest rate and *reduced* the window guid-ance loan growth limit, then with this policy-mix, the bubble would not have developed. But in reality, interest rates were reduced and window guidance was very relaxed. Thus the money supply rose by 10 per cent, up to 13 per cent. The question why they didn't close the window guidance more is extremely puzzling. (. . .) All the banks tried to use their loan growth quotas until the maximum and did all they could to give out loans. But the loans did not go to normal cor-porations, such as steel, automobiles, but instead to construction, non-bank financial institutions [which engaged in real estate speculation]. This became the bubble (Bank of Japan official 5).

This was confirmed by interview subjects from private-sector banks, such as the following:

> I worried a lot about the policy of the authorities . . . If they had taken a little tighter policy in the window guidance, this kind of phenomenon, the bubble, would have been prevented . . . If the Bank of Japan had wanted to tighten, it would have achieved a lot (bank officer 2).[10]

Thus the solitary statement by a senior Bank of Japan officer quoted in the Japanese financial press in 1992, that the 'bubble' was created by the Bank of Japan through its window guidance credit controls, seems to have been accurate (Nikkei, 1992).

Concerning the decision-making process and thus responsibility for the creation of the bubble of the 1980s (and hence the subsequent long-lasting recession), it was found that the 'window guidance' credit quotas were decided solely by the Bank of Japan, and that the key decision makers during the late 1980s, when the bubble was created, were Mr Yasushi Mieno, the deputy governor, and the Director of the Banking Department of the Bank of Japan, which operated the window guidance and forced the banks to increase their lending excessively; the latter post was held from 1986 to 1989, the years of the bubble economy, by Mr Toshihiko Fukui (Werner, 2003).

It is of interest that during the 1980s Mieno and Fukui also gave indica-tions that they were aware of what they were doing, including the potentially dire consequences that excessive real estate lending was likely to result in. Both justified their actions with reference to the need to implement 'far-reaching structural changes', even a 'structural transformation', which was unlikely to take place without sufficient pressure or a sense of crisis. This conclusion is seconded by other researchers. Posen (2000) concluded that the 'BoJ wants to use monetary policy to induce structural reforms. . . . It is clear that "creative destruction", invoked and praised repeatedly in [Bank of Japan governor] Hayami's speeches, is the motivating ideology' (pp. 205f).

Such sentiments, combined with disastrous policy actions, are reminiscent of IMF and World Bank policies in many developing countries. In many cases, banking crises were used to force deep structural changes on these countries, without these changes having any merit in terms of economic performance. But in most cases the structural changes opened the economies and financial markets to foreign financial interests. As the World Bank staff so aptly put it, '[a] crisis can be a window for structural reform', and it can 'be an opportunity to reform the ownership structure in the country' (Claessens et al., 2001, p. 13). Leading IMF and World Bank staff pursuing such policies that advanced the interests of Wall Street firms would often be rewarded with lucrative posts upon their departure from the international organizations. Professor Joseph Stiglitz, who saw the internal operations of the IMF and World Bank at close hand as World Bank chief economist, suggested: 'Looking at the IMF *as if* it were pursuing the interest of the [US] financial community provides a way of making sense of what might otherwise seem to be contradictory and intellectually incoherent behaviors' (2002, p. 209).

In Japan the key roles played by two individuals (Fukui and Mieno) over the quarter-century beginning in 1985 seem to rule out suggestions of policy mistakes due to personnel changes. It would appear that the well-documented commitment of leading central bank figures to an ideological and preconceived policy agenda (namely to implement deregulation, liberalization and privatization, although there is no empirical evidence that such reforms are in the interest of improved economic performance) has influenced their monetary policy decision making such that a string of disastrous policies was adopted which first created the bubble of the 1980s, and then one of the longest recessions among industrialized countries in modern history.

V WHAT LESSONS CAN BE LEARNED FOR THE ROLE OF CENTRAL BANKS?

From our findings it is clear that the Japanese central bank has throughout the period since 1985 acted far too independently and without appropriate accountability for its monetary policy. A main problem has been the widespread ignorance of the true nature of central bank monetary policy, which has been perpetuated by the central bank itself (nowhere in its official publications or research organs has the central bank in the past 20 years acknowledged the true role of 'window guidance' or quantitative credit creation policies). The legal change in the Bank of Japan Law in 1998 further worsened the situation, as it made the central bank less accountable to the government. It is clear from Japan's experience, as well as that of many other countries, that central banks that are not subject to close government scrutiny are likely to engage in sub-optimal monetary policy. It is thus recommended to change the Bank of Japan Law again and make the central bank subject to the supervision of the Ministry of Finance. Alternatively, Milton Friedman's (1982) suggestion could be adopted, namely to abolish the central bank and run monetary policy with one person who has one desk inside the Ministry of Finance – technically a distinct possibility. That Fukui, promoted to the position of governor of the Bank of Japan in 2003, proceeded to encourage bank lending and thus – very belatedly – stimulated a recovery in Japan does not absolve him from his responsibility. In the words of Posen (2000): 'no Japanese citizen elected the BoJ to pursue this policy of promoting restructuring, and in fact no elected official delegated this task to the BoJ or put the goal of "encouraging creative destruction" into its mandate' (pp. 206f). Yet it is astonishing how bold Fukui has become in acknowledging his role in creating and exacerbating the recession in order to engineer structural change in public. In 2004, he said in a public speech, 'While destroying the high growth [economic] model [of the 1960s], I am building a model that suits the new era. Now the fruits are beginning to show.'[11]

VI WHAT ARE THE LESSONS CONCERNING METHODOLOGY IN ECONOMIC RESEARCH AND THEORY?

Research based on deductive, axiomatic theories is far less likely to further knowledge than research that adopts the scientific research methodology of inductivism. Economic theory that is only built on deductive approaches must be considered inferior to theory that has been derived inductively. The fact that the majority of economists have no idea about the realities of bank credit creation serves to illustrate how irrelevant mainstream academic economics has become. Certainly there is little reason to heed any policy advice advanced on the basis of deductive mainstream economic theory, as such policy advice cannot be relevant to the world we live in: it was designed, based on, and can only be useful within, a theoretical dream world.

Had inductive and empirical research methodology been more widespread in economics – at the moment it is a sheer exception – then the problems with central banks would have been recognised earlier and past lessons would have been heeded.

NOTES

1. They found that productivity growth slowed from 0.96 per cent in the period of 1975–90 to 0.61 per cent during the period of 1990–95, but rose to 1.04 per cent during the period of 1995–2000.
2. Hayashi and Prescott (2002) assume that all factors of production were fully employed and then proceed to measure the productivity of the work force, instead of the actually employed work force. Fukao et al. (2003) have shown that Hayashi and Prescott (2002) therefore incorrectly count as productivity decline what in fact was a fall in factor utilization.
3. They argue that, as long as their open market liabilities are imperfectly substitutable with managed liabilities, a credit effect remains. They find that, during tight-money periods, when open-market interest rates rise, the prime rate rises by more. They note that this is difficult to distinguish from a balance sheet channel, where a tightening of monetary policy leads to a simultaneous worsening of both banks' and borrowers' balance sheets.
4. There is no evidence that the decline in land prices in Japan during the 1990s was due to firms selling their land holdings, as Kiyotaki and Moore (1997) postulate. Ogawa (2000) reports empirical support for the balance sheet channel, working through land used as collateral by firms, while land prices themselves are said to depend on interest rates. However, lower interest rates during the 1990s did not raise land prices. Consequently, Ogawa has merely replaced one puzzle (why interest rates have failed to boost the economy) with another (why interest rates have failed to boost land prices). While Ogawa reports that, in his empirical study, interest rates have long-lasting effects on investment, this finding is based on the observation period from 1975 to 1990. Based on these, Ogawa estimates by how much investment by firms would have increased in the 1990s, if the same relationships as in the pre-1990s period had prevailed. It is found that investment rose by less than expected. That, however, is merely restating the puzzle that requires an explanation, without offering any insights. Further, Ogawa, citing Ueda (1993), uses the call rate as the sole measure of monetary policy. This is erroneous (see Werner, 2002). There are further problems, beyond the scope of this chapter.
5. See, for instance, Vittas et al. (2002), Levine and Renelt (1992) and Levine (1997), Gurley and Shaw (1955, 1960), Goldsmith (1969), Shaw (1973), McKinnon (1973) and Fry (1978, 1980, 1984).
6. Total volume of transactions $PQ = \Sigma p_i q_i$. Fisher used T to represent the quantity of transactions.
7. This tradition started with Pigou (1917).
8. The dangers of adopting the deductive research methodology are illustrated well by the case of credit theory. As the 1911 edition of the *Encyclopaedia Britannica* shows, credit-based macroeconomic theories were common at the time: 'The immense growth of credit and its embodiment in instruments that can be used as substitutes for money has led to the promulgation of a view respecting the value of money which may be called the Credit Theory. According to the upholders of this doctrine, the actual amount of metallic money has but a trifling effect on the range of prices, and therefore on the value of money. What is really important is the volume of credit instruments in circulation. It is

on their amount that price movements depend. Gold has become only the small change of the wholesale markets, and its quantity is comparatively unimportant as a determinant of prices. The theory has some connection with the view of Money as consisting in the loanable capital of the market, taking shape in the cheques that transfer liabilities' (*Encyclopaedia Britannica*, 1911 edn). Today, this knowledge has been largely lost.

9.   In line with Werner (1991, 1992, 1997).
10. Both quotations as cited in Werner (2005).
11. Nichigin sōsai, kuni ya chihō no zeikin no tsukaikata 'hontōni heta', *Nikkei Net*, 18 September 2004 (obtained on that day at: http://www.nikkei.co.jp/news/keizai/ 20040918AT1F1 800E18092004.html, but now deleted by Nikkei).

ACKNOWLEDGEMENT

This contribution draws on earlier works by Werner, as cited, and in particular reproduces a number of figures, as well as abridged excerpts from Richard A. Werner, *New Paradigm in Macroeconomics*, 2005, Palgrave Macmillian, with kind permission from the publisher.

BIBLIOGRAPHY

Bernanke, Ben S. (1993), 'How important is the credit channel in the transmission of monetary policy? A comment', Carnegie-Rochester Conference Series on Public Policy, **39**, December, pp. 47–52.
Bernanke, Ben S. and Alan S. Blinder (1988), 'Credit, money and aggregate demand', *American Economic Review, Proceedings*, **78**, May, 435–9.
Bernanke, Ben S. and Mark Gertler (1995), 'Inside the black box: the credit channel of monetary policy transmission', *Journal of Economic Perspectives*, **9**(4), Fall, 27–48.
Boughton, James M. (1991), 'Long-run money demand in large industrial countries', IMF Staff Papers, **38**(1) (March), 1–32.
Calomiris, Charles W., Charles P. Himmelberg and Paul Wachtel (1995), 'Commercial paper, corporate finance, and the business cycle: a microeconomic perspective', Carnegie-Rochester Conference Series on Public Policy, **42**, 203–50.
Claessens, Stijn, Daniela Klingebiel and Luc Laeven (2001), 'Financial restructuring in banking and corporate sector crises – what policies to pursue?', NBER, April (available at http://www.nber.org/books/mgmtcrises/claessens 4-24-01.pdf).
Engle, R.F. and C.W.J. Granger (1987), 'Co-integration and error-correction: representation, estimation and testing', *Econometrica* 55, 251–76.
Fisher, Irving (1911), *The Purchasing Power of Money, Its Determination and Relation to Credit, Interest and Crises*, New York: Macmillan.
Friedman, Milton (1956), 'The quantity theory of money – a restatement', in Milton Friedman (ed.), *Studies in the Quantity Theory of Money*, Chicago, IL: University of Chicago Press.
Friedman, Milton (1982), 'Monetary policy, theory and practice', *Journal of Money, Credit and Banking*, **14**(1), February, 98–118.
Fry, Maxwell J. (1978), 'Money and capital or financial deepening in economic development', *Journal of Money, Credit and Banking*, **10**(4), November, 464–75.

Fry, Maxwell J. (1980), 'Saving, investment, growth and the cost of financial repression', *World Development*, **8**(4), April, 317–27.

Fry, Maxwell J. (1984), 'Saving, financial intermediation and economic growth in Asia', *Asian Development Review*, **2**(1), 82–91.

Fukao, Mitsuhiro (2003), 'Financial sector profitability and double gearing', in Magnus Blomstrom, Jenny Corbett, Fumio Hayashi and Anil Kashyap (eds), *Structural Impediments to Growth in Japan*, Chicago: University of Chicago Press.

Gertler, Mark and Simon Gilchrist (1993), 'The role of credit market imperfections in the monetary transmission mechanism: arguments and evidence', *Scandinavian Journal of Economics*, **109** (May), 309–40.

Goldfeld, Stephen M. and Daniel E. Sichel (1990), 'The demand for money', in B.M. Friedman and F.H. Hahn (eds), *Handbook of Monetary Economics*, vol. I, Amsterdam: North-Holland, pp. 300–356.

Goldsmith, Raymond W. (1969), *Financial Structure and Development*, New Haven, CT: Yale University Press.

Goodhart, Charles A.E. (1989), 'The conduct of monetary policy', *Economic Journal*, **99** (June), 293–346.

Gurley, J.G. and E.S. Shaw (1955), 'Financial aspects of economic development', *American Economic Review*, **45**(4) Sept., 515–38.

Gurley, J.G. and E.S. Shaw (1960), *Money in a Theory of Finance*, Washington, DC: Brookings Institution.

Handa, Jagdish (2000), *Monetary Economics*, London and New York: Routledge.

Hayashi, Fumio and Edward C. Prescott (2002) 'The 1990s in Japan: a lost decade', *Review of Economic Dynamics*, **5**(1), 206–35.

IMF (2002), Japan: Staff report for 2002 Article IV consultation, Washington, DC.

Jorgenson, Dale W. and Kazuyuki Motohashi (2003), 'The role of information technology in economy: comparison between Japan and the United States', prepared for RIETI/KEIO Conference on Japanese Economy: Leading East Asia in the 21st Century?, Keio University, 30 May.

Kashyap, Anil K. (2002), 'Sorting out Japan's financial crisis', *Economic Perspectives*, Q4, **26**(4), Chicago, IL: Federal Reserve Bank of Chicago, 42–55, also published as NBER Working Paper 9384, Cambridge: National Bureau of Economic Research, December. (The paper can be downloaded at http://www.chicagofed.org/publications/economicperspectives/2002/4qepart4.pdf).

Kashyap, Anil K. and Jeremy C. Stein (1993), 'Monetary Policy and Bank Lending', NBER Working Papers 4317, National Bureau of Economic Research.

Keynes, John Maynard (1930), *A Treatise on Money*, Vol. 1, London: Macmillan.

Kiyotaki, Nobuhiro and John Moore (1997), 'Credit cycles', *Journal of Political Economy*, **105**, 211–48.

Krugman, Paul (1998), 'It's Baaack: Japan's slump and the return of the liquidity trap', *Brookings Papers on Economic Activity*, **2**, 137–205.

Levine, Ross (1997), 'Financial development and economic growth: views and agenda', *Journal of Economic Literature*, **35** (June), 688–726.

Levine, Ross and David Renelt (1992), 'A sensitivity analysis of cross-country growth regressions', *American Economic Review*, **82**(4), 942–63.

Mateut, Simona, Spiros Bougheas and Paul Mizen (2003), 'Trade credit, bank lending and monetary policy transmission', Economics working papers ECO2003/02, European University Institute, Florence.

McKinnon, Ronald I. (1973), *Money and Capital in Economic Development*, Washington, DC: Brookings Institution.

Meltzer, A.H. (1995), 'Monetary, credit (and other) transmission processes: a monetarist perspective', *Journal of Economic Perspectives*, **9** (Fall), 49–72.

Newcomb, S. (1885), *Principles of Political Economy*, New York: Harper.

Nikkei (1992), 'Nagoya shitenchō ga keiken, zaitech toraburu nichigin nimo sekinin', 26-12-92, p. 7.

Ogawa, Kazuo (2000), 'Monetary policy, credit and real activity: evidence from the balance sheet of Japanese firms', *Journal of the Japanese and International Economies*, **14**, 385–407.

Phillips, Chester A. (1920), *Bank Credit*, New York: Macmillan.

Pigou, Alfred C. (1917), 'The value of money', *Quarterly Journal of Economics*, **32** (November), 38–65.

Posen, Adam S. (2000), 'The political economy of deflationary monetary policy', in Ryoichi Mikitani and Adam S. Posen (eds), *Japan's Financial Crisis and its Parallels to US Experience*, Institute for International Economics special report 13, Washington, DC, September.

Shaw, Edward S. (1973), *Financial Deepening and Economic Development*, New York: Oxford University Press.

Stiglitz, Joseph E. (2002), *Globalisation and its Discontents*, New York: W.W. Norton.

Ueda, Kazuo (1993), 'A comparative perspective on Japanese moentary policy: short run monetary control and the transmission mechanism', in K. Singleton (ed.), *Japanese Monetary Policy*, Chicago, IL: University of Chicago Press.

Vittas, Dimitri, Gerard Caprio and Patrick Honohan (eds) (2002), *Financial Sector Policy for Developing Countries: A Reader*, Oxford: Oxford University Press, The World Bank.

Werner, Richard A. (1991), 'The great yen illusion: Japanese capital flows and the role of land', Oxford Applied Economics Discussion Paper Series, No. 129, December.

Werner, Richard A. (1992), 'Towards a quantity theorem of disaggregated credit and international capital flows', paper presented at the Royal Economic Society Annual Conference, York, April 1993, and at the 5th Annual PACAP Conference on Pacific–Asian Capital Markets in Kuala Lumpur, June 1993.

Werner, Richard A. (1993), 'Japanese-style capitalism: the new collectivist challenge? An analysis of the nature and origin of Japan's political economy and social order', paper presented at the Fifth Annual International Conference of the Society for the Advancement of Socio-Economics (SASE), 26–8 March, New School for Social Research, NYC.

Werner, Richard A. (1994a), 'Japanese foreign investment and the bubble', *Review of International Economics*, **2**(2), June, Blackwell, Oxford, 166–78.

Werner, Richard A. (1994b), 'May edition, Liquidity Watch', Jardine Fleming Securities, Tokyo.

Werner, Richard A. (1995a), 'Bank of Japan: start the presses!', *Asian Wall Street Journal*, Tuesday, 13 June.

Werner, Richard A. (1995b), 'June edition, Liquidity Watch', Jardine Fleming Securities, Tokyo.

Werner, Richard A. (1995c), 'Keiki kaifuku, ryoteki kinyū kanwa kara', Nihon Keizai Shinbun, Keizai Kyoshitsu, 2 September.

Werner, Richard A. (1995d), 'Q3 1995: Japan at the crossroads', *Economic Quarterly*, September, Jardine Fleming Securities, Tokyo.

Werner, Richard A. (1996a), 'Liquidity no nobi, kasoku', Nikkei Kinyū Shinbun, 28 February.

Werner, Richard A. (1996b), 'The BoJ prolonged Japan's recession', *Asian Wall Street Journal*, Thursday, 13 June.

Werner, Richard A. (1996c), 'Nichigin Manipulation, Ronso Toyokeizai', Part I: July, pp. 64–73; Part II: September, pp. 130–39; Part III: November, pp. 190–95, Toyo Keizai Shinposha (in Japanese).

Werner, Richard A. (1996d), 'Q2 1996', *Economic Quarterly*, Jardine Fleming Securities: Tokyo.

Werner, Richard A. (1997), 'Towards a new monetary paradigm: a quantity theorem of disaggregated credit, with evidence from Japan', *Kredit und Kapital*, **30**(2), 276–309, Berlin: Duncker und Humblot.

Werner, Richard A. (2002), 'Monetary policy implementation in Japan: what they say vs what they do', *Asian Economic Journal*, **16**(2), (June), Blackwell, Oxford, 111–51.

Werner, Richard A. (2003), *Princes of the Yen: Japan's Central Bankers and the Transformation of the Economy*, Armonk, New York: M.E. Sharpe.

Werner, Richard A. (2004), 'No recovery without reform? An empirical evaluation of the structural reform argument in Japan', *Asian Business and Management*, **3**(1), 7–38.

Werner, Richard A. (2005), *New Paradigm in Macroeconomics: Solving the Riddle of Japanese Macroeconomic Performance*, Basingstoke: Palgrave Macmillan.

Werner, Richard A. (2006), 'Aspects of German monetary and development economics and their reception in Japan', in George Stathakis and Gianni Vaggi (eds), *Economic Development and Social Change: Historical Roots and Modern Perspectives*, London: Routledge.

Wicksell, Knut (1907), 'The influence of the rate of interest on prices', *Economic Journal*, **17**, 213–20.

4. Transnational monopoly capitalism, the J-mode firm and industrial 'hollowing out' in Japan

Keith Cowling and Philip R. Tomlinson

I INTRODUCTION

The 1990s were known as Japan's 'lost decade', a long period of stagnation and relative economic decline. The crisis brought an end to Japan's long period of economic growth and prosperity that had begun in the immediate aftermath of World War II. Although there has been some recent improvement in the Japanese economy, particularly in terms of economic growth, its performance remains below its long-run potential and future prospects for manufacturing in particular are uncertain. In trying to explain the crisis, many commentators have sought to blame Japan's economic woes upon overregulation, interventionist industrial policies and the country's 'antiquated' financial and industrial institutions. For instance, Japanese employment practices have been regarded as being a barrier to generating new business, while the nature of Japan's industrial groupings has been blamed for 'excessive investment' and poor returns to capital. Many Western commentators have advocated that Japan undertakes major structural reforms and move towards an Anglo-American style of capitalism (see, for instance, Katz, 1998).

Our view is that such mainstream approaches are misconstrued and consequently are unlikely to provide any long-term solutions. This is because they ignore the fundamental characteristic that underpinned the Japanese crisis and which was common to economic crises that have afflicted industrial nations elsewhere (including the USA and Western Europe): that of rising industrial concentration and the dominance of giant corporations within the economy. These corporations have long played the key role in the development path of economies, particularly in the industrialized world (see, for instance, Chandler, quoted in Teece, 1993), often shaping industrial structures to meet their own strategic interests at the expense of other actors in society (Cowling and Sugden, 1999). Moreover, the growth of corporate power can often lead to long periods of stagnation as predicted by the monopoly capitalism literature, while the concentration of economic power and strategic decision making suppresses economic democracy (see section II). In the case of Japan, the growth of its giant transnational corporations has led to a significant 'hollowing out' of its industrial base with adverse consequences for both its micro and macro economy (see section V).

In this chapter, we build upon our earlier work (see also Cowling and Tomlinson, 2000, 2002, 2003a, 2003b) and argue that, rather than the Japanese crisis being unique to Japan, the economy was experiencing the deficiencies that are typically associated within a system of transnational monopoly capitalism. The Japanese case is particularly interesting in that, for a long period in the twentieth century, the Japanese state was able to nullify the effects of monopoly capitalism through a proactive industrial policy, while the growth-maximizing behaviour of Japanese corporations and their preference for internal growth over acquisitions (see Odagiri, 1992) appeared to suit the long-term ambitions of Japan.[1] We will argue that the breakdown of this apparent consensus in Japan (during the 1990s) illustrates the danger in pursuing (economic) policies which tie the wider public interest to the ambitions of the corporate sector.

The remainder of this chapter is set out as follows. In section II, we introduce the basic tenets of the monopoly capitalism argument and set out the strategic decision-making approach to industrial organization. Using this theoretical framework, we then begin to explore the Japanese case, beginning, in section III, with a reappraisal of the literature on the Japanese corporation: the so-called 'J-mode'. This is important since the J-mode is often purported to be a significantly different entity than its Western counterpart, and is often regarded as the main source of Japan's post-war competitive advantage (see Aoki, 1990). Section IV reconsiders the role of industrial policy and explores the growth of corporate Japan and its role shaping the country's economic development. Section V identifies the roots of Japan's industrial stagnation and presents some evidence on the 'hollowing out' of Japanese manufacturing. Although our prime focus is upon the industrial sector, we argue that much of our analysis explains Japan's wider malaise during the 1990s. Finally, section VI concludes.

II   TRANSNATIONAL MONOPOLY CAPITALISM: A BRIEF OVERVIEW

The basic premise in the monopoly capitalism literature is that the increasing monopolization of the (domestic) economy, by giant firms, has fundamental implications for price–cost margins, the distribution of income and aggregate demand.[2] In particular, rising concentration in markets leads to an increase in prices relative to marginal costs, which is sustained by effective collusion between firms, strategic entry deterrence and a reduction in the price elasticity of demand as a consequence of advertising expenditures/product differentiation by the leading firms. This, in turn, raises the potential for an increase in the share of profits in national income. Yet whether this potential is realized depends upon the impact of the monopolization process upon aggregate demand. In the first instance, rising monopolization is associated with a decline in planned investment in line with a planned reduction in the rate of output within those sectors where the degree of monopoly power has risen, since higher prices are associated with a lower level of sales. Furthermore, the corollary for potential profits to rise is a simultaneous reduction in the relative income share of labour.[3] This is likely to depress sales further since labour forms the principal consumer group. Taken together, the reduction in aggregate investment and declining consumption leads to a reduction in the level of profits in the whole system, which in turn generates a cumulative process of decline and stagnation.

The problem is essentially one of sustaining effective demand so as to ensure that a crisis can be avoided and potential profits can be realized. In this respect, one might consider whether export markets and/or government initiatives such as a Keynesian expansion can take up the slack within the economy and provide a possible outlet for firms.[4] Yet these options are only likely to provide a temporary reprieve. In the case of exports, over time a net export surplus is unlikely to be sustainable: indeed the evidence suggests that, while rising domestic concentration might lead to growing exports, these are likely to be countered by rising levels of imports (Koo and Martin, 1984). Furthermore, faced with international competition, giant domestic firms are likely to evolve into transnational corporations as a strategic response to counter international rivalry and to take the opportunity to attain lower labour/supplier costs via global outsourcing. In the first instance, the transnational base provides dominant firms with greater degrees of freedom to engage in reciprocal exchanges of threats with (international) rivals and secure accommodation in an international oligopolistic environment while smaller, weaker rivals are squeezed out. In the second, transnationality allows firms to engage in 'divide and rule' tactics whereby the credible threat of relocation enhances their bargaining position *vis-à-vis* world governments (in the pursuit of favourable tax regimes and subsidies and/or domestic legislation) and their international workforce and supply base (thus placing downward pressure upon wage and supplier costs). For the domestic economy, the substitution of overseas for home production has adverse consequences such as initiating the 'hollowing out' of industrial capacity and exacerbating decline (see section V). A Keynesian expansion may well alleviate some of the demand deficiencies within the system in the short term but, in the long run, the pressures placed upon the economy's fiscal position are unlikely to be tenable. Indeed, with increasing globalization, the 'twin deficits' scenario is increasingly likely with expansionary fiscal policies generating balance of payments deficits more quickly and fiscal crises more generally, as domestic expansions are satisfied by transnationals sourcing products from overseas locations.

Moreover, the globalization process and the growth in the power of the corporate sector have significant implications for economic development, democratic governance and the public interest. This is because transnational corporations are the central actors in the (global) economy (UNCTAD, 1993) with the tentacles of their control often extending beyond their legal boundaries to include not only in-house activities but also subcontracting and global outsourcing. The essence of these corporations is captured in the strategic decision making approach to industrial organization: typically, modern corporations are governed by elite corporate hierarchies and it is their strategic decisions (on key economic variables such as investment, employment and output) which ultimately determine the direction of (economic) development in regions and nation states. This raises the spectre of 'strategic failure': a situation that occurs when the strategic decisions of the elite conflict with the wider public interest, with no available mechanism for society to redress the balance and achieve what it regards as a socially desirable and efficient outcome (Cowling and Sugden, 1999).

The deficiencies of transnational monopoly capitalism are well documented and there is substantial evidence to suggest that its emergence as the dominant form of capitalism in the twentieth century has been detrimental to the performance of economies in the industrialized world.[5] Yet, for a long period, Japan appeared immune to the crises of monopoly capitalism. Indeed, Japan was often regarded by commentators as a model for sustainable economic and industrial development, with the country's superior economic performance – over the post World War II period – providing an alternative to traditional Western modes of capitalism (Johnson, 1982). Furthermore, Japanese firms were also regarded as being 'flexible' in production, enabling them to be more resilient and successful than their Western rivals in the face of international crises (see Kenny and Florida, 1988, 1993). Let us now reconsider these propositions in the light of recent evidence.

III THE JAPANESE CORPORATION (THE J-MODE)

In analysing the earlier success and recent failures of the Japanese economy, it is instructive to begin with an understanding of the Japanese corporation. The reasoning is twofold. First in the monopoly capitalism and the related strategic decision-making literature it is the giant corporations that control the economic system and ascertaining their role in the process is crucial in tracing the development path of the economy. Second, and particularly pertinent in the Japanese case, we follow Aoki (1990: 2) who remarked that 'one of the important sources of the industrial strength (and weaknesses in certain respects) of the Japanese economy can be found in the micro-micro (internal) structure of firms'. Indeed, in a number of influential articles and books, Aoki (1984, 1988, 1989, 1990, 1994) has sought to portray the Japanese firm – the so-called J-mode – as a unique entity, one that is distinctly 'less hierarchical' in its organization and outlook than its Anglo-American counterpart (which Aoki describes as being 'hierarchical' and subsequently labels the 'H-mode'). The main differences between the J-mode and the H-mode refer to the management of production activities, employer–labour relations and finance and equity arrangements. For writers such as Aoki and others, the J-mode has underpinned the Japanese economy: the 'flexibility' and 'non-hierarchical' modes employed by Japanese corporations being seen as the source of Japan's competitive advantage and (earlier) economic success.[6]

If the J-mode is a significantly different entity from its Western counterpart, then this may raise serious doubts about the validity of our central hypothesis (see section II). This would particularly be the case if, as Aoki suggests, the J-mode represents a wider set of interests than those pursued by profit-maximizing Western corporations.

However, a close inspection of Aoki's J-mode reveals some remarkable similarities in its command and control structures with those one generally associates with Western corporations. In drawing this observation, let us briefly reassess the J-mode through the lens offered by the strategic decision-making approach, which seems appropriate given that Aoki's (and also our own) focus is upon hierarchy and governance within giant corporations. First consider the J-mode's management of vertical supply chains, the so-called *keiretsu* networks. It is through these networks that Japanese corporations organize and manage their production activities via an extensive set of subcontracting arrangements. The general consensus in the management literature is that Japan is unique in establishing and sustaining long-standing cooperative relationships between *keiretsu* firms, based upon 'trust' and the (relatively) 'free exchange' of information and technology between firms. The nature of these relationships and Japan's apparently vertically de-integrated industrial structure is often portrayed as being markedly different from that observed in the West (see for instance, Womack et al. (1990), Smitka (1991), Gerlach (1992) and Scher, 1997). These and earlier commentaries in the management literature provide the basis for Aoki's (1990) claim that the J-mode is 'non-hierarchical' in production.

This depiction of the J-mode is, however, misleading, particularly when one considers the well-documented evidence that Japan's giant corporations often exercise considerable control over their smaller *keiretsu* partners. For instance, consider the automobile industry, which has the largest and widest set of *keiretsu* networks in Japan and is used as the reference point for Aoki's thesis. The first point to note here is that at the pinnacle of the industry's hierarchy the giant Japanese assemblers typically hold significant equity stakes in both their core and – along with their major *keiretsu* partners – lower-tier suppliers.[7] These equity holdings have allowed the giant assemblers to place former senior employees in key positions throughout the supply chain, a move that establishes direct lines of communication and facilitates the dissemination of corporate strategy (from the assemblers' hierarchies) throughout the production and supply chain. Yet, while equity holdings have undoubtedly provided assemblers with direct control over their lower tier-partners, due account should also be paid to other control levers that are perhaps less obvious but are exercised outside the corporation's legal boundaries and through the locus of its strategic decision making. These are considered in some detail by Ruigrok and Van Tulder (1995: 51–4) and include the subjugation of *keiretsu* partners by assemblers dictating contract conditions and imposing technologies and processes upon them. Moreover, Japanese assemblers employ a form of 'divide and rule' through the extensive use of the multiple sourcing of components, which further weakens the relative bargaining of *keiretsu* partners, three-quarters of whom typically depend upon one assembler for over 50 per cent of their orders (Dodwell, 1997: 11).[8] Indeed, the transactional hierarchy of the Japanese automobile industry has led Ruigrok and Van Tulder (1995: 53) to describe the situation as one where there is 'a one-way dependency of suppliers on the end producers'. Similar sentiments have also been expressed by industry practitioners.[9]

If the reality of the J-mode's external relations is that they do not fit Aoki's 'non-hierarchy' thesis then what about internal relationships? In this regard the literature emphasizes how Japanese corporations regard workers as integral to their competitive strength and that they are duly rewarded through a 'rank hierarchy' system which provides financial incentives for length of service and good performance as opposed to the 'status' rewards associated with the seniority promotion system in Western corporations. The distinctive nature of the Japanese incentive system is said to allow for a greater delegation of decision making, which in turn encourages wider on-site information and problem solving and horizontal coordination across departments, thus facilitating positive learning externalities throughout the firm (Aoki, 1988, 1990). Moreover, relating the incentive structure to length of service also enables Japanese firms to retain workers with firm-specific skills, which explains the long-standing tenure of Japanese employment. Indeed, the arrangements within Japanese corporations have led some writers to argue that they favour employees, who could be considered as the J-mode's most important stakeholders (see Abegglen and Stalk, 1985; Miwa, 1996).

On the surface, the picture presented here is clearly at odds with the strategic decision-making approach, where workers are excluded from participating in corporate decision making. Yet, while there may well be differences in management styles between corporations (whether Japanese and/or Western), it is our contention that strategic decisions are and always have been concentrated within Japan's corporate elite.[10] References in the literature to a decentralization of decision making within the J-mode typically refer to operational decision making which affect the day-to-day running of the firm as opposed to those decisions that govern its strategic orientation. This point appears to be accepted by Aoki (1990: 13–16) who is quite clear in this respect that workers are subordinate to management authority (who are in turn monitored and are answerable to the major shareholders). Indeed, if we also consider the lack of a veto by Japanese workers (or their representatives) on the recent globalization activities of Japan's giant corporations, which have worsened employment prospects in Japan (see section V), then it is apparent that the J-mode's main stakeholders are its corporate elite and not its workers.[11]

We could, of course, elaborate much further upon these and other points regarding Aoki's J-mode and its perceived differences from its Western counterpart: a full critique of the J-mode is provided by Coffey and Tomlinson (2003a, 2003b). What is clear is that Aoki's description of the J-mode as a 'non-hierarchical' entity is highly questionable. The reality is that governance systems within the so-called J-mode are remarkably similar to those that exist in its Western counterpart: in essence, control is exercised by a corporate elite from one centre of strategic decision making. Moreover, the concentration of economic power within corporate Japan has had significant implications for the direction and the performance of the Japanese economy during the 1990s. We will now take up this point in sections IV and V.

IV INDUSTRIAL POLICY, CORPORATE JAPAN AND GLOBALIZATION

Perhaps the most important factor behind the extraordinary post-World War II success of the Japanese economy was the role played by MITI (see Johnson, 1982). During the post-war era, MITI was proactive in strategically planning and nurturing a market economy: this provided the basis for Johnson's 'developmental state'. This included selecting and promoting industries that were identified as being 'strategic' from the perspective of the national economy: in the 1950s and 1960s these comprised the heavy industries (iron and steel, shipbuilding and electric power), in the 1970s and 1980s, consumer durables (automobiles and semiconductors) and, in the 1990s, the higher technology sector (advanced electronics and computer research). A range of policy measures were introduced, including the regulation of foreign trade to protect domestic 'infant industries' and the provision of export subsidies. MITI also encouraged the importation of foreign technology, but this was closely regulated along with both inward and outward foreign direct investment (FDI).[12] The strict FDI regulations reflected MITI's concerns that (1) US-led transnationals would enter and dominate Japan's domestic markets at the expense of nationally owned companies and (2) outward FDI and offshore production would encourage 'reverse exports' and harm Japanese domestic industry (Bailey et al.: 1994). Finally, these measures were supplemented by the growth of the banking *keiretsu*, which provided finance to industry at preferential rates of interest, thereby encouraging long-term investment. Through pursuing an interventionist industrial policy, Japan was able to quickly overcome the devastation left by World War II. Indeed, within a few years, during the industrialized world's 'Golden Age' (1956–73), Japan began to outperform her main international rivals on almost all of the key economic indicators and, by the early 1980s, the country had become, in terms of GDP, the world's second largest economy (Graham and Seldon, 1990).

For Johnson (1982), Japan's 'economic miracle' was a testament to the country's institutions and the role afforded to state strategic planning in a market economy, a view that we generally concur with, in that we see a positive role for institutions and a proactive industrial policy. However, a close examination of MITI's industrial strategy reveals that, within it, it ultimately carried the seeds of Japan's decline that occurred during the 1990s. In making this claim, we draw upon Piore and Sabel's (1984) observation that MITI's policies contained a clear prejudice in favour of promoting its giant corporations, often at the expense of the smaller *keiretsu* firms: indeed industrial strategy was based upon the *keiretsu* being subservient to the strategic interests of the giant corporations (see section III).[13] MITI also approved a programme of cartelization, which further raised the level of industrial concentration and reduced domestic competition (see Schaede, 2000). Moreover corporate Japan developed and maintained close links with MITI, to the extent that it was able to influence the higher echelons within the ministry, often being successful in lobbying for changes in national policy to pursue its own strategic interests (see for example, Johnson, 1982: 68–74). This influence was particularly apparent in MITI's concession to relax the restrictions on outward FDI in 1971 (Mason, 1994: 21–5). In short, Japanese industrial policy was geared towards the promotion of Japan's corporate giants (its 'national champions') who were increasingly encouraged to compete internationally with their rivals from the USA and Europe.

Since the early 1970s, corporate Japan has expanded its interests throughout the globe. The lifting of the FDI restrictions provided the catalyst for Japan's transnationals to increasingly shift their production activities offshore in order to enhance their bargaining power with labour ('divide and rule') and take subsequent advantage of lower labour costs, to overcome rising trade barriers and to compete strategically with their domestic and global rivals.[14] This overseas expansion was particularly prominent during Japan's halcyon years of the 1980s and continued until well into the mid-1990s: for instance, between 1981 and 1995, Japanese FDI amounted to over $470 billion, representing a fourfold increase (in real terms) over the period and the highest average growth rate (22 per cent) in overseas investment of any G8 industrial nation (UNCTAD, 1997). And while the growth rate in Japanese FDI has since fallen slightly, corporate Japan has continued to pursue an internationalization strategy. This increasing internationalization of Japanese industry is perhaps best reflected in the continued growth of Japan's overseas production ratio. This ratio measures the proportion of total (Japanese) manufacturing output produced offshore:[15] in 1985, it was 3 per cent of domestic output, by 2002, it had risen sixfold, to 18.2 per cent. Furthermore, in 2002, Japan's transnationals produced 37.2 per cent of their total output overseas, again up from 8.7 per cent in 1985.[16] In 2002, Japan's transnationals directly employed approximately 3.14 million foreign employees – up from just over 1.1 million in 1992 – in their offshore affiliates around the globe (all data from METI, 2003; Ito, 2003).

The reported data are indicative of the growing extent to which Japan's corporate giants have become involved in transnational production networks – sometimes referred to as the 'new (overseas)' *keiretsu*. These networks primarily involve production linkages across the economies of Asia, North America and Europe through the operations of Japanese-affiliated and group companies. It is through these networks that Japan's corporations have been able to exercise their corporate power and engage in the 'divide and rule' of both world governments and international labour (see section III).[17] Moreover, the global expansion of corporate Japan has – as we shall argue – been detrimental for the performance of Japan's domestic welfare, but it has nullified the ability of MITI and the Japanese state to successfully manage the direction of the Japanese economy.

V INDUSTRIAL STAGNATION AND 'HOLLOWING OUT'

The first consequence of the globalization of Japanese industry is that it is likely investment expenditures have been diverted away from Japan's industrial regions in favour of overseas locations, thus reducing the future potential for indigenous growth within Japan. Given that corporate Japan now takes a global view in allocating its limited investment expenditures, this is likely to be significant. These investment funds are limited in supply since the majority of Japanese corporations rely upon net earnings as the major source of net finance for new industrial investment (Corbett and Jenkinson, 1996; Yaginuma, 1997). Moreover, with imperfect capital markets, transnational firms are likely to distribute their internally generated funds between competing international locations (Stevens and Lipsey, 1992). In this respect, cost considerations are likely to be a key determinant and the evidence suggests that this is indeed the case. For instance, in Japan's highly important machinery sector, the behaviour of domestic investment (and employment) is highly sensitive to international wage differentials: both domestic investment and employment functions being relatively elastic with respect to variations in international wages (Tomlinson, 2002). Concerns were also raised during the mid-1990s that a substantial number of Japanese firms had been investing in low-cost offshore facilities in East Asia at the expense of domestic sites (MITI, 1996). This situation has continued with China, where wage costs are approximately one-thirtieth of those for comparable employment in Japan (Kobayashi, 2004), becoming the main substitute for Japanese investment in Asia (JETRO, 2004). In summary, for corporate Japan, overseas investment opportunities are increasingly more attractive than in Japan as reflected in the ever-rising overseas investment ratio (the proportion of Japanese capital invested annually overseas): 8.8 per cent in 1992, and up to 20 per cent in 2001 (METI, 2003).

In the long run, the diversion of investment in favour of cheaper overseas sites diminishes both the level and the quality of Japan's capital stock, and thus initiates and exacerbates a cumulative process of decline in Japan's industrial regions. Furthermore, given the discrepancy in the outward to

inward stock of Japanese FDI of 12:1, it is unlikely that any inward investment flows will reverse the process.[18] The growing evidence is that corporate Japan's overseas investments are primarily a substitute for domestic
production rather than a means to support complementary production
activities. A consequence of this has been the dramatic decline in employment within Japan's domestic manufacturing industry over the past decade,
with registered manufacturing employment falling from 15.69 million in
1992 to 12.22 million to 2003; over the same period, employment in overseas Japanese manufacturing plants rose by approximately two million (see
section IV). Ito (2003) reports that an estimated 600 000 of the decline in
numbers of Japan's domestic manufacturing employment during the 1990s
was a direct result of global outsourcing: his estimate takes account of the
(positive) export induction effect (sales of capital and intermediate goods
from Japan to overseas affiliates) and the (negative) export substitution
(where overseas production replaces exports) and reimportation effects[19]
(goods produced by overseas Japanese affiliates and reimported into
Japan).[20] The largest declines in domestic employment were in the machinery sector (in which Japan has long held a comparative advantage), which
has seen the greatest expansion in overseas production (Ito, 2003).

A further consideration is the effects of globalization upon Japan's small
firm sector, particularly the small *keiretsu* firms, who have become increasingly isolated and placed in a weaker bargaining position as their main contractors have resorted to the global outsourcing of intermediate goods and
services. Indeed, since the early 1990s, surveys have consistently shown that
these small firms have experienced a significant fall in their order book
volumes and been under pressure to accept lower profit margins, making it
difficult for them to earn sufficient revenue to repay long-term borrowing
commitments (see for instance, MITI, 1998, 1999). These pressures are
reflected in small firm gross profit margins in Japanese manufacturing,
which have fallen from an average of 3.5 per cent in the late 1980s (1986–91)
to zero in the period 1999–2002, while the return on capital employed has
more than halved, from an average of 5.6 per cent to 2.2 per cent over the
same time-frame. A further indicator of the pressures afflicting Japanese
small businesses is the number of small firm bankruptcies, which have continued to be extraordinarily high, averaging around 17 000 for three years
to 2003 (data obtained from the *Japanese Statistical Yearbook*, 2005).
Moreover, since the early 1990s, the exit rate of firms in Japanese manufacturing has significantly exceeded the number of business start-ups. For
Acht et al. (2004: 14) the increasing closure rate is a result of industrial
restructuring and 'hollowing out' and, in discussing the prospects for entrepreneurship in the Japanese economy (where, in contrast to most other
OECD countries, business ownership rates have been in long-term decline)

they worryingly note that 'the safe haven for small firms has disappeared and it has not been adequately replaced with an alternative institutional structure stimulating new venture creation'.[21]

The problems afflicting the *keiretsu* and the 'hollowing out' of Japanese manufacturing have been widespread across Japan: during the 1990s, all prefectures and industrial sectors experienced a significant decline in real output (approximately 10 per cent), the number of business establishments (a fall of 15 per cent) and employment (a fall of 15 per cent). The large industrial belts of Kanagawa, Tokyo, Osaka and Saitama, regions that have traditionally relied upon corporate Japan for their economic prosperity, have, not surprisingly, been particularly adversely affected. The industrial capacity of these regions fell dramatically throughout the1990s, and they experienced higher levels of unemployment than the national average (for further details and data on these and other regions, see Cowling and Tomlinson, 2003a). It is our view that the problems of deindustrialization in Japan's industrial regions significantly weaken the country's prospects for long-term economic recovery and renewal, the decline in small firm activity and entrepreneurship along with the actual and potential loss of 'vitality' and 'innovative' capacity within small firm networks being particularly detrimental to future economic growth (see also Acht et al., 2004).

The 'hollowing out' of Japanese industry has occurred despite Ozawa's (1991, 1992) optimism that the internationalization of Japanese industry would be an opportunity for Japanese industry to restructure and upgrade its manufacturing technology through the redeployment of resources into the development of higher value-added products, with traditional, declining industries being moved offshore. Ozawa envisaged that this would lead to a 'flying geese formation' of production, where advanced technological work was completed in Japan, medium value-added work is done in the newly industrialized economies (NIEs) and so on throughout Asia, the benefits of this pattern being seen as a combination of rising technological standards and the extension of product life cycles beyond Japanese and Western markets. Unfortunately for Japanese manufacturing, this does not appear to have been borne out by events. As we have argued, corporate Japan has pursued its own strategic interests, and its offshore affiliates have been increasingly used as a direct substitute for domestic production and, in some cases, product development. In the latter case, it is interesting to note Beamish et al. (1997: 26) who report a notable change in the strategy of Japan's transnationals, from establishing offshore 'assembly (plants), using parts sourced in Japan, to full manufacturing, to, in some cases, R&D located in the host country'. The *Nikkei Weekly* (18/6/2001: 4) have also reported upon the rising technological competence of the NIEs, which has led 'to an increasing number of (Japanese) firms transferring research and development activities, once considered the epitome of Japanese excellence, to (Asian) offshore affiliates'. Finally, Whittaker (1997: 58) has also noted that, in production, it now only takes a matter of months before the latest Japanese-designed, sophisticated products are able to be manufactured offshore, in East Asia, to serve both Japanese and Western markets. In short, the purported benefits of the internationalization of Japanese industry have not been realized.

We turn, finally, to the issue of the various 'negative shocks' that have afflicted Japan's macroeconomy over the last decade and a half and which are often cited by commentators as being the main factors behind Japan's economic malaise during this period. In this regard, the 'negative shocks' primarily referred to are (a) the yen–dollar realignment arising from the Plaza Accord in the mid-1980s, which had the effect of reducing both asset and production costs in the USA and other countries relative to Japan and is seen as precipitating the outflow of Japanese FDI (Kogut and Chang, 1996) and the subsequent 'hollowing out' of Japanese manufacturing (JSBRI, 1996);[22] and (b) various fiscal and monetary policy mistakes such as the Hesei boom in the late 1980s, which encouraged a speculative asset price 'bubble' and the subsequent 1989 Tokyo stock market crash and the 1991 property market collapse. We would agree that such events have undoubtedly played a part in Japan's economic stagnation during the 1990s, adversely affecting both business confidence and expectations within the Japanese economy. Yet it is our contention that a focus upon the real economy and the activities of corporate Japan (and the pursuit of its own strategic and commercial interests) in particular, reveals more fundamental insights: it allows us to explore the roots of Japan's economic decline. In the aggregate, it is the micro-activities of Japan's giant corporations which have the most impact upon the behaviour of (Japanese) macroeconomic variables, and it is this that underpins many of the strategic failures of the Japanese economy during the 1990s.

In this regard, the apparent failure of successive expansionary fiscal and monetary policies to halt Japan's deflationary spiral during the 1990s was a direct consequence of Japan's changing industrial structure, which – as we have argued – has been shaped by its corporate elite. For instance, the growth in overseas production has had an overall negative effect upon domestic output and employment, while the increase in global outsourcing has left Japan's small business sector increasingly vulnerable, bereft of profitable business opportunities. As has been all too apparent in the Japanese case, low business and consumer confidence renders looser monetary policy and/or Keynesian fiscal expansions ineffective. Until these structural issues are addressed, Japan is unlikely to return to a more stable, long-run development path.

VI CONCLUSIONS

Japan's economic crisis during the 1990s was a classic example of the deficiencies associated with transnational monopoly capitalism. The seeds of this crisis were sown during an earlier stage of Japan's economic development, with Japanese industrial policy, however well intentioned, containing a fundamental flaw in that it generally favoured the growth and expansion of corporate Japan. Over time, MITI's ability to influence the direction of industry in the public interest diminished, with economic power effectively being yielded to Japan's giant corporations. These corporations shaped the country's industrial structure and economic development to suit their own strategic interests with production being organized, contrary to popular perceptions in the management literature, along hierarchical lines and control (within the Japanese corporation) being exercised by an elite corporate group of strategic decision makers. This corporate elite has, for some time now, pursued a strategy of global expansionism, developing and extending its own transnational production networks, to the extent that such activities are no longer compatible with the wider Japanese public interest: a situation we have described as 'strategic failure'.

Japan is, of course, not alone in being afflicted by 'strategic failure'. Both the USA and Europe have continued to suffer periodic crises associated with rising industrial concentration and transnational monopoly capitalism. These crises create long-term problems that have a real impact upon the fabric of society and economic development: persistently high unemployment in the case of Continental Europe and growing income and wealth inequalities (with its adverse consequences) in the UK and the USA. Furthermore, with increasing globalization, other countries have not been immune to such crises: the Pacific Rim economies appear to have lost their former vitality (with countries such as Taiwan and South Korea also now experiencing 'hollowing out' (see Ito, 2003)), the so-called developing world continues to underperform, while South America and the former Soviet Union have experienced similar problems. The common denominator in all these situations has been one of growing corporate power and global expansionism by transnational corporations and a genuine lack of economic democracy. The Japanese case does, however, provide a salutary lesson for industrial policy insofar as policy initiatives that attempt to marry the strategic interests of the corporate sector with the wider public interest are likely to end in an unhappy divorce, with society being the ultimate loser.[23]

At a fundamental level, the challenge for Japanese industrial policy (and elsewhere) in the twenty-first century is to seek ways to diffuse the concentration of strategic decision making away from the corporate elites towards a system that encourages wider social and economic participation. Overcoming 'strategic failure' is no easy task, although we have suggested in our other work that a starting point might be to consider exploring the possibility of promoting non-hierarchical modes of production, perhaps along the lines of the traditional 'industrial district' (see Cowling and Tomlinson, 2003a, 2003b). It is beyond the scope of this chapter to consider this possibility in detail here, although we note that the relative economic success of this type of industrial structure in regions of Italy and Germany, where horizontal networks of small firms have successfully been able to challenge the dominance of the giant transnationals (see Best, 1990) suggests an alternative mode of production might be viable. For Japan (and indeed other countries), exploring such a possibility may offer the chance to transform the economy and allow the country to move towards a more stable and sustainable development path, while also serving the wider public interest.

NOTES

1. Internal growth provides a widening span of opportunities for both managers and other employees and is suggested to reflect a wider concern with the human resources of the firm (see Odagiri, 1992).
2. The early monopoly capitalism literature is primarily attributed to Steindl (1952), who had, in turn, been strongly influenced by Kalecki (1939, 1971). Further analysis is contained in Baran and Sweezy (1966), which is updated and extended by Cowling (1982). For an application of the arguments in an international context, see Cowling and Sugden (1987, 1994), with a more recent update provided by Cowling and Tomlinson (2005).
3. The ability of labour to reverse this process has been increasingly nullified by the corporate sector over the decades (see Cowling and Tomlinson, 2005).
4. A reduction in the domestic household propensity to save and/or an increase in household debt levels are other possibilities by which effective demand might be sustained. However, given the empirically observed low propensities to save (see Ruggles, 1993) and high levels of personal indebtedness in the industrialized world, such measures are unlikely to be sustainable in the long run.
5. For some recent evidence on the deficiencies of transnational monopoly capitalism, see Cowling and Tomlinson (2005).
6. For other contributions on this theme see, for instance, Abegglen and Stalk (1985) and Kenny and Florida (1988, 1993).
7. This issue, along with relevant data, is explored in further detail by Coffey and Tomlinson (2003a: 125–32). Drawing upon earlier work by Cusumano (1985), they argue that, if one considers an assembler's controlling equity stake in a supplier to be 20 per cent (as suggested by Berle and Means, 1932), rather than the standard 50 per cent ownership threshold, then it could be construed that the degree of vertical integration in the Japanese automobile industry is actually higher than that recorded in the North American assemblers.
8. Indeed, it is worth noting that Japanese assemblers rely upon multiple-sourcing of production to a far greater extent than their North American competitors. For instance, Womack et al. (1990: 157) report that, for Japan, just over 12 per cent of parts were single-sourced by assemblers, compared to almost 70 per cent in the USA: this refers to

the situation for first-tier suppliers, although it is recognized that multiple sourcing is also the norm further down the chain.

9. For instance, Adio Kodani, a former Nissan-appointed President of the Nissan-affiliated supplier Ikeda Bussan, notes that 'the keiretsu served to create a comfortable vertical supply structure for Nissan, rather than as a structure to make affiliates stronger' (*Nikkei Weekly*, 21 August 2000). A similar perspective is offered by Kono (1984: 127) who remarks that the keiretsu supplier 'perceives that Toyota's policy is "not to kill, neither to keep alive easily"'.

10. In terms of shareholdings, analysis by Sheard (1994: 310) argues that the major shareholders of Japanese corporations are concentrated among a few shareholders who exercise joint control.

11. We might also point out that, in terms of employment conditions, the benefits and privileges afforded to Japanese workers have tended to be only available to those in the leading firms: those employed in lower-tier subcontractors are excluded and typically endure worse employment conditions (Ruigrok and Van Tulder, 1995: 25, 46–51). Moreover, in the automobile industry, Womack et al. (1990: 158–9) applaud the use of Japanese assemblers using multiple sourcing strategies to mitigate the threat of trade union militancy, a strategy that suppresses the ability of workers to bargain effectively for better employment conditions (see also note 9).

12. Johnson provides the most comprehensive review of Japanese industrial policy in the post-war period. A summary is provided by Cowling and Tomlinson (2000: F362–4).

13. On this, it is also worth considering Ruigrok and Tate's (1996) account of activities within MITI's publicly funded testing and research centres for small firms in the automotive industry. The authors reveal that these centres ultimately became the preserve of Japan's giant assemblers and a mechanism by which to exert further control over their suppliers.

14. The nature of competition has predominantly been one of regional and global oligopolistic interdependence and it is interesting to note in this regard the behaviour of Japanese corporations insofar as, like their Western rivals, they have strategically undertaken both 'aggressive' and 'defensive' investments to expand and protect their local, regional and (ultimately) global market share. Some evidence of this so-called Knickerbocker (1973) effect for Japanese corporations is provided by Yu and Ito (1988), in the case of Japanese investments in the US tyre and textile industries, Dunning (1994) for the entry of Japanese machinery firms in Europe, and Tomlinson (2005) for the global entry patterns of Japanese automotive corporations.

15. The overseas production ratio (as with the overseas investment ratio discussed in section V) is calculated using data from METI's annual survey of Japanese transnationals. Given that these surveys are typically vulnerable to variance in coverage and response rates, it is wise to treat such statistics with caution (Ramstetter, 1996). Nevertheless, in the absence of alternative data sources, and taken in conjunction with the other evidence presented here, the overseas production ratio is a useful indicator of the internationalization of the Japanese economy.

16. In contrast, over a period (1985–99) for which comparable data are available, overseas production rose less significantly in other major industrialized countries, such as Germany and the USA (MITI, 1999).

17. A case in point was Toyota's ability (in the late 1990s) successfully to play off both the UK and French governments in the pursuit of a 'lucrative' investment package for their new European production site (which was eventually built in Lens, Northern France). As far as the 'divide and rule' of workers is concerned, James (1989) notes that, by locating new production units in areas characterized by low trade union density, low wages and high unemployment, Japanese transnationals have successfully been able to play the 'international wage game'. Further evidence on the divide and rule of workers by Japanese transnationals is also provided in Coffey and Tomlinson (2003b: 13–14).

18. Indeed, inward FDI might even exacerbate deindustrialization in Japan. For instance, Renault's purchase of a controlling interest in Nissan and General Motors' increased equity participation in Isuzu led to automobile plant closures and substantial redundancies in Japan's major industrial belts.

19. According to METI (2003), 85 per cent of reimports are from low-cost Japanese affiliates based in East Asia.
20. If we also consider the indirect effects of global outsourcing, the loss of jobs in Japanese manufacturing due to overseas expansion is likely to be much greater than 600 000.
21. The 'safe haven' here refers to the traditional *keiretsu* structure which, although highly exploitive (see section III), at least to some extent provided (for the majority of subcontractors) a minimum guaranteed income stream.
22. In contrast, we would argue that it is unlikely that (short-run) exchange rate fluctuations are the prime driver behind overseas Japanese FDI, since transnationals typically base their long-run international production decisions upon economic fundamentals, such as access to lower wages and foreign markets (Dunning, 1988). Thus, while, the Yen's appreciation following the 1985 Plaza Accord (a realignment that, to a large extent, reflected the earlier success of corporate Japan's export expansion), may well have affected the timing of subsequent overseas Japanese investments, it is unlikely to have had much impact upon corporate Japan's long-run moves towards global expansion via international production.
23. In this respect, there are some interesting parallels between Japan's crisis and those experienced in Sweden. In the Swedish case, industrial policy was one of 'social corporatism', where the state sought cooperation between the corporate sector and trade unions to pursue various labour market and welfare policies to minimize the threat and impact of severe unemployment during the global economic downturn of the 1970s and 1980s. Yet, while such cooperation was generally effective during this period, the price was that industrial policy was engineered in favour of Sweden's transnational corporations at the expense of the small business sector. The subsequent breakdown of the Swedish model has led to lower levels of entrepreneurship and innovation, lower productivity growth and higher unemployment (for further details see, Blomström and Kokko, 1997).

REFERENCES

Abegglen, J.C. and G. Stalk (1985), *Kaisha, the Japanese Corporation*, New York: Basic Books.

Acht, J.V., J. Stam, R. Thurik and I. Verheul (2004), 'Business ownership and unemployment in Japan', Tinbergen Institute discussion paper, TI 2004-036/3.

Aoki, M. (1984), 'Aspects of the Japanese firm', in M. Aoki (ed.), *The Economic Analysis of the Japanese Firm*, Amsterdam: North-Holland, pp. 3–43.

Aoki, M. (1988), *Information, Incentives and Bargaining in the Japanese Economy*, Cambridge: Cambridge University Press.

Aoki, M. (1989), 'The participatory generation of information rents and the theory of the firm', in M. Aoki, B. Gustafsson and O.E. Williamson (eds), *The Firm as a Nexus of Treaties*, London: Sage, pp. 26–51.

Aoki, M. (1990), 'Toward an economic model of the Japanese firm', *Journal of Economic Literature*, **28**(1), 1–27.

Aoki, M. (1994), 'The Japanese firm as a system of attributes: a survey and research agenda', in M. Aoki and R. Dore (eds), *The Japanese Firm, Sources of Competitive Strength*, Oxford: Oxford University Press, pp. 11–40.

Bailey, D., G. Harte and R. Sugden (1994), *Transnationals and Governments, Recent Policies in Japan, France, Germany and the USA and Britain*, London: Routledge.

Baran, P.A. and P.M. Sweezy (1966), *Monopoly Capital*, Penguin: Harmondsworth.

Beamish, P.W., A. Delios and D.J. Lecraw (1997), *Japanese Multinationals in the Global Economy*, Cheltenham, UK and Lyme, US: Edward Elgar.

Berle, A.A. and G.C. Means (1932), *The Modern Corporation and Private Property*, New York: Macmillan.

Best, M.H. (1990), *The New Competition*, London: Polity Press.

Blomström, M. and A. Kokko (1997), 'Sweden', in J.H. Dunning (ed.), *Governments, Globalisation and International Business*, Oxford: Oxford University Press, pp. 359–76.

Coffey, D. and P.R. Tomlinson (2003a), 'Globalisation, vertical relations and the J-mode firm', *Journal of Post Keynesian Economics*, Fall, **26**(1), 117–44.

Coffey, D. and P.R. Tomlinson (2003b), 'Co-ordination and hierarchy in the Japanese firm: the strategic decision making approach vs. Aoki', in M. Waterson (ed.), *Competition, Monopoly and Corporate Governance, Essays in Honour of Keith Cowling*, Cheltenham, UK and Northampton, MA, USA: Edward Elgar, pp. 3–19.

Corbett, J. and T. Jenkinson (1996), 'The financing of industry, 1970–1989: an international comparison', *Journal of the Japanese and International Economies*, **10**(1), 71–96.

Cowling, K. (1982), *Monopoly Capitalism*, London: The Macmillan Press.

Cowling, K. and R. Sugden (1987), *Transnational Monopoly Capitalism*, Brighton: Wheatsheaf.

Cowling, K. and R. Sugden (1994), *Beyond Capitalism, Towards a New Order*, London: Pinter.

Cowling, K. and R. Sugden (1999), 'The wealth of localities, regions and nations: developing multinational economies', *New Political Economy*, **4**(3), 361–78.

Cowling, K. and P.R. Tomlinson (2000), 'The Japanese crisis: a case of strategic failure?', *The Economic Journal*, **110**(No. 464), F358–81.

Cowling, K. and P.R. Tomlinson (2002), 'Revisiting the roots of Japan's economic stagnation: the role of the Japanese corporation', *International Review of Applied Economics*, **16**(4), 373–90.

Cowling, K. and P.R. Tomlinson (2003a), 'The problem of regional hollowing out in Japan: lessons for regional industrial policy', in R. Sugden, R.H. Cheung and G.R. Meadows (eds), *Urban and Regional Prosperity in a Globalised New Economy*, Cheltenham, UK and Northampton, MA, USA: Edward Elgar, pp. 33–58.

Cowling, K. and P.R. Tomlinson (2003b), 'Industrial policy, transnational corporations and the problem of "hollowing out" in Japan', in D. Coffey and C. Thornley (eds), *Industrial and Labour Market Policy and Performance*, London: Routledge, pp. 62–82.

Cowling, K. and P.R. Tomlinson (2005), 'Globalisation and corporate power', *Contributions to Political Economy*, **24**, 33–54.

Cusumano, M.A. (1985), *The Japanese Automobile Industry: Technology and Management at Nissan and Toyota*, Cambridge, MA and London: Harvard University Press.

Dodwell Marketing Consultants (1997), *The Structure of the Japanese Auto-Parts Industry*, Tokyo: Dodwell.

Dunning, J.H. (1988), 'The theory of international production', *The International Trade Journal*, **3**, Fall.

Dunning, J.H. (1994), 'The strategy of Japanese and US manufacturing investment in Europe', in M. Mason and D. Encarnation (eds), *Does Ownership Matter? Japanese Multinationals in Europe*, Oxford: Clarendon Press, pp. 59–86.

Gerlach, M.L. (1992), *Alliance Capitalism: The Social Organisation of Japanese Business*, Berkeley, CA: University of California Press.

Graham, A. and A. Seldon (1990), *Government and Economies in the Post-War World, Economic Policies and Comparative Economic Performance 1945–1985*, London: Routledge.

Ito, M. (2003), 'Hollowing out of the Japanese manufacturing industry and regional employment development', Japan Institute for Labour Policy and Training Research Paper.

James, B.G. (1989), *Trojan Horse: The Ultimate Japanese Challenge to Western Industry*, London: Mercury.

Japan Small Business Research Institute (JSBRI) (1996), *The Age of Small Business: The Foundation for Reconstruction of the Japanese Economy*, Tokyo: MITI.

Japan Statistics Bureau (2005), *Japanese Statistical Yearbook*, Tokyo: Japan Statistical Association.

Japanese External Trade Organisation (JETRO) (2004), 'Expanding Japanese presence in East Asia reflects shift to offshore production', JETRO Working Paper, no.1 (January), JETRO, Tokyo.

Johnson, C. (1982), *MITI and the Japanese Miracle: the growth of industrial policy 1925–1975*, Stanford, CA: Stanford University Press.

Kalecki, M. (1939), *Essays in the Theory of Economic Fluctuation*, London: Allen and Unwin.

Kalecki, M. (1971), *Selected Essays on the Dynamics of the Capitalist Economy*, Cambridge: Cambridge University Press.

Katz, R. (1998), *Japan the System that Soured – the Rise and Fall of the Japanese Miracle*, New York: M.E. Sharpe.

Kenny, M. and R. Florida (1988, 1993), 'Beyond mass production: production and labour processes in Japan', *Politics and Society*, **16**(1), 121–58.

Kenney, M. and R. Florida (1993), *Beyond Mass Production: the Japanese System and its Transfer to the US*, New York: Oxford University Press.

Knickerbocker, F.T. (1973), *Oligopolistic Reaction and Multinational Enterprise*, Cambridge, MA: Harvard University Press.

Kobayashi, H. (2004), 'Responses of South Korea, Taiwan and Japan to the hollowing out of industry', mimeo, Waseda University.

Kogut, B. and S.J. Chang (1996), 'Platform investments and volatile exchange rates: direct investment in the US by Japanese electronic companies', *Review of Economics and Statistics*, **79**, 221–31.

Kono, T. (1984), *Strategy and Structure of Japanese Enterprises*, London: Macmillan.

Koo, A.Y.C. and S. Martin (1984), 'Market structure and US trade flows', *International Journal of Industrial Organisation*, **2**(3), September, 173–97.

Mason, A. (1994), 'Historical perspectives on Japanese direct investment in Europe', in M. Mason and D. Encarnation (eds), *Does Ownership Matter? Japanese Multinationals in Europe*, Oxford: Clarendon Press, pp. 1–38.

Ministry of Economy, Trade and Industry (METI, formerly MITI) (2003), *Summary of the 32nd Annual Survey of Overseas Business Activities of Japanese Companies*, Tokyo: METI.

Ministry of International Trade and Industry (MITI) (1996), *Highlights of the Corporate Survey on Overseas Operating Strategy*, Tokyo: MITI.

Ministry of International Trade and Industry (MITI) (1998), *Summary of the 27th Annual Survey of Overseas Business Activities of Japanese Companies*, Tokyo: MITI.

Ministry of International Trade and Industry (MITI) (1999), *Small Business in Japan*, White Paper on Small and Medium Enterprises in Japan, Tokyo: MITI.

Miwa, Y. (1996), *Firms and Industrial Organisation in Japan*, New York: New York University Press.

Nikkei Weekly (21/8/2000), 'Nissan steps up dismantling of keiretsu', Nihon Keizai Shimbun Inc., New York.

Nikkei Weekly (18/6/2001), 'Japanese R&D trickling overseas: skilled, cheap work forces in other Asian nations attracting Japanese firms', Nihon Keizai Shimbun Inc., New York.

Odagiri, H. (1992), *Growth through Competition: Strategic Management and the Economy of Japan*, Oxford: Clarendon Press.

Ozawa, T. (1991), 'Japan in a new phase of multinationalism and industrial upgrading: functional integration of trade, growth and FDI', *Journal of World Trade*, **25**, 43–60.

Ozawa, T. (1992), 'Cross investments between Japan and the EC: income similarity, technological congruity and economies of scope', in J. Cantwell (ed.), *Multinational Investment in Modern Europe: Strategic Interaction in the Integrated Community*, Aldershot, UK and Brookfield, US: Edward Elgar, pp. 13–45.

Piore, M. and C. Sabel (1984), *The Second Industrial Divide: Possibilities for Prosperity*, New York: Basic Books.

Ramstetter, E.D. (1996), 'Estimating economic activities by Japanese transnational corporations: how to make sense of the data', *Transnational Corporations*, **5**(2), 107–43.

Ruggles, R. (1993), 'Accounting for saving and capital formation in the United States 1947–1991', *Journal of Economic Perspectives*, **7**(2), 3–17.

Ruigrok, W. and J.J. Tate (1996), 'Public testing and research centres in Japan: control and nurturing of small and medium sized enterprises in the automobile industry', *Technology Analysis & Strategic Management*, **8**(4), 381–401.

Ruigrok, W. and R. Van Tulder (1995), *The Logic of International Restructuring*, London: Routledge.

Schaede, U. (2000), *Co-operative Capitalism: Self-Regulation, Trade Associations and the Antimonopoly Law in Japan*, Oxford: Oxford University Press.

Scher, M.J. (1997), *Japanese Inter-firm Networks and their Main Banks*, London: Macmillan.

Sheard, P. (1994), 'Interlocking shareholdings and corporate governance', in M. Aoki and R. Dore (eds), *The Japanese Firm, Sources of Competitive Strength*, Oxford: Oxford University Press, pp. 310–49.

Smitka, M.J. (1991), 'Competitive ties: subcontracting in the Japanese automotive industry', Columbia University, New York.

Steindl, J. (1952), *Maturity and Stagnation in American Capitalism*, Oxford: Oxford University Press.

Stevens, G.V.G. and R.E. Lipsey (1992), 'Interactions between domestic and foreign investment', *Journal of International Money and Finance*, **11**, 40–62.

Teece, D.J. (1993), 'The dynamics of industrial capitalism: perspectives on Alfred Chandler's scale and scope', *Journal of Economic Literature*, **31**, 199–225.

Tomlinson, P.R. (2002), 'The real effects of transnational activity upon investment and labour demand within Japan's machinery industries', *International Review of Applied Economics*, **16**(2), 107–29.

Tomlinson, P.R. (2005), 'The overseas entry patterns of Japanese automobile assemblers, 1960–2000: globalisation of manufacturing capacity and the role of strategic contingency', *International Journal of Automotive and Technology Management*, **5**(3), 284–304.

United Nations Conference on Trade and Development (UNCTAD) (1993), *World Investment Report*, New York: UN.
United Nations Conference on Trade and Development (UNCTAD) (1997), *World Investment Report*, New York: UN.
Whittaker, D.H. (1997), *Small Firms in the Japanese Economy*, Cambridge: Cambridge University Press.
Womack, J.P., D.T. Jones and D. Roos (1990), *The Machine that Changed the World*, New York: Rawson Associates.
Yaginuma, H. (1997), 'Fixed investments and finance sources: from a national to a global perspective', in JCIP (ed.), *Report of the Japan Commission on Industrial Performance JCIP, Made in Japan – Revitalising Japanese Manufacturing for Economic Growth*, Cambridge, MA: MIT Press, pp. 311–34.
Yu, C.M.J. and K. Ito (1988), 'Oligopolistic reaction and foreign direct investment: the case of the US tire and textile industries', *Journal of International Business Studies*, **19**, 449–60.

5. Globalization and the Japanese subcontractor system

Ulrike Schaede

I INTRODUCTION: GLOBALIZATION OF PRODUCTION AND 'HOLLOWING OUT'

When Japanese companies began to build plants outside Japan in the 1970s and 1980s, the media coined a frightening term for what was considered a new, dooming trend: *kūdōka*, the 'hollowing out' of Japan's industrial base. With ongoing globalization in the 1990s, the prophecies became ever more menacing: in 2002, the Fuji Research Institute estimated that, between 2002 and 2010, domestic production would fall by ¥8.8 trillion (roughly $85 billion), GDP would fall by 1.7 per cent and employment by 1.25 million (cited in SD, 2002). In 2003, the Japan Research Institute forecast that, if the current growth rate in imports from Asia were to continue, by 2005 alone another 300 000 jobs in Japan would be lost in addition to the two million already displaced by foreign production throughout the 1990s.[1] In the same year, a government council warned, not entirely tongue-in-cheek, that if the current rate of overseas FDI (foreign direct investment) by Japanese firms were to continue, no manufacturing plants would be left in Japan by 2018.[2]

The debate is similar to that of 'off-shoring' in the USA, albeit with the important difference that the USA is a large recipient of FDI in manufacturing, such as for car and electronics plants by Japanese and Korean companies, whereas Japan is not. Even in Japan the doomsday prophesies of 'hollowing out' are perhaps intended, not to cause panic but simply to draw attention to a phenomenon that is fundamentally affecting Japan's industrial structure, in terms of both employment and industrial organization, in particular as it pertains to Japan's highly appraised system of subcontracting.

Not all observers agree that hollowing out is necessarily negative. To help in this evaluation, Kwan (cited in *The Japan Times*, 2003) differentiates between 'good' and 'bad' hollowing out: the former refers to investments abroad with clear economic efficiency goals that eventually contribute to increased productivity and profitability in the industry, thus contributing to economic growth and the necessary reorientation of Japan's economic activities towards higher value-added activities. FDI coming into China with the goal of reducing labour costs by relocating simple assembly processes, while reinvesting the profits into R&D centres in Japan would be an example of 'good' FDI. In contrast, 'bad' hollowing out refers to FDI abroad in reaction to trade barriers and other market-disturbing mechanisms; an example is a car plant abroad that serves the single purpose of adhering to local content rules and avoiding tariffs. Little overall economic gain is reaped from such an investment, and the effect on Japan is negative.[3]

Proponents of the negative view, in contrast, argue that it matters in which country employments and profits are generated, partly because of the diversity of the labour force in each country: not all labour can move into higher value-added activities such as R&D (leaving alone intricate corporate strategy issues of necessary co-location of manufacturing and R&D), so that relocating a car plant to China in order to save on labour costs will negatively impact local employment, regardless of the move's macroeconomic efficiencies. Neither can loss in employment and wages simply be compensated by cheaper import prices. Thus, given that labour is not perfectly mobile in terms of skill change, hollowing out is leaving Japan with large numbers of displaced, structurally unemployed workers. Moreover, the negative view also warns of a vicious cycle set in motion if Japan's basic economic logic is challenged by the shrinking economy and trade surplus, including prospects of increasing long-term interest rates, a weakening of the exchange rate and a collapse of the stock market (Sd, 2002: 30).

In 2003, the research department of Shōkō Chūkin, the small firm bank, conducted a study in which it graphed differences in positive versus negative effects of globalization by industry (Shoko Research Institute (SRI), 2003). Figure 5.1 replicates this concept, in which the two axes represent import penetration and labour productivity. Protected industries with decreasing labour productivity are considered in long-term decline, whereas industries that experience rising import penetration and decreasing labour productivity are in 'hollowing out' status. In contrast, industries in which global production has led to increased labour productivity are referred to as 'level up' industries. In calculating the rate of change in productivity and imports from 1995 to 2001, SRI (2003) shows that textiles, precision machinery, general machinery, plastics and metal products, and the kiln industries (cement, glass) are being 'hollowed out', whereas electronics, non-ferrous metals, chemistry and paper and pulp are being 'levelled up' thanks to increased productivity with increased imports. Meanwhile, automobiles, steel and petroleum/mining are found to continue to benefit from rather closed domestic markets while experiencing productivity increases. One

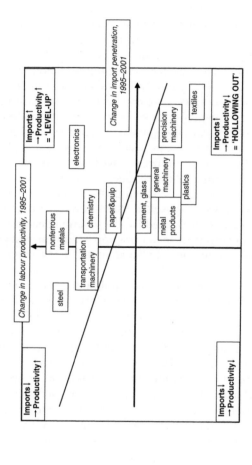

Note: Import penetration is scaled between −8 per cent and 14 per cent; labour productivity from −3 per cent to 6 per cent. The trendline indicates an overall increase in imports and decrease in labour productivity during this period.

Source: Adapted from SRI (2003:33).

Figure 5.1 Globalization effects on Japanese industry, by import penetration and labour productivity

should note, however, that 'automobiles' is a somewhat complicated category, because many Japanese makers received substantial foreign capital injections during this period (Nissan by Renault, Mazda by Ford and Mitsubishi Motors by DaimlerChrysler). Although import penetration may have stagnated or decreased during this period, globalization of this industry has nevertheless been pushed forward dramatically.

One problem with evaluating the implications of hollowing out for domestic employment is that the effects are noisy, in particular in Japan, where the big push abroad occurred during the extended recession of the 1990s. To what extent, then, is the doubling of Japan's unemployment rate in that period due to hollowing out rather than the recession? For example, Itami (2004) argues that the main reason for declining employment in manufacturing in the 1990s is not hollowing out, but rather the combination of depressed Japanese consumption with increased labour productivity. At the same time, increased production abroad has triggered exports, both of specialized plant and equipment, and of parts and materials. Moreover, increased imports from Asia have created new jobs (anything from longshoremen to trading company employees) so that hollowing out needs to be appreciated for the spark it has given non-manufacturing jobs in Japan (see, for instance, Ryan, 2003).

Rather than taking sides in the employment discussion, this chapter draws attention to another ramification of 'hollowing out': the challenges it poses to one pillar of Japan's industrial organization, the subcontractor system. The special features of Japan's long-term, stable outsourcing system have been analysed in detail, and the system is considered one of the great contributors to Japan's long-term success in manufacturing (see Aoki, 1988; Asanuma, 1989; McMillan, 1990; Smitka, 1991). The entire Toyota Production System is characterized as hinging on an array of large numbers of long-term, exclusive subcontractors that deliver parts just-in-time so that flow can be smoothed, waste minimized and production efficiency maximized, all the while building quality improvements into the production process in real time (see Monden, 1993; Cole, 1983, 1994; Dyer, 2000; Nishiguchi, 1994; Liker, 2004).

The question, then, is what changes we can observe in terms of subcontractor relations in those industries most affected by globalization. During the 1990s, Japan witnessed a pronounced decline in the rate of small firms that were subcontractors for large manufacturers. The two main explanations for this surprising development (in light of the amount of studies praising the subcontractor system's advantages for high-quality production) are related to globalization. First, as the large manufacturers moved their plants abroad, they built new suppliers in that locality (as would be necessary for just-in-time delivery). Large, important Japanese suppliers were asked to open subsidiaries abroad to continue the relationships, whereas the lesser ones were simply left behind. Second, as globalization increased world price competition for the Japanese manufacturers, suddenly the subcontractor system was considered too expensive, even within Japan. As FDI into Japan (in addition to the cheaper reimports from China) increased competition in the home market, machinery, electronics, textiles and car makers had to re-evaluate, and greatly reduce, their subcontractor line-up.

This chapter analyses these two observed phenomena associated with globalization in terms of Japan's subcontractor system, by presenting data on both trends. It finds that the ongoing shift of production abroad has coincided with new global cost pressures in manufacturing that have also affected production processes within Japan. The exclusive subcontractor system that has made Japan famous has become a strategic disadvantage, and Japanese firms have opened this system up to more competition. Just as in the labour market, the deindustrialization process is not all negative, for it helps the weeding out of outdated, insufficiently productive suppliers from Japan's industrial base. Survivors remain all the stronger for it. It is left for further studies to show just how the Toyota Production System (and its variants in other industries) is affected by this basic change in industrial organization.

II GLOBALIZATION

In 1999, Japan's outward-bound FDI totalled ¥74 trillion, and its total foreign production ¥50 trillion. This compared with exports of ¥48 trillion; in other words, Japan was producing more abroad than it was exporting (Kobayashi, 2003: 75). Perhaps more impressive still is the overall trend, in particular the recent China boom. What is important to note, however, is that this is not a new development, but rather the next stage in a process that began in the 1970s when the main exporting industries opened plants in South East Asia, Europe and the USA. What is new in this current phase is that it has triggered new competition within Japan (for example, through the Nissan–Renault tie-up), such that it is beginning to affect Japanese production processes at home. A look at the data highlights these developments.

The Overall Picture

Figure 5.2 shows Japan's exports and imports over time and by region. Over the past 30 years, Japan's trade focus has shifted from the United States to East Asia, as Asia now accounts for more than 43 per cent of Japan's imports and exports, whereas trade with the USA accounts for less than a quarter of both. To be sure, an important reason for the decline in exports

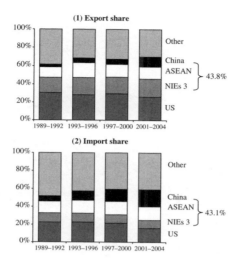

Source: Adapted from *Trade Statistics of Japan* (www.customs.go.jp/toukei/suii/html/time_e.htm).

Figure 5.2 Exports and imports, by region

to the USA is Japan's continuing high rate of FDI into the USA, meaning that Japanese products sold in America are increasingly made there. Still, the shift of Japan's trade towards Asia over the last 30 years is clear. During this time, globalization has also greatly advanced, and it has affected Japan in three main ways. First, with the appreciation of the Yen after 1985, overall exports have declined and imports increased, which has reduced Japan's trade surplus. As shown in Figure 5.3, the import penetration ratio (mining and manufacturing only) has risen from roughly 7 per cent to over 12 per cent, overseas production has reached 17 per cent of total production and the investment in outward-bound FDI accounts for more than a quarter of all corporate plant and equipment investments. Second, households have benefited from this trend in that more imports mean lower prices and more choices, which has reduced the cost of living in Japan and created new demand for services. Third, overseas production has led to vertical specialization (that is, increased intra-industry trade), which has increased competition within industries and affected Japan's industrial organization (Cabinet Office (CO), Government of Japan 2004, Section I).

As for foreign direct investment, one has to differentiate between inbound and outbound, as well as between manufacturing versus financial. Japan's 'financial openness' (the ratio of GDP over accumulated foreign investment) has increased greatly in recent years, and foreign investors now

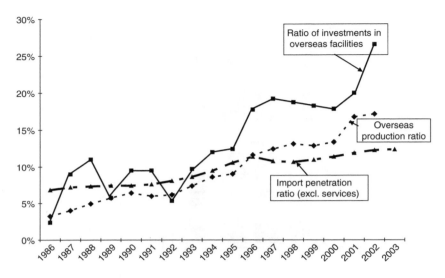

Source: Adapted from CO (2004).

Figure 5.3   *Globalization: outward-bound investments, overseas production and import penetration, 1986–2003*

own more than 25 per cent of the stock traded at the Tokyo Stock Exchange (as compared to only 7 per cent in the USA), although only 4 per cent of Japanese government bonds are in foreign hands (as compared to 41 per cent for the USA) (CO, 2004). In contrast, Figure 5.4 shows that FDI into Japan continues to be low, in particular outside the finance industries: while it has increased significantly since 1998, it is still less than half the amount of outward-bound FDI.

There are also clear patterns of Japanese FDI by country. Figure 5.5a shows that the vast majority of Japanese FDI has flown into North America (39 per cent), followed by Europe (27 per cent). Figure 5.5b looks at only the 11 largest recipient countries for the period 1989–2003, which includes the years of the 'China boom' in the late 1990s. It highlights that, in terms of cumulative investments, the USA accounts for 61 per cent of investments, and the Netherlands for 11 per cent, whereas China has received only 5 per cent of investments in that period.

Japanese Production Abroad

The hollowing out trend began in the late 1970s, and reached a peak in 1995, when a total of 1016 new Japanese establishments were opened

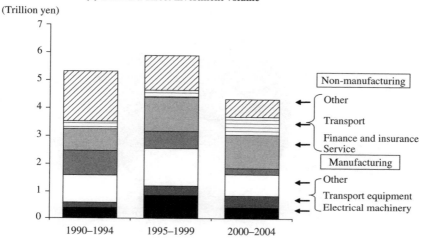

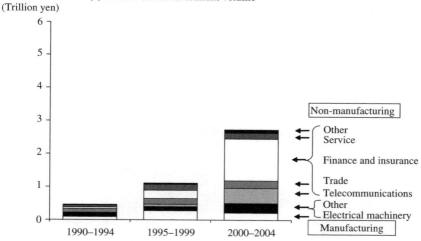

Source: Cabinet Office, Annual Report on the Japanese Economy and Public Finance (at http://www5.cao.go.jp/zenbun/wp-e/wp-te04/04-00302.html).

Figure 5.4   Trends in Japanese FDI, by industry

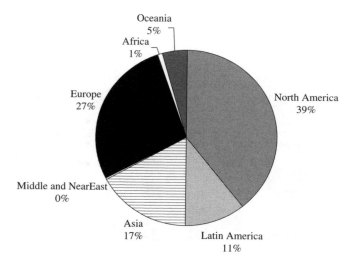

Source: Calculated from Ministry of Finance web site, 'Statistics', www.mof.go.jp.

Figure 5.5(a)   Japanese cumulative outward FDI, 1989–2003, by region (total outward FDI in that period was ¥83.8 trillion.)

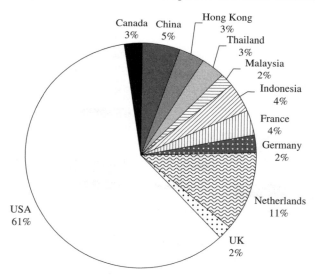

Source: Calculated from Ministry of Finance web site, 'Statistics' (www.mof.go.jp).

Figure 5.5(b)   Japanese cumulative outward FDI, 1989–2003, by country (most important recipient countries only)

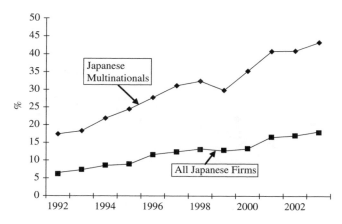

Source: *Monozukuri Haknsho* (2004), Figure 121–8.

Figure 5.6   Trends in overseas production

abroad. Since then, the number has steadily declined, to a total of 340 new openings abroad in 2001. As a result of this long-term trend of relocating production abroad, about 18 per cent of total sales by Japanese firms are now produced outside Japan; if counting only sales by Japanese firms that have overseas subsidiaries, 44 per cent of all sales are produced abroad (see Figure 5.6).[4] We have already seen, in Figure 5.3, that more than 15 per cent of total Japanese production is now located outside Japan. Figure 5.7 adds to this the insight that 28.5 per cent of all large firms in Japan, and 13 per cent of all small manufacturing firms, have overseas subsidiaries. Whereas for large firms, the level has been steadily over 25 per cent through-out the 1990s, in the small firm sector the percentage of companies with foreign subsidiaries has almost doubled.

Various surveys conducted by METI (the Ministry of Economics, Trade and Industry) in the early twenty-first century found that firms that are larger, have a higher equity ratio, higher labour productivity and higher R&D intensity are more likely to engage in FDI (Small and Medium Enterprise Agency (SMEA) 2004: 136–45). While this sounds rather plau-sible,[5] what is surprising is the relatively high rate of small firms moving production abroad. This trend is indicative of the fact that large firms are taking subcontractors with them as they build factories abroad.

One survey also indicated that, for the fiscal year 2001, 30 per cent of Japanese overseas subsidiaries were located in the USA, 25 per cent in South East Asia, 18 per cent in China and 15 per cent in the NIEs (SMEA, 2004: 136). Two-thirds of the subsidiaries in North America and Europe

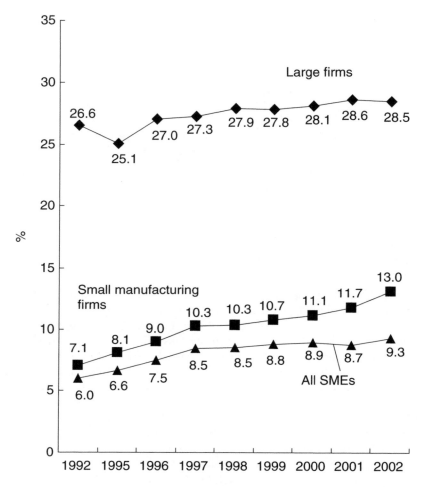

Note: 'Overseas subsidiaries' are overseas firms in which a Japanese company owns at least 20%.

Source: SMEA (2004), Figure 2-2-2.

Figure 5.7   Proportion of Japanese firms with overseas subsidiaries

were established with the goal to cater for the overseas market (that is, to circumvent trade regulations, such as local content rules and tariffs), whereas more than 60 per cent of subsidiaries in China and the NIEs were explicitly operated in order to reimport cheaper products into Japan. In particular, in South East Asia the main role of foreign subsidiaries was seen to be providing parts to the local Japanese affiliates. In other words, they operated within well-established supplier relationships with Japanese assemblers that also operated in those countries.

In 2004, Japan witnessed what one observer labelled the 'anti-hollowing out', a sudden increase in plant and equipment investment by Japanese firms in Japan.[6] After a long hiatus, Japanese firms opened plant after plant in various regions in Japan. Three possible reasons can be given for this movement (Rowley and Tashiro, 2004). First, given that the share of Japanese production capacity abroad is now at over 43 per cent (similar to the USA with 50 per cent), it may be the case that the potential gains from relocation of production have already occurred; in other words, the cost structure of Japanese manufacturers is similar to that of their rivals. Second, it is possible that the cost advantage of producing in, say, China is not as great as it is sometimes presented. Any savings on labour costs are often exceeded by other costs such as high worker turnover, quality problems, unreliable power supply and so on. Finally, protecting intellectual property continues to be difficult in some of these countries, capping the type of production that can safely be moved into those places.

Although this may indicate a reversal towards more new investment in Japan, the fact remains that almost one-fifth of total Japanese production, and 45 per cent of production by Japan's multinationals, has moved abroad. This development will invariably influence Japan's domestic industrial organization over time.

China

Between 1998 and 2003, China's exports grew by 77 per cent, and in 2002 alone they jumped by 22 per cent. In 2002, Japan registered its first trade deficit with China, as imports of $62 billion were not matched by exports of $40 billion. Moreover, in 2001 alone, 69 major Japanese firms shut down a total of 120 factories in Japan; 70 per cent of these were moved to China (Ryan, 2003). These developments have caused a 'China fear' in some Japanese circles, triggering everything from 'hollowing out deliberation councils' to highly protectionist policy proposals.

However, many observers warn of exaggerated interpretations (for instance, Kwan, cited in the *Japan Times*, 2003). For one, the share of China in Japan's imports has grown to 18.3 per cent of total, but total Japanese imports remain small, accounting for less than 1.5 per cent of Japan's GDP. Second, half of China's exports are produced by overseas firms; in the case of Japan, 60 per cent of its imports from China are reimports from Japan's electronics, car, textiles and other manufacturers (Ryan, 2003). As we saw in Figure 5.1, in some industries this has resulted in productivity gains. A third argument against the 'China angst' is that Japan's commitment in China is dwarfed by its commitment in the USA, as already shown in Figure 5.5 above. Even in the China angst period of 1998–2001, Japanese firms invested more in the USA than in China. And, to the extent that there are worries about a new trend, these should be alleviated somewhat by the above-mentioned reversal to investments within Japan.

Looking at the FDI data from China's perspective, Japan is indeed not a large factor: in the late 1980s, Japan accounted for 16 per cent of total FDI into China, and for only 7 per cent in the late 1990s (Lincoln, 2002). Historically, most of Japan's FDI was 'bad hollowing out'; that is, it was intended to escape protectionism. Some argue that Japanese FDI into China is of the 'good hollowing out' type, in that it pressures non-competitive sectors in Japan rather than replacing competitive ones. However, even if China occupies only a comparatively small cumulative piece of Japan's overall global production map, China is important for Japan in that it brings a new type of competition: price and choice. Japan's FDI into the USA, being of the anti-protectionism type, affected employment in Japan negatively but did not challenge domestic price structures and the distribution system. Japanese production in China, in contrast, does exactly that: it has rocked Japan's domestic pricing structures, and therefore has also affected Japan's domestic production processes.

III SUBCONTRACTING

The Origins and Logic of the Subcontractor System

Japan's small manufacturing firms can be broadly divided into three categories: (1) independent firms with a strong technology base that sell to multiple buyers; (2) exclusive suppliers to one buyer that are often dependent on that buyer for technological and management know-how; and (3) independent firms with a weak base that cater to narrow local demand, without significant entrepreneurial activity or growth prospects. Of these, the second category are referred to as '*shita-uke*' (usually translated as 'subcontractor', lit.: 'lower level order taker'), which might be defined as small 'companies that produce goods, half-goods, parts and materials based on orders for a larger company' (Aoyama, 2001: 123). The subcontractor production system, epitomized by the Toyota Production System but equally widespread in electronics, general machinery and other manufacturing industries, is characterized by the assembler making explicit orders for the layout, quality, design and so on of an item, and by just-in-time delivery of these items for highly efficient assembly. Thus the subcontractor produces to very specific order and typically invests in asset-specific equipment (machinery that cannot be readily used for other purposes). The relationship is one of dependency, which in the best case is mutual but can be oppressive for very small firms. In all cases, the strictly vertical hierarchy among suppliers is clear, and all depend on the buyer.[7]

In essence, Japan's subcontractor system is an outsourcing system whereby the buyer has mitigated problems of asymmetric information, uncertainty and potential threat of hold-up by making the suppliers dependent. A long list of historical reasons explains how Japanese manufacturers happened upon this system after World War II and now depend on outsourcing to a much greater extent than US firms. These include the initial lack of capital (outsourcing being less risky and cheaper); labour relations (strikes were frequent in the immediate post-war era); and a significant wage differential between long-term employees at large and small firms. By the time the capital and labour constraints began to ease, Japanese firms had built an entire production system and cooperation logic around the supplier structure (for instance, Toyota launched its new production methods in 1963). It had also become clear that outsourcing was beneficial in terms of dampening the business cycle when, in the early 1960s, the increasingly institutionalized system of lifelong employment made labour force adjustments difficult for large firms. When rapid growth led to large-scale mergers among large firms and a labour shortage in the late 1960s, the vertical *keiretsu* and the supplier system were tied together even closer and became institutionalized, to discourage supplier turnover and poaching of talent by competitors.

In the process, a bifurcation within the suppliers began to materialize. Inflows of new technologies and capital allowed the first- and second-tier suppliers to thrive, leaving the smaller, low-tech suppliers behind. For these smaller suppliers, guidance from the buyer could be quite uncomfortable, and small firms usually saw their profits squeezed to a stable margin, even when the buyer's profits were soaring.[8] There was only limited upward mobility for lower-tier suppliers. To be sure, exclusive, long-term supplier relationships offered advantages for small firms as well. They enjoyed a stable, long-term order flow; that is, comparatively high certainty of income through the business cycles. They saved greatly in sales and marketing, which was essentially unnecessary. There was little outside pressure on management, unless a firm failed the buyer's quality or cost requirements. In such a case, the buyer might invest in technological improvements to keep the family of suppliers lined up in stable ways.

Clearly the biggest shortcoming in this system for the very small firms was the total dependency on their buyers. In 1987, more than half of all small firms identified themselves as 'subcontractors', and 81.5 per cent of these depended on only one buyer (Aoyama, 2001: 124; see also below), which obviously greatly increased the bargaining power of that buyer. Even if a buyer did not insist on exclusivity, the small firm often limited its sales to one firm in order to achieve economies of scale, given that the buyer would cap prices. During recessions, buyers were known to squeeze their suppliers in two ways: by reducing the prices they were willing to pay, and by delaying payment for a long time. In the early postwar period, the government had passed legislation prohibiting non-payment of bills by more than 180 days and other forms of exploitation.[9] In the 1970s, small suppliers began to form cooperative supplier groups (*kyōryoku-kai*) and began to receive subsidies and other support measures from the government. After buyer transgressions were aggravated greatly during the recession of the 1990s in what was labelled 'subcontractor bullying' (*shita-uke ijime*), in early 2003 the government introduced more 'subcontractor protection' rules, and expanded coverage to more firms and industries. Next to proactive supportive measures such as financing guarantees, the new regulations expanded the list of what constitutes 'prohibited behaviour' (ranging from forced 'contribution monies' to be paid by the supplier, forced dispatching of redundant workforce to the supplier, to denying that a delivery had been received and refusing to pay for it); increased penalty fees; and began publishing information on abusive buyers to create reputation deterrents.[10] But, while the protection of subcontractors was increasing, numbers decreased as functions changed.

Hollowing Out: Quantitative Changes in the Subcontractor System

The subcontractor system received its first shock with the onset of trade frictions with the USA and Europe in 1982. Until then, Japan had achieved rapid growth through highly aggressive exporting, but the increasingly protective stance by the two largest target markets forced Japanese firms to consider moving production into these countries and use locally produced input materials to fulfil 'local content' requirements. Many automobile makers did this by convincing most important first-tier suppliers to open up shop with them in foreign places; that is, by replicating parts of the subcontractor structure abroad. Over time, however, the share of parts bought from non-Japanese suppliers in these places grew, and not all of the local products were necessarily inferior or more expensive.

The 'hollowing out' of the 1990s further increased the threat towards small, inefficient firms in Japan. When buyers moved more and more production capacity abroad, they offered suppliers a choice: either move with them, or go their own way. Only the financially strong firms were able to follow buyers abroad, which left many small firms behind in Japan, with asset-specific production tools geared specifically to the previous buyer yet nobody to supply to. Some may label this 'good hollowing out', in the sense that high-cost Japanese suppliers were replaced by lower-cost suppliers outside Japan, but the effects on Japan's employment and society were severely felt, beginning in the late 1990s.

Every six years, between 1966 and 1987, METI has conducted a Basic Survey on the Manufacturing Industries (Kōgyō jittai kihon chōsa); and together with the 1996 Survey on Subcontractors (*Shitauke torihiki-tō jittai chōsa*) and the 1998 Manufacturing Industries Survey (*Shōkōgyō jittai kihon chōsa*), these surveys draw a clear picture of the rise and decline of Japan's subcontractor system over the postwar period (see Figure 5.8). Whereas in 1966, about 53 per cent of SMMs identified themselves as *shita-uke*, members of a clear hierarchy of subcontractors to a large buyer, by 1981 this number had hit a high point with 66 per cent (almost 90 per cent in automobiles) but has since fallen to an average of only 48 per cent in 1998.

Figure 5.8 highlights this drop in the ratio of small firms that consider themselves parts of subcontractor families. Note the differences across industries. At the low end (not shown here), we find the food and beverages

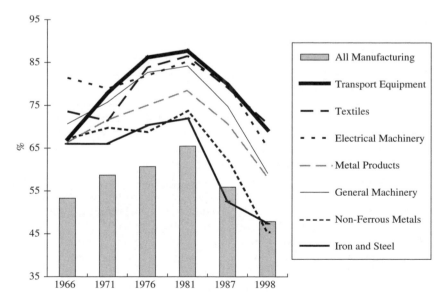

Source: SMEA (2003), Figure 2-4-1.

Figure 5.8   Trends in subcontracting

industries with subcontractor ratios of less than 10 per cent, whereas textiles and transport equipment (including cars) still boasted over 70 per cent as recently as in 1998. Moreover, survey data suggest that an increasing number of firms sell to more than ten buyers, and the share of the main buyer has been declining steadily (Aoyama, 2001: 124).

As powerful and perhaps surprising as these trends may be, in a comparative perspective Japan's system continues to be characterized by strong supplier relations. As Figure 5.8 shows, almost half of all small manufacturing firms in Japan continue to be members of a subcontractor family. Thus the claim here is not that the Japanese subcontractor system is being replaced altogether; rather, it is to show that the system is changing and adapting to the new challenges of the twenty-first century. Perhaps even more important than the quantitative changes outlined so far are the qualitative changes in Japan's subcontractor organization.

Globalization: Qualitative Changes in Subcontracting

Globalization has brought new challenges within Japan from foreign manufacturers. Until the 1990s, the Japanese market was greatly protected from hostile takeovers by foreigners. Even in the few instances where foreigners attempted to overcome all obstacles, the government intervened at the last minute by identifying a Japanese white knight.[11] In the 1990s, however, faced with a huge non-performing loan problem and multiple de facto bankrupt banks and firms, Japan eventually could not or would not resist foreign investments any longer. The first two big cases, in the manufacturing industries, were Mazda and Nissan. It should be noted that the automobile industry has long been considered the 'poster child' for subcontracting in Japan, as car parts account for about 70 per cent of value added in car manufacturing (Kobayashi, 2003: 82). However, what used to be a completely domestic industry has turned into perhaps the most global of all Japanese industries: more than 38 per cent of Japanese cars are now produced outside Japan (METI SKS, 2001). As for car parts, by early 2002 imports into Japan had reached ¥145.3 billion, which represented an increase of 19 per cent over 2001 (in particular, car part imports from China increased by 45 per cent in that one year; Kobayashi, 2003: 79).

While some of this development can be attributed to the global consolidation among major car companies to address cost pressures in world markets, much of the qualitative change in subcontracting within Japan was triggered by Nissan's new competitive push. One of the first announced measures of Renault executive Carlos Ghosn, when he arrived at Nissan in 1999, was to cut the supplier base by half, which meant releasing 600 companies. This initially caused great resistance by Toyota (also at the time the leader of Keidanren, the large firm lobbying umbrella) and others as to its detrimental effects on Japan's industrial organization and social fabric, but as Nissan could not be deterred these companies began to act likewise in order to compete. This episode, which earned Ghosn the label 'Le Cost Killer', highlighted one aspect of subcontractor-based production largely ignored previously: its potential to build up slack and cost over time. While Toyota has long been considered a master in squeezing its suppliers with a friendly smile, Nissan and others had been much less effective at keeping their supplier structure on the edge. Ghosn succeeded in reducing part costs by 30 per cent within two years, simply by modifying its supplier system and squeezing the remaining firms (Ghosn and Ries, 2005). Arguably, this was possible only because Nissan had its back against the wall, and neither the Japanese government (with its emphasis on employment-saving strategies) nor the suppliers themselves had any choice but to accept the squeeze. Likewise, when Ford took over Mazda, it reduced the 'C30' programme, nice-speak for slashing prices on all parts by 30 per cent; subcontractors that refused to go along were bid good-bye. While the foreign car makers did all this under the spotlight, quietly the electronics makers such as Hitachi, Mitsubishi Electrics and others underwent similar transformations, beginning in the late 1990s. In industry after industry, employment and subcontractor structures were reconsidered.

Thus the reason for the large-scale reorganization of subcontractor line-ups across industries was that the system was suddenly revealed to introduce a high-cost structure that hurt the assemblers' global competitive advantage. Many buyers began to dissolve their cooperative supplier groups in order to drive their subcontractor hierarchy apart. Some large firms were even said to have issued 'orders against *settai*' (clubby drinking outings aimed at bonding to cement long-standing business relations) in an attempt to break open their circle of suppliers and open the door to new firms (Aoyama, 2001).

A separate, but equally important, factor contributing to the consolidation and increased competition of automobile suppliers was a change in the way automobiles are built, towards modulization: rather than outsourcing shock absorbers, for example, from one supplier and brakes from another, the auto makers now order complete modules that contain both parts but are already pre-assembled. This greatly reduces the number of parts to be outsourced, as well as complications at the final assembly stage, thus reducing costs for the assembler. It also puts the burden of innovation and quality improvements squarely on the suppliers' shoulders: those that can upgrade their technologies and capabilities will compete, but they are also likely to free themselves from dependencies on one buyer and instead supply to multiple car companies. Internet-based procurement processes, moreover, allow car makers to procure from whoever is cheapest around the globe (Kobayashi, 2003: 82–3).

Finally, cost pressures have affected the logic of protection against abuse in subcontracting. Previously, a large firm would order most parts from at least two firms, to reduce dependency on a single supplier (that is, the threat of hold-up by one single firm as well as the exposure to risk of fire and other interruption of production or quality problems) (see, for example, Asanuma and Kikutani, 1993). The price of this insurance was efficiency losses in scale of production. In the 1990s, this approach began to change: to achieve economies of scale, more assemblers began to order one part from one supplier only, which was most likely the one with lowest bid rather than the one with the longest-standing business relation (Aoyama, 2001: 136).

The new system of price-based subcontracting is referred to as 'open kompe', which stands for 'open competition'. Started by the electronics makers as early as in the late 1980s, it is now integral to part procurement in cars, machinery and other Japanese industries where the subcontracting remains substantial.[12] According to one analysis, this open pricing system (where suppliers must submit bids, and the best bidder wins the contract) can lead to cost savings of 3–4 per cent if existing suppliers are used, and savings of 15–30 per cent if new firms enter the market (Aoyama, 2001: 135).

These qualitative changes in subcontracting constitute a departure from the former closed and 'wet' system of supplier relations towards a greater emphasis on price and innovation, based on 'dry', arm's-length relations. In other words, this new approach to supplier pricing is exactly the system that the Detroit automakers were so derided for using in the 1980s. Certainly, this does not mean that Detroit was doing the right thing in the 1980s, but rather that different systems work well at different times, and the Japanese subcontractor system may no longer be as contributive to competitiveness as it was in the 1980s.

The New Subcontractor

To the extent that Japan's subcontractor system continues to exist in terms of long-term relationships, it is morphing into a globally adaptive, more competitive and fluid structure. With reduced exports from Japan and increased price competition worldwide, subcontractors have changed their calculations as to what it takes to satisfy their buyers in the long run. This includes being flexible and open to change, and moving abroad.

One backdrop to this transformation is how subcontractor families developed historically. In the 1960s, many large assemblers (especially but not exclusively in cars, electronics and machinery) began to open new plants in rural areas of Japan (such as Yamagata, Aomori, Iwate and Kyushu). Around these plants, cities of subcontractors sprang up ('jōka-machi', 'castle towns', referring to the historical development of cities in Japan whereby manufacturers, vendors and other service providers located around castles to cater to the samurai). When, in the 1990s, these plants were either closed owing to recession or moved overseas, they literally left full cities behind with nothing to do or produce.[13] At the same time, Japanese castle towns are springing up around the globe, from Ohio to Shanghai. Once there, Japanese suppliers have to compete with local ones, and the best are also courted by competing buyers, thus increasing their bargaining power.

Most importantly, for suppliers to survive the shift towards moduliza-tion, fewer suppliers, and production at the location of sales, mean they have to become more efficient, innovative and technologically competitive. In 2002, Toyota introduced 'open competition' for robotics. The company likewise cut the number of its suppliers by either dismissing or consolidat-ing suppliers that are inefficient and then working with those suppliers it needs on efficiency improvements. Dependencies were reduced by encour-aging suppliers to work with more than one buyer.[14] To maintain compet-itive advantage over world competitors, suppliers have to uphold their technological edge. Japanese suppliers are no longer captive, controlled executors of their buyers' strategies. They are becoming more aggressive, independent and strategic for their own good.

In the process, the bifurcation between strong and weak supplier firms has become ever more pronounced. Only the strong suppliers that are able to charge ahead with their buyers will remain suppliers, and they are becoming ever stronger as a result. On the other hand, weak firms are increasingly unable to compete in the 'open kompe' system.

IV CONCLUSIONS

This chapter has discussed the effects of globalization – both the trend among Japanese multinationals to produce outside Japan and the new cost competition within Japan – on Japan's industrial organization. The effects of 'hollowing out' on employment in Japan are somewhat ambiguous, for they are mixed up with the decade-long recession that struck Japan in the 1990s. However, the effects on industrial organization are much clearer, as 'hollowing out' has reshaped Japan's long-standing subcontractor system in both quantitative and qualitative terms. We observe a clear trend, in all industries, away from the previous long-term, 'wet' relations based on repeated interaction, loyalty and cooperation, towards open price competition in components.

'Hollowing out' in Japan is not just media-induced hysteria; it is a real and ongoing process with critical implications for Japan's industrial organization. About one fifth of all Japanese production has been moved abroad since the late 1980s. At the same time, unlike Europe and the USA, there is hardly any inflow of manufacturing FDI into Japan. This means that there is no replacement for the manufacturing that is being moved abroad, and no entry of new customers for existing supplier firms. The estimated 2.5 million workers displaced by 'hollowing out' are therefore unlikely to find new job openings in their industries. Most of the job losses occur at the supplier level. Even if in macroeconomic terms this may be a positive, even much-needed, weeding out of Japan's small firms, the long-term negative effects on employment are undeniable.

Second, 'hollowing out' is exerting a great impact on the structure and logic of Japan's subcontractor system. Whereas, 20 years ago, about 80 per cent of small manufacturing firms identified themselves as subcontractors and parts of a large vertical supplier *keiretsu*, this ratio has now dropped to less than 50 per cent. What is more, new cost pressures have forced buyers to introduce elements of competitive bidding into their supplier networks. Innovative suppliers are getting stronger in the process, whereas smaller, less competitive ones fall by the wayside. Figure 5.1 showed that some Japanese industries benefit from this new cost competition, in particular electronics and automobiles. Industries unable to move to cost competition and thus hit hardest by 'hollowing out' include, first and foremost, textiles, followed by machinery, plastics and kiln (glass, cement). 'Hollowing out' increases the bifurcation of Japanese industries into those thriving with globalization and those being done in by it.

It is as yet unclear how, exactly, these changes will affect Japan's production processes, as epitomized by the Toyota Production System. However, it is already apparent that 'hollowing out' has irrevocably changed the relations between buyers and suppliers in Japan. This has happened in parallel with the reorganization of other pillars of the Japanese industrial system, such as the main bank system and the horizontal *keiretsu*. The logic of Japan's supplier networks, as we used to know it, has been altered.

NOTES

1. METI (2002), White Paper on International Trade and Investment.
2. Interview with a high-ranking government official, Tokyo, Spring 2003. The doomsday proponents were wrong, as Japan witnessed a trend reversal in 2004; see section II, Japanese Production Abroad.

3. Note that this interpretation is not unanimously shared even among economists. Bailey (2003, p. 4) describes the 'tariff-hopping' and 'tariff-preventing' FDI as having much less serious implications for Japan's economy, as opposed to the labour-cost reducing FDI into Asia. This view is echoed by Itami (2004), who suggests that the former are complementary to Japanese production because they are extensions of existing production into new markets (such as the USA and EU), whereas the latter are 'donut-type' FDI in that they deindustrialize Japan (leaving a hole in Japan).

4. In official Japan government statistics, a 'Japanese foreign subsidiary' is considered as any subsidiary in which a Japanese firm owns more than 20 per cent.

5. In contrast to the USA, where the equity ratio decreases with the size of the firm, small firms in Japan have lower equity ratios than large firms. See SMEA (2004).

6. Jesper Koll, cited in Rowly and Tashiro (2004).

7. The literature on this topic is extensive; one short description can be found in Aoyama (2001: 123–36), but see also McMillan, 1990; Smitka, 1991; Nishiguchi, 1994.

8. This was accomplished by means of the 'after-sales price adjustment' system (atogimeseido), whereby the buyer determined the price for the part after the product had been sold to the end consumer, thus allowing for flexible adjustment of supplier margins; see Schaede (2000).

9. These are the 'Subcontracting Charges Law' (Law to prevent extension and so on of payments to subcontractors) and the 'Law on the Promotion of Subcontracting SME', revised in 2003.

10. *Nikkei* daily newspaper, 9 February 2003, 'Shita-uke Protection to Include Services Industries; METI wants to expand coverage; 700,000 initially'. To facilitate SME financing, the government supports SME lending backed by account receivables by offering an insurance or guarantee system. The biggest change in 2003 was that subcontractors in the services industries (such as software development, shipping and building maintenance), where abusive buyer behaviour was apparently common, are now also covered by these rules against abuse, which extends total coverage of these policies to over one million small firms.

11. Perhaps the most famous case of not being able to overcome systemic obstacles of protection is T. Boone Pickens' attempt to purchase, and then control, a majority stake in Koito Manufacturing, a supplier in the Toyota *keiretsu*. Although the purchase succeeded, the control never materialized.

12. See Hoetker (2004) on differences in the subcontracting industry between electronics and automobiles.

13. See SD (2002) for a vivid account of ghost towns that used to produce for large buyers all over Japan.

14. Recent newspaper and magazine articles describing these qualitative changes in the automobile industry include: Ekonomisuto, 29 July 2002: 28–30 and 3 February 2004: 4–5; Nihon Keizai Shinbun, issues of 15 May 2002 (p. 11), 12 July 2002 (p. 1), 22 August 2002 (p. 13), 25 June 2003 (p. 1), 14 May 2004 (p. 13), 9 November 2004 (p. 13).

REFERENCES

Aoki, M. (1988), *Information, Incentives, and Bargaining in the Japanese Economy*, Cambridge: Cambridge University Press.

Aoyama, K. (2001), Shinpan-Kaimei Chūshō Kigyo ron (Understanding Medium-sized Enterprises in Japan, revised edition), Tokyo: Doyukan.

Asanuma, B. (1989), 'Manufacturer–supplier relationships in Japan and the concept of relation-specific skill', *Journal of the Japanese and International Economies*, **3** (March), 1–30.

Asanuma, B. and T. Kikutani (1993), 'Risk absorption in Japanese subcontracting: a microeconometric study on the automobile industry', Stanford, Center for Economic Policy Research, no. 218.

Bailey, D. (2003), 'Explaning Japan's kudoka (hollowing out): a case of government and strategic failure?', *Asia Pacific Business Review* **10**(1), 1–20.

CO (Cabinet Office, Government of Japan) (2002), 'Annual report on the Japanese economy and public finance, 2001–2002: no gains without reforms II' (translation of Keizai Zaisei Hakusho, 2002), Tokyo.

CO (Cabinet Office, Government of Japan) (2004), 'Annual report on the Japanese economy and public finance, 2003–2004: no gains without reforms IV' (translation of Keizai Zaisei Hakusho, 2004), www5.cao.go.jp/zenbun/wp-e/wp-je04/04-00302.html, Tokyo.

Cole, R.E. (ed.) (1983), 'Automobiles and the future: competition, cooperation, and change', Ann Arbor, Center for Japanese Studies, University of Michigan.

Cole, R.E. (1994), 'Different quality paradigms and their implications for organizational learning', in M. Aoki and R. Dore (eds), *The Japanese Firm: The Source of Competitive Strength*, New York: Oxford University Press, pp. 66–83.

Dyer, J. (2000), *Collaborative Advantage: Winning Through Extended Enterprise Supplier Networks*, Oxford: Oxford University Press.

Ghosn, C. and P. Ries (2005), *Shift – Inside Nissan's Historic Revival*, New York: Currency Doubleday.

Hoetker, G. (2004), 'Same rules, different games: variation in the outcomes of "Japanese-style" supply relationships', *Advances in International Management* **17**, 187–214.

Itami, H. (2004), ' "Nihon-sei" de katsu (Winning with "Made in Japan"): (1) "Sangyō kūdōka" ron wa koko ga machigatte ita (How the "hollowing out" thesis got it wrong), *Ekonomisuto*, 27 July, 24–6.

JT (*Japan Times*) (2003), Japan needs to see China as ally, not threat, economist says (www.japantimes.co.jp/cgi-bin/getarticle.p 15?nn20030206d20030202.htm).

Kobayashi, H. (2003), *Sangyō kūdōka no kokufuku* (Overcoming industrial hollowing out), Tokyo: Chūō kōronsha.

Liker, J.K. (2004), *The Toyota Way: 14 Management Principles from the World's Greatest Manufacturer*, New York: McGraw-Hill.

Lincoln, E.J. (2002), 'On Japan: "Hollowing Out" in Newsweek Japan', 28 August 2002.

McMillan, J. (1990), 'Managing suppliers: incentive systems in Japanese and United States industry', *California Management Review*, **32**(4), 38–55.

METI (Ministry of Economy, Trade and Industry), (2002), 'White paper on international trade and investment' (www.meti.go.jp.).

METI (Ministry of Economy, Trade and Industry), MHLW (Ministry of Health, Labor and Welfare), MEXT (Ministry of Education, Culture, Sports, Science and Technology) (eds) (2004), *Seizō kiban hakusho, 'Monotsukuri Hakusho' Heisei 11 nendo* (2003 Manufacturing White Paper), Tokyo: Japanese Government.

METI SKS (Sangyō Kōzō Shingikai, Shinseichō seisaku bukai) (2001), 'Inobeeshion to jūyō no kojunkan no keisei ni mukete' (Report on Constructing Positive Feedback Cycles in the Demand for Innovation), report of the Subcommittee on New Growth Policies, Industrial Structure Council, Government Report, Tokyo.

Monden, Y. (1993), *The Toyota Management System: Linking the Seven Key Functional Areas*, Cambridge: Productivity Press.

Nishiguchi, T. (1994), *Strategic Industrial Sourcing: The Japanese Advantage*, Oxford: Oxford University Press.

Rowley, I. and H. Tashiro (2004), 'So much for hollowing out', *Business Week* online (www.businessweek.com/print/magazine/content04_41/b3903069.htm.

Ryan, P. (2003), 'Is China exporting deflation globally, hollowing out Japan?', Marubeni Corporation Economic Research Institute (www.marubeni.co.jp/research/eindx/0303).

Schaede, Ulrike (2000), *Cooperative Capitalism: Self-Regulation, Trade Associations, and the Antimonopoly Law in Japan*, Oxford: Oxford University Press.

SD (Shūkan Daiyamondo) (2002), 'Kūdōka: hontō no kyōfu' (The real dangers of hollowing out)', special issue of *Shūkan Daiyamondo*, 12 January, 26–43.

SMEA (Small and Medium Enterprise Agency) (ed.) (2003), 'Chūshō kigyō hakusho 2003 nenpan: Saisei to "kigyōka shakai" e no michi', *White Paper on Small and Medium Enterprises in Japan: The Road to Regeneration and the Creation of an Entrepreneurial Society*, Tokyo, Gyōzai.

SMEA (Small and Medium Enterprise Agency) (ed.) (2004), 'Chūshō kigyō hakusho 2004 nenpan', *White Paper on Small and Medium Enterprises in Japan: The Limitless Potential of the Diversity of Small Firms*, Tokyo: Gyōzai.

Smitka, M.J. (1991), *Competitive Ties – Subcontracting in the Japanese Automotive Industry*, New York: Columbia University Press.

SRI (Shoko Research Institute, Shōkō Chūkin Chōsabu) (2003), 'Sangyō kūdōka to chūshō kigyō – kaigai seisan no zōka ga chūsho kigyō ni ataeru eikyō' (Industrial hollowing out and small firms: how the increase in production abroad has influenced small firms), *Shōkō Kinyū*, **5**, 16–38.

6. Institutionally driven growth and stagnation – and struggle for reform

Terutomo Ozawa

I SEA CHANGE

As recently as the 1980s, Japan was still considered an industrial jugger-
naut, often riding roughshod over the world market. Its economic prowess
was both admired and feared. The picture, however, has changed dramatically ever since the bursting of Japan's asset bubble of 1987–90 that set off
a banking crisis and more than a decade of stagnation. The Japanese
economy has come to be looked at – or even down on – as an anaemic
economy that is scraping along by exporting (that is, depending on
someone else's markets) instead of growing by dint of its own domestic
spending. Recently, however, there are some promising signs of economic
turnaround, especially in the wake of reformist Prime Minister Koizumi's
landslide victory in the lower-house elections of 11 September 2005.

The leitmotif of this chapter is that a particular set of institutional
arrangements Japan crafted to achieve rapid catch-up growth in the early
postwar years (which is often referred to as 'Japan Inc.') proved to be
effective for a particular stage of growth, but that it has been suffering from
the subsequent sclerosis of institutions ('the Japanese disease') caused by
the very success of economic growth that those institutions were once able
to foster. This trap of institutional obsolescence is the inevitable cost of the
way Japan's catch-up strategy itself was organized and carried out.
Institutions have their own logic of tenacious existence with highly charged
sociopolitical values and often yield self-contradictory dialectical outcomes in the end.

More specifically, the themes of this chapter are (i) that postwar Japan
was largely tolerated for pursuing its dirigiste catch-up policy because of
America's geopolitical needs during the Cold War, (ii) that the end of the
Cold War, as well as Japan's own economic success, drastically altered the
global political economy environs for itself, (iii) that the asset bubble of
1987–90 was symptomatic of institutional sclerosis, (iv) that Japan's
initial aversion to inward FDI (foreign ownership of domestic industry)

has recently and paradoxically morphed into an 'eagerness' to seek help from and depend on foreign multinationals' participation in corporate Japan as a renovator of its obsolete institutions – that is, obsolete both in terms of its own needs and in the light of the current zeitgeist of globalization, and (v) that Koizumi's victory is likely to create a tipping point for the Japanese economy to go through a critical institutional alteration.

In what follows, we will first briefly describe the 'political trilemma' model of economic management as a general framework for our analysis, and then examine how Japan's dirigiste catch-up regime worked, how institutional obsolescence has set in, and how its economy now struggles to renovate its domestic set of institutions and practices.

II   THE POLITICAL TRILEMMA MODEL

The notion of a 'Golden Straitjacket' (Friedman, 1999) has recently gained general currency. It describes the newly emerged institutional requirements for countries to survive and thrive in this age of globalization that has replaced the era of the Cold War. The Cold War era divided the world into the Free World, the Soviet Communist bloc and the Third World which played the game of pitting the US and Soviet superpowers against each other. Japan as a designated bulwark against communism was one of the most fortunate beneficiaries of the Cold War era (Ozawa, 2005). When the Berlin wall tumbled down, Chalmers Johnson aptly observed: 'the Cold War is over, Japan has won'.

The collapse of the USSR created an entirely new world, in which the US suddenly found its total hegemony and began to mould the global environs in its own image. Thatcher–Reaganism was first aimed at deregulation and marketization at home, but soon to spread overseas in the post-Cold War period. This forced other countries to wear the Golden Straitjacket if they were to partake of the benefits of global capitalism (stepped-up economic integration). The rules of the Golden Straitjacket (which is also known as 'the Washington Consensus') are fiscal and monetary austerity, privatization, market liberalization and opening of the domestic markets for trade and investment – all the hallmarks of market capitalism.

Rodrik (2000) incorporates the idea of the Golden Straitjacket into what is called 'the political trilemma of the world economy', a trilemma stemming from three policy choices: economic integration (that is, globalization), nation-state (economic growth maximizer) and mass/local politics (interest groups), as illustrated in Figure 6.1. The trilemma allows us to

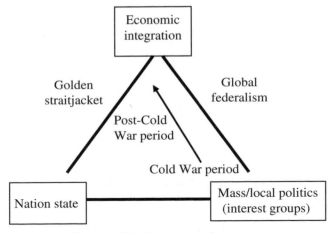

Bretton Woods compromise

Source: Based on Rodrik (2000) with modifications.

Figure 6.1   The political trilemma model

choose a combination of two choices, not all three, If we want true international economic integration, we have to go either with the nation-state,
in which case the domain of national policies will have to be significantly
restricted, or else with mass politics, in which case we will have to give up
the nation-state. If we want highly participatory political regimes, we have
to choose between the nation-state and international economic integration
(Rodrick, 2000: 180).

In the early postwar period, all the war-devastated nations (in Europe and
Japan) devoted themselves to reconstructing their economies by concentrat-
ing on the 'nation-state-cum-mass-politics' axis. This is because the original
Bretton Woods regime permitted the member countries to put restrictions on
trade and capital flows (that is, protection from the forces of economic integration in favour of national economic interests), although the overall trend
was in the direction of freer exchange of goods, services and financial assets.
Hence the 'nation-state-cum-mass-politics' axis is named the 'Bretton
Woods compromise' in the trilemma model. Furthermore, Cold War geopolitics was such that US key allies (notably Japan and the NIEs, so far as Asia
is concerned) were allowed to pursue their own dirigiste and protectionist
growth strategies. In the post-Cold War period, however, the full force of economic integration was suddenly unleashed, calling for acceptance of the
Golden Straitjacket: that is, yielding to the forces of globalization and adhering to the 'integration-cum-nation-state' axis.

The trilemma model is basically about a new tug of war between the national economy and the outside world in this age of globalization where national economic autonomy (jurisdiction) is often at the mercy of the forces of global markets, and global institutions, such as the IMF, the World Bank and, more recently, the WTO. NGOs are also going global. (These supranational institutions operate on the 'integration-cum-mass-politics' axis as sort of 'global federations'.) The developing countries in particular are under reform pressure from the 'Washington Consensus', so long as they engage in international commerce with the United States and receive economic aid and preferential trade treatment, as evidenced in the African Growth and Stabilization programme, the Central American Free Trade Agreement (CAFTA) and bilateral free trade agreements.

A Matrix of Institutions

In this regard, the notion of 'a matrix of institutions' introduced by North (1990) is relevant. He stresses that the overall economic performance of a given economic unit is largely determined (enhanced or retarded) by its institutional regime. Such a regime can also be called 'an institutional matrix that defines the incentive structure of society' against the backdrop of 'the belief system' that connects 'reality' to the institutions (North, 1999). In addition, the belief system is a product of local mores and traditions in the individual country. In fact, the incentive structure of a society consists of 'formal rules (constitutions, laws and rules)', 'informal constraints (norms, conventions and codes of conduct)', and their enforcement characteristics (North, 2005).

North is thus talking about the role of an institutional matrix in a given individual country; that is, an inner/domestic set alone. However, his concept of an institutional matrix can be extended to the outside world as well. The global economy has its own matrix of institutions, an outer set that defines the 'integration-cum-nation-state' axis. And each nation's inner matrix of institutions that is originally built on the 'nation-state-cum-mass-politics' axis interacts with a prevailing outer matrix.

In today's world economy, the outer set (a global institutional matrix) is designed to maintain global stability largely under the hegemonic leadership of the United States (the Pax Americana). Especially, ever since the collapse of the Soviet Union, the Pax Americana has been ruling the world with the ideology of global capitalism embedded in the Anglo-American belief system of market liberalism and free enterprise. In this age of hegemon-led globalization (Ozawa, 2005), therefore, the outer set is dominant over the inner set, forcing accommodation and compliance of the latter with the norms of the former. Hence, the inner matrix of institutions is compelled to 'renovate' itself as much as is practical so as to be in line with the outer matrix: that is, to swing toward the 'integration-cum-nation-state' axis.

Some inner institutions, however, retain their own logic of survival, resisting changes. As stressed by Gerschenkron (1962), developing countries in particular, as latecomers to industrialization, tend to become reliant on state involvement and institutional arrangements rather than on the market, for the very simple reason that the market mechanism itself has yet to be developed. And immediate postwar Japan that was war-ravaged was in such a situation.

Let us explore how early postwar Japan was able to pursue national goals along the 'nation-state-cum-mass-politics' axis, the goals that were quite ethnocentric and even nationalistic at the cost of international economic integration (that is, protecting domestic industries and controlling capital flows across borders). As will be explained below, Japan's ethnocentric dirigiste catch-up policy turned out to be effective mostly during the Bretton Woods-cum-Cold War period.

III   DIRIGISME IN POST-WAR JAPAN

We will first look at how early postwar Japan manoeuvred to set up its own inner set of institutions. In the early postwar period America's geopolitics was such that Japan was able to pursue its dirigiste (that is, government-guided) catch-up growth policy. Japan's strategy was to restrict inward FDI as much as practical in order to keep its industries not foreign-controlled but nationally owned, yet to import and absorb advanced industrial knowledge from the West under licensing agreements and through other non-equity (non-FDI) channels (Ozawa, 1974).

Right after the war, the occupation authorities completely overhauled Japan's old inner matrix of feudalistic institutions in order to turn Japan into a democratic society that was compliant with the outer matrix of institutions established by Western democracy. Japan's political system in particular was remade so as to eliminate any feudalistic remnants of the prewar years. Once the communist thread emerged, moreover, a conservative government was quickly handpicked by the US. Nobusuke Kishi (who became prime minister in 1957), a former minister of munitions in Tojo's cabinet, was freed of war crime charges and released from prison, along with others. Furthermore, the occupation authorities used the Japanese bureaucracy as implementers of their democratization and economic revitalization policies, thereby legitimizing its authority. Many wartime economic planners, who once were engaged in the Greater East Asian Co-Prosperity Sphere programme, came back to Japan's dirigiste bureaucracy and started to plan a series of industrial reconstruction policies.

As soon as Japan regained political autonomy under the San Francisco Peace Treaty of 1951, furthermore, the government and corporate Japan were able to modify and remould the occupation-imposed inner set of institutions in such a way as to suit its own purpose of state-orchestrated economic development. As a consequence, there emerged numerous unique institutional set-ups such as *keiretsu* formation, the main bank system, the stakeholder (instead of shareholder) model of capitalism, the widespread practice of cross-shareholding among affiliated companies, postal savings and insurance, and the like. And all these institutional arrangements were designed to reconstruct the Japanese economy and regain industrial competitiveness on world markets by way of a dynamic infant-industry protection policy: that is to say, by initially protecting domestic industries but sooner or later developing them into export-competitive industries. Indeed, this sequence of industrial development is the fundamental formula of the so-called 'flying-geese' catch-up strategy, a strategy that early postwar Japan pursued (Ozawa, 2005).

The end result was the establishment of a unique inner matrix of institutions designed and crafted by early postwar Japan for the purpose of catching up with the West (or what is popularly dubbed 'Japan Inc'.). There are many idiosyncratic features of this catch-up regime. For the purpose of elucidating the process of institutional sclerosis, however, we will concentrate on three major ones: (i) state-augmented bank-based finance, (ii) *keiretsu* formation, and (iii) protectionism and 'pork-barrel' politics.

Each of these characteristics has already been extensively explored in many studies, but their interactions and evolutionary developments in the context of Japan's catch-up growth and recent economic malaise remain largely unexamined. As will be detailed below, these structural set-ups have eventually evolved and converged in a sequential and path-dependent fashion to cause some critical institutional misalignments (incongruities), which culminated in the asset bubble of 1987–90, hence in the post-bubble banking crises and economic stagnation. These developments are the vicissitudinary outcomes of Japan's once phenomenal catch-up growth propelled by such an inner set of institutions. The resultant institutional misalignments have been caused by the combined forces of the fast-changing market conditions that Japan's postwar matrix of institutions itself was responsible for and the ossification of such a matrix *à la* Olson (1982). In the recent past, therefore, Japan has been struggling to extricate itself from the trap of institutional obsolescence. All these evolutionary developments that have transpired are sketched in Figure 6.2.

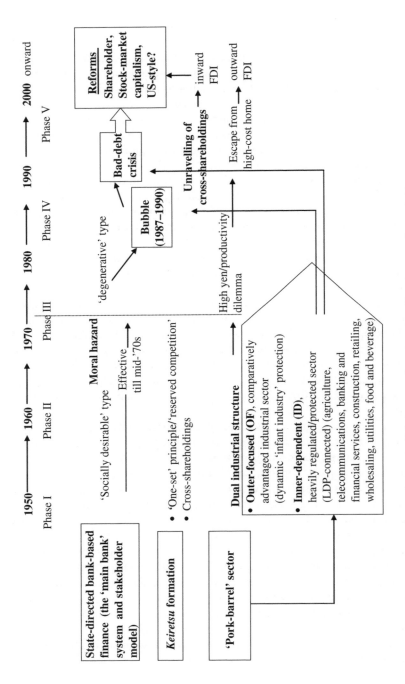

Figure 6.2   The dénouement of Japan's dirigiste catch-up regime ('institutional matrix')

Bank-based Finance and Repressed Capital Markets

As is typically true of any developing countries, Japan once resorted to and maximized the use of bank-based finance for catch-up growth instead of capital market-based finance. In this scheme, Japan also used 'central bank-provided finance' (the Bank of Japan created funds internally) rather than 'current-account deficit-derived finance' (that is, borrowings from overseas to finance the current excess in spending over savings) (Ozawa, 1999, 2001). These two, but especially the latter, are the crucial financial aspects of Japan's successful catch-up growth.

At the start of postwar growth the stock market initially was a relatively important source of funds for corporate investment in Japan. Soon, however, bank loans were deliberately promoted as the essential financial source for capital formation under dirigisme, since such finance could be effectively controlled and managed by the government. Equity finance, therefore, quickly became secondary to bank loans. In order to govern credit expansion, moreover, the government prohibited corporations from issuing bonds. A bond-issuing privilege was granted only to those state-run financial institutions (mainly, three long-term credit banks) and utilities that were specifically designed to finance long-term public-purpose projects (Patrick, 1994a). Consequently, there was early on no choice on the part of corporations but to borrow mostly from banks.

Dependence on bank loans thus became the critical mechanism through which a policy of financial repression was implemented by keeping interest rates low, controlling market competition (via entry regulations), and channelling capital to policy-prioritized sectors and projects, notably in capital-intensive heavy and chemical industries. Under the close supervision and control of the Bank of Japan, which was virtually a policy arm of the Ministry of Finance, the six major *keiretsu* banks (Mitsui, Mitsubishi, Sumitomo, Fuji, Sanwa and DKB) played the role of 'main banks' for their respective groups in investing the capital injected by the central bank to modernize prewar-built heavy and chemical industries (Aoki, 1994; Aoki and Patrick, 1994; Teranishi, 1994). In those days, the strength of the main bank system was 'its strong information collecting, related monitoring capabilities, and management consulting', reducing uncertainty and increasing commercial information, although it was accompanied by weaknesses such as preferential access to information among participants, secretive and opaque relationship banking, and limited public disclosure (Patrick, 1994b: 359).

Furthermore, bank-created money (both the central bank's credit and the banking industry's multiple-expansion of deposits and loans) did not lead to any serious inflation, because (i) the funds were carefully invested in supply-increasing industrial projects, (ii) the monetary spigot was turned off as soon as Japan encountered a balance-of-payments deficit, a deficit caused by such an expansionary monetary policy (Wallich and Wallich, 1976), (iii) during Japan's high-growth period (from the early 1950s to the early 1970s) domestic savings increased dramatically, and were channelled into business investment (instead of consumer credit, whose facilities were still repressed), and (iv) the government maintained a balanced budget, hence the absence of open-market operations to monetize national debts (Patrick, 1994b). That central bank-augmented credit creation for growth was a classic case of development finance in the early stage of industrial capitalism as envisioned and theorized by Schumpeter (1934), who even called the banks 'the headquarters of the capitalist system'.[1]

Capital markets were given a supplementary role, and the bond market in particular was even discouraged to develop until the mid-1980s; corporate issues and the development of a secondary market were severely discouraged (Patrick, 1994a). Furthermore, the stock market was often 'influenced' by the government in terms of administrative guidance and occasional involvements (purchases and sales) in the market. Interestingly enough, for example, until the mid-1980s, the share prices of major Japanese banks remained nearly constant for long periods of time, because regulators wanted 'to limit stock price fluctuations in an effort to influence the public's perception of risk at banks' (Genay, 1999).

The state-augmented banking system naturally produced a moral hazard effect because high-risk investments were encouraged and the commercial banks were equally protected under the scheme popularly referred to as a 'convoy system', in which strong banks were obliged to guard weak ones. The result was that banks' operations became extremely asset-expansive as they eagerly extended loans, especially in the context of inter-*keiretsu* oligopolistic rivalry as the *keiretsu* competed vigorously with each other in setting up a similar set of industries, a phenomenon that came to be called the 'one-set' principle (Miyazaki, 1980).

Banks – and their *keiretsu* customers – were thus all the more willing to take risks because they could count on government help. Moral hazard was actually needed as an inducement to promote large-scale investments in capital-intensive, scale-driven industries, which imposed high financial risks on the private sector. Without government support and the *keiretsu* formation, individual enterprises alone might have been reluctant to plunge into new large-scale ventures during Japan's heavy and chemical industrialization (from the mid-1950s to the early 1970s). A rise in national output capacity (aggregate supply) had to be induced to match the liquidity (aggregate demand) pumped into the economy by the central bank-augmented credit creation in order to prevent inflation (as emphasized by Schumpeter). This type of moral hazard, then, can be identified as the socially justifiable type (Ozawa, 1999), because it induced socially desirable investments in the modern sector, thereby facilitating a swift industrial transformation. Indeed, this was the financial side story of Japan's inner matrix of institutions and practices, which led to high growth during the stage of heavy and chemical industrial modernization characterized by the so-called 'investment-feeding-investment' growth.

Logic of Internal Funds

Ironically, the very success of dirigiste bank-based capitalism came to undermine the privileged position of banks. It was a self-destructive system. Thanks to the low-cost capital made available under such a system, big corporations, mostly in the *keiretsu*, grew quickly and accumulated internal reserves, along with a sharp rise in debt–equity ratios: for example, from 0.78 in 1961 to 5.67 in 1964; that is, over only three years (Arisawa, 1967). Both retained earnings and bank loans were needed to finance the development of capital-intensive heavy and chemical industries. The rapid accumulation of internal funds was soon made possible, however, because corporate investment was quite profitable during the high-growth period and, moreover, because companies did not need to pay out many dividends (post-tax payments) and paid mainly a fixed amount of interest (pre-tax expenditure payments) without regard to profitability.

The inevitable accumulation of internal funds under bank-based finance is theorized by Tsuru (1993) in terms of the sources and uses of funds for a main bank-affiliated firm as follows:

$$D - R + S = V \tag{6.1}$$

where D is depreciation allowances, R is replacement investment, S is internal funds (retained earnings) and V is new investment.

When the firm is on a rapid growth path, D is necessarily larger than R, creating a surplus (internal funds). Its rapid growth also brings in profits, part of which is retained as S. But its need for funds to finance V during a high-growth period will be greater than $D - R + S$. Hence, long-term bank loans (L) are required:

$$V = D - R + S + L \tag{6.2}$$

Eventually, the firm successfully grows to a point where $S - V$ become positive, creating 'net internal surplus (NS) of the firm', namely

$$(NS > 0) = (D + S) - (V + R) \qquad (6.3)$$

Now that the firm has accumulated a substantial amount of NS over a high-growth period, how to use NS becomes an important decision. NS can be used for a variety of activities, including (i) repayment of debt to banks, (ii) R&D expenditures, (iii) direct foreign investment, (iv) diversification of business activities, and (v) financial investment in securities and land. 'When we view the entire economy, composed of numerous firms, the aggregate of NS found its destinations in *all* these directions as the high-growth period progressed' (Tsuru, 1993: 185, emphasis added). The most important result, however, is a reduced dependence on banks through (i) and (v).

Unravelling of Bank-based Finance

Consequently, once Japan's economic growth slowed down after the first oil crisis of 1974, the accumulated internal reserves began to serve as an emancipator from dependence on banks. In other words, the once-effective main bank system itself was destined ironically to make the banks' clients less and less dependent on loans, hence, less susceptible to monitoring and more autonomous in investment decisions (Ozawa, 2000). (As will be seen below, Japanese companies on the whole soon developed a habit of accumulating large amounts of retained earnings without distributing much to their shareholders. And this is attracting a lot of takeover bids, including hostile ones these days, and energizing the stock markets.)

Moreover, as Japan entered the subsequent phase of assembly-based, components-intensive industries, notably automobiles and electronics, leaving behind heavy and chemical industries, there soon emerged new world-class manufacturers of consumer durables. Many of these manufacturers actually did not originate as *keiretsu* firms that were supposedly best coached by their main banks. These new companies started out as outsiders (non-*keiretsu* upstarts) and largely remained as such.

A prime example is Toyota Motor Corporation, now the world's most efficient car maker, which has had no affiliation either with any *zaibatsu* or with *keiretsu* since its establishment in 1937. In fact, the company persistently avoided external debts. Its internal reserves became enormous, so much so that Toyota itself came to be known as the 'Toyota Bank'. Another example is Honda, which in its infancy (during the 1950s) had a hard time securing bank loans because of its initial status as an independent upstart. It originated as a bike repair shop in the early postwar period. Only later on did the company become 'affiliated' with the Mitsubishi Bank (now Tokyo-Mitsubishi Bank). Likewise, Matsushita Electric Industries quickly amassed huge internal funds and has ever since been practically free from external debt. It is also often called the 'Matsushita Bank'. Sony was another example of a non-*keiretsu* firm.

In addition, some successful Japanese corporations were soon able to tap both the bond market at home and the international capital markets for their financial needs at low cost as the former was deregulated and as restrictions on borrowings from abroad were lifted with the amendment of the Foreign Exchange Control Law in 1980. For example, 'As a fraction of all securities issued by Japanese companies, overseas issues [reached] nearly 50% by 1985' (Kester, 1991: 188). The less regulated overseas bond market soon became more popular than its still regulated domestic counterpart: 'within three years of the revision of the Law, the value of bonds issued abroad exceeded the value of bonds issued domestically' (Weinstein and Yafeh, 1998: 637).

Moreover, 'Interestingly, not only were most of these bonds underwritten by Japanese financial institutions, they were purchased by Japanese insurance companies and other Japanese institutions. This was because such foreign issue was far cheaper and easier because of persisting Ministry of Finance (MOF) restrictions on domestic bond issue. MOF has been a slow learner when major transformations are occurring' (personal communications with Hugh Patrick, June 2001). Thus, for a while, Japanese corporate finance had to make a U-turn trip overseas through the international capital market.

As a result of ever-increasing internal funds and the opportunities to raise capital abroad, there was consequently no reason for Japan's successful large corporations to remain subservient to their banks and to be dictated to about how to run their own businesses by bank officials. Besides, the main bank system might not have been as beneficial for the affiliated firms as made out to be by its proponents, who emphasized the magic of the system in solving the problems of information asymmetry and transaction costs. One empirical study (Weinstein and Yafeh, 1998) revealed that the cost of capital of bank-affiliated firms was higher than that of their peers (non-bank-affiliated ones), and that most of the benefits from relation banking were appropriated by the banks. No wonder, then, that the 'departure from banks' syndrome intensified. Japan's main bank system was effective in capital allocation only during the early stages of Japan's postwar catch-up – at most, until the early 1980s with 1975 as its watershed year.

The Asset Bubble and its Aftermath

It was against the backdrop of this rapid structural change in the market environment that the asset bubble of 1987–90, stemming from, and fed by, speculative investments in real estate and stocks, occurred. The easy monetary policy was adopted to combat the so-called 'high-yen recession' after the Group Five (G5) Plaza Accord of 1985, and the banks consequently became awash in liquidity. However, they began to be 'departed from' by big corporations mainly because of the deregulation and development of a corporate bond market, as explained above, and found themselves in need of searching for new, smaller, more risky borrowers, such as small- and medium-sized enterprises, real estate firms, distributors (both wholesalers and retailers) and construction companies. The share of this new group of borrowers soon accounted for as much as one-third of total bank loans. Real estate firms alone, who were engaged in speculative investments, were responsible for one-quarter of the total. In addition, the banks channelled loans through non-blank banks (for example, housing-loan companies and consumer credit firms) because these intermediaries were less strictly regulated than the banks themselves. The non-blank bank loans came to account for as much as 37.8 per cent of the total loans the real estate industry secured during the asset bubble (Noguchi, 1992).

Low interest rates and the abundance of liquidity fuelled the rising prices of stocks and real estate. With the soaring share prices and property values, firms and individuals alike borrowed even more because they used their assets as collateral. Both lenders and borrowers failed to realize that they were under the illusion of non-declining property values, which had actually kept soaring over the preceding 40 years (1950–90). Thus a speculative spiral set in. The dirigiste bank-based finance brought about the problem of moral hazard, but this time the moral hazard effect was of the degenerative type as it inflated the bubble (in contrast to the earlier socially justifiable one).

The bursting of the bubble began in early 1990, following the rise in the discount rate. The Bank of Japan was intent on popping the bubble because of the undesirable income redistribution effect in favour of the haves (asset holders) and against the have-nots (ordinary company employees). The stock market peaked on the last trading day of 1989, and the urban land price started to fall later. The débâcle was a disaster for speculative borrowers in real estate, construction, distribution and finance, as well as for banks as lenders. The latter came to be saddled with the ever-rising amounts of bad loans – the initial cause of Japan's prolonged banking crisis – and more than a decade-long stagnation. In early 2001, the value of outstanding bad loans was estimated to be somewhere between $337.9 billion ('non-performing loans' only) and $1.23 trillion (including 'problem loans'), thus all depending on how 'bad loans' are defined.[2] It is only as recently as 31 March 2005 that bad loans had declined to $226 billion (as reported by the Financial Services Agency) and that bad debt disposal efforts were finally no longer so frequently negated by loans newly turning bad.[3] Japan's banking sector has at last succeeded in bringing the outstanding amounts of bad loans to a manageable level.

Postal Savings System as a Major Source of Investment Funds

It would be amiss if we failed to mention the role of Japan's postal savings system (now called 'Japan Post') in financing catch-up growth. In addition to the main bank system the Japanese government used another financial set-up specifically designed to encourage private savings and to finance state-planned investments, a huge postal savings and insurance programme. The system was modelled on the British Postal Savings system and established in 1875. With ¥386 trillion ($3.6 trillion) in assets in 2004, Japan Post became the world's biggest financial institution, with close to 25 000 branches around the country (in contrast to only 2606 branches run by Japan's seven nationwide banks combined). Its savings deposits alone, of about $2 trillion, which account for 34 per cent of household savings, are some three times those of Japan's largest private bank, Mitsubishi Tokyo Financial Group. Its life insurance represents 30 per cent of the Japanese industry.

In the postwar period this state-run savings programme came to play a significant role in promoting thrift among small savers, notably in rural areas, and complementing the private sector's investments by way of building up industrial infrastructure (such as communications, transportation, port facilities and industrial parks), electrical power, coal mining and other key basic industries (such as iron and steel, petrochemicals, machinery and electronics). Prior to March 2001, the savings collected by the Postal Savings system were deposited into the Trust Fund Bureau of the Ministry of Finance and were in turn lent to the Ministry's Fiscal Investment Loan Programme (FILP). And the FILP parcelled out funds for policy-targeted projects. The government-run financial institutions devoted to Japan's economic growth, such as the Japan Import-Export Bank, the Japan Development Bank and the Japan Finance Corporation for Small Businesses, were some of the major recipients of FILP disbursements.[4]

In the face of financial uncertainties and insecurity brought about in the aftermath of the asset bubble of 1987–90, the postal savings system became very popular among the public, so much so that its savings deposits came to exceed all of Japan's commercial banks combined. This unique institution, however, began to be criticized as unfair government involvement and even regarded as an obsolescent institution standing in the way of market efficiency. It is clearly a left-over from the days of the 'nation-state-cum-mass-politics' axis. It provides vital rural postal services to farmers, who constitute a powerful voting bloc for the ruling Liberal Democratic Party (LDP). It employs 400 000 postal workers, who also comprise a strong lobbying group. Furthermore, Japan Post has funnelled money to politically connected public works such as construction of roads and bridges. In fact, politicians shamelessly used their influence to direct the funds toward pork barrel projects in their own constituencies.

As will be seen below (in section V on protectionism and pork-barrel politics), the LDP itself was split over the plan to privatize Japan Post for good political (if not economic) reasons. There are actually nine other government financial institutions (such as the already partially reformed Government Housing Loan Corporation, the Development Bank of Japan and the Shoko Chukin [Small and Medium Business Finance] Bank), some of which definitely need to be privatized in order to unwind what *The Economist* calls 'Japan's pervasive system of financial socialism'.[5]

IV *KEIRETSU* FORMATION AND CROSS-SHAREHOLDING

The main bank system was organized with *keiretsu* formation, which emphasized collective collaboration not only within each *keiretsu*, but also between the *keiretsu* and the government in industrial development. The *keiretsu* was part and parcel of Japan's industrial dirigisme, serving as the critical vehicle through which state-created capital was channelled into investment projects considered essential under industrial policies. The *keiretsu* served as an effective mechanism to reduce 'coordination failure' in large-scale investment projects (Okazaki, 1997), while business firms individually were not willing or able to take risks. Only a collective investment could realize the potential of increasing returns, linkages and complementarities (dynamic external economies and indivisibilities) simultaneously in both supply and demand capabilities and spillovers. (This is a classic case of market failure once debated in academia in the 1960s when the notions of 'big push' and 'balanced growth' were advanced as a strategy for economic development.)

Another feature of the main bank-led *keiretsu* system is cross-shareholdings among affiliated banks and firms. Mutual holdings of shares were practised as a way of cementing the business ties among intra-*keiretsu* firms and reducing transaction costs (especially the costs of the principal–agent problem and opportunism). The main bank owned shares of its affiliated corporations and other affiliated (usually smaller) banks (up to the legal limit of 5 per cent), and vice versa (no limit for non-financial firms, so long as they own other non-financial firms). The banks' holdings of stocks were said to serve as an important means of influencing the course of business in their client firms, while intercorporated stockholdings on the non-banking sector were also a symbol of mutual trust (and hostage exchange) and long-term relations.

In fact, the interlocking of stock ownership and directorship is what characterized the *keiretsu* system, of both the financial (*kinyu*) and the industrial (*sangyo*) types. It was supposed to serve as a mutual monitoring mechanism, but in reality it largely deepened the entrenchment of management, because hostile takeovers were hindered under this cross-shareholding arrangement. 'Friendly and patient' capital was thus created. Some 10 to 25 per cent of each constituent firm's stock was held by other firms within the group. In addition, two-thirds of these firms had full-time executives dispatched from affiliated firms, resulting in interlocked directorships.

The rise of cross-shareholdings steadily continued. In 1950, for example, individual investors used to own as much as 60 per cent of total value of stocks, financial institutions (mainly banks and insurance companies) had about 12 per cent, and corporations 11 per cent. By the latter half of the 1980s (that is, about 40 years later, during the 1987–90 bubble), however, individual investors' share had declined to 24 per cent, while financial institutions' and corporations' shares had risen to more than 40 per cent and 28 per cent, respectively. That is to say, cross-shareholdings had come to account for no less than 70 per cent. Investment trusts (the Japanese equivalent of mutual funds), foreign investors and pension funds owned relatively small portions, all less than 10 per cent, respectively, at any point in time over the 1950–94 period (Ozawa, 2000). Cross-shareholdings at 481 of Japan's biggest companies stood at 46 per cent at the end of January 1997.[6] In short, the intercorporate holdings of stocks by banks and corporations became quite dominant in the late 1980s.

Loosening Ties

A drastic change has occurred since the bursting of the bubble in 1990 and throughout the 1990s (so-called Japan's 'lost decade'). Interestingly, individual investors' share has been hovering around 20 per cent since 1990. Most importantly, the share of foreign investors began to climb, from 5 per cent in 1990 to 23.7 per cent in 2004 – and is expected to rise further. In fact, some of Japan's major corporations are now being increasingly owned by foreign investors. At the end of March 2005, for example, foreign ownership accounted for as much as 57.2 per cent of Orix's shares, 55.6 per cent of Hoya's shares, 51.7 per cent of Canon's shares, 48.7 per cent of Fuji Photo Film, and 48.1 per cent of Sony's shares. And foreign shareholders have been actively exercising their rights at shareholders' meetings, influencing the management decisions. At Fanuc Ltd's annual meeting on 29 June 2005, its shareholders (whose 43.7 per cent is owned by overseas investors) voted down a proposal to more than double the number of authorized shares to 900 million lest the value of their shares to be diluted. Similar shareholder activism is now observable at other increasingly foreign-owned Japanese firms.[7]

In short, the cross-shareholdings and *keiretsu* formation has been unravelling in the aftermath of the bubble burst, aggravating downward pressure on share prices as a large number of shares were put on the block. The *keiretsu* system also came to cause (i) the overcapacity, overdiversification and overstaffing of productive facilities in the non-financial sector (manufacturing, construction, wholesale and retailing and other services) with too many unprofitable subsidiaries and too many employees to be profitable; and (ii) the excessive number of banks (too many banks to be profitable). The former has contributed to the recent deflationary pressure, while the latter aggravated the unprofitable (as yet not fully restructured) banking sector. Thus the needs for business and financial restructuring arose out of Japan's once phenomenal growth. And this set the stage for the recent spate of M&As (mergers and acquisitions), as will be detailed below.

V   PROTECTIONISM AND PORK-BARREL POLITICS

Any economy has two opposite sectors in terms of their exposure to international competition: the traded goods (tradable) sector and the non-traded goods (nontradable) sector. By definition, the former is subjected to the vigour of international competition, while the latter is protected from it. Japan's tradable sector was developed under dynamic infant-industry protection: that is, a policy of import substitution-cum-export promotion. On the other hand, the nontradable sector produced solely domestic market-oriented goods and services largely because they were protected from imports and inward investment but also because some goods and services were by nature less susceptible to foreign competition. During the course of catch-up economic development, however, these two sectors became even more different from each other, evolving into a dual industrial structure.

As far as the tradable sector is concerned, Japan started out with labour-intensive industries such as textiles and toys in the early postwar years. From there, Japan quickly developed competitiveness in a ladder-climbing fashion: first in capital-intensive industries such as steel, ships, heavy machinery and chemicals during the 1960s; in small compact automobiles and early-generation electronics (for example, colour TVs and calculators) during the 1970s; and in robotics, new materials, microchips and higher-end automobiles – and then on to latest-generation electronics (for example, lap-tops, speciality microchips and play-stations) during the 1980s and up to the mid-1990s. Japan is now eagerly catching up in new Internet-driven, information technology-based industries (Ozawa, 2005).[8]

And all these stage-delineated competitive industries have come to con-stitute what may be called the outer-focused (OF) sector. This sequential development of export industries was accomplished largely by way of dynamic infant-industry protection strategy, initially involving heavy pro-tection and subsidization of domestic industries. Some industries such as consumer electronics, however, developed more autonomously (that is, without any government support) by absorbing the latest technologies from the West mostly under licensing agreements. Japan was fully bent on build-ing nationally-owned (not foreign-controlled) industries at home, but was clearly much dependent on imported technologies on climbing up the ladder of development.

In the meantime, however, Japan ended up creating a slew of once heavily regulated and protected inefficient industries (protected from competition). Foreign competition from imports and inward FDI was fended off, not only by outright legal restrictions, but also by the built-in bias of regula-tions and red tape, as well as of *keiretsu*-based industrial organization. These industries, which may be called the inner-dependent (ID) sector, are agriculture, food and beverage, telecommunications, transportation, wholesale and retailing, construction, health care, banking, finance, insur-ance, real estate and other domestic market-focused services.

These bifurcated sectors were under the jurisdiction of different govern-ment ministries. The OF sector was mainly under the purview of the Ministry of International Trade and Industry (MITI). The ID sector, on the other hand, was under the supervision of a variety of inner-focused min-istries such as the Ministry of Agriculture, Forestry and Fisheries, the Ministry of Construction, the Ministry of Health and Welfare, the Ministry of Posts and Telecommunications, and so on. These ID-supportive min-istries were the home of the interventionists promoting the development of domestic industries under their respective jurisdictions.

As dynamic comparative advantages were acquired in the OF sector, Japan's rising trade surplus began to cause a sharp appreciation of the Yen. Up to 1971, the Yen was nominally fixed at 360 to the dollar. This meant a continuous real depreciation (namely undervaluation) of the Yen as Japanese industry gained export competitiveness. However, once exchange rates were subject to market forces, the Yen quickly began to appreciate. To cope with the ever-rising Yen, the OF sector had to keep raising productivity to remain export competitive. As the sector succeeded in this endeavour, however, it again faced another round of Yen appreciation because the ID sector did not absorb imports sufficiently to relieve the upward pressure on the currency. In other words, the OF sector came to be trapped in a treadmill, a vicious cycle running from a struggle for productivity improvement and a greater trade surplus, to an ever-appreciating Yen, and to an even greater need for cost cutting.

The 'Japanese Disease' and Outward FDI

This intersectoral effect by way of the foreign exchange market is the Japanese version of the 'Dutch disease'. Imports should have become available to Japanese consumers at cheaper and cheaper prices in Yen terms, but they were either hindered by trade and inward FDI barriers or not delivered to consumers at cheaper retail prices (that is, the foreign exchange gains were simply pocketed by the highly regulated and protected distribution sector). In other words, a stronger Yen was a hidden subsidy for the ID sector. As a consequence, the OF sector began to escape from the disadvantages of producing at home by shifting production abroad through outward FDI. The high Yen also subsidized this investment outflow. The upshot was a one-sided imbalance in Japan's FDI account: a huge investment outflow but a miniscule investment inflow.

The 'price distortion' effect of the foreign exchange rate was thus the primary cause of the sharp growth in Japan's outward FDI in the 1985–95 period. Put differently, so far as this period is concerned, Japan became a high-cost country, and many Japanese firms moved offshore, not so much because they were genuinely attracted to overseas host countries that offered promising local markets or truly favourable industrial milieus but because they had to escape from the ever-increasing cost burden of home-based production. This anomaly was caused by the overregulated structure of the ID sector.

ID: the Pork-barrel Sector

What made things worse was that, instead of letting competitive forces rationalize the ID sector, the government held onto – and even reinforced through administrative guidance – its regulatory involvement to further shelter the ID sector. The reason was that this sector as a whole (but especially agriculture, construction, distribution, health and finance) was the key political power base and financial source of the Liberal Democratic Party (LDP), Japan's long-reigning political regime ever since 1955. In this respect, the ID sector can be most appropriately identified as a 'pork-barrel' sector, a political economy institution developed basically as a legacy of the occupation authorities that succeeded in installing the conservative administration. This was the core of Japan's mass/local politics, one of the three basic elements of the trilemma model.

This characteristic is most pronounced particularly in agriculture, construction and small and medium businesses. Early on (for example, in 1955), agriculture was the major political base of the LDP when that sector provided employment for as much as 39 per cent of Japan's work force and yielded 21 per cent of GDP. In fact, this pork-barrel was created as a result of a drastic land reform introduced by the occupation authorities to emancipate peasants. Under this reform, up to 1950, about 1.5 million landlords lost their farmland, while about four million peasant households acquired new land. Consequently, the tenant farmers all but disappeared. The occupation authorities under General MacArthur also converted the prewar and wartime hierarchy of agricultural associations into a democratic agricultural cooperative system. These well-organized agricultural cooperatives eventually became a powerful conservative political bloc on a par with other lobbying groups such as labour unions.

Thus agricultural regions themselves, along with their surrounding semi-urban farm-linked areas (where farm-related activities such as dairy, food processing, farm supplies and services are centred), became a major political power base for the LDP. In addition, throughout Japan, but especially in the urban districts, construction firms and their workers (estimated to be over six million workers, approximately about 10 per cent of Japan's labour force) have been staunch supporters of the LDP. Indeed, many LDP politicians came to represent these interest-group constituents, and have received nicknames such as a 'construction tribe', a 'farm tribe', a 'road tribe', and so on.

Moreover, small businesses in both manufacturing and distribution (wholesale and retail) constitute an important political base for the LDP, as Japan's primary sector contracted while the secondary and tertiary sectors expanded – *pari passu* with rapid economic growth. Wholesale and retail businesses (including restaurants) have been squarely in the highly protected and regulated ID sector. In short, it is thus important to realize how the ID sector was built up as the pork-barrel of LDP politicians.

There has recently occurred a great sea change in Japan's farm policy, however. The Japanese government is now reorienting its policy away from its traditional support in terms of heavy price supports, subsidies and protection toward a greater emphasis on value and efficiency, specifically on self-sufficiency and self-survival. The farm sector should not and cannot remain comparatively disadvantaged; Japan has already begun to see an expanding (hence potentially large) export market in China for high-quality, high-priced Japanese farm goods such as apples, peaches and pears. It can engage in intra-agricultural trade on the basis of comparative advantage. Furthermore, the number of Japanese farmers used to be around eight million back in 1975, but had been cut in half by 2000 – and it keeps declining. Besides, the proportion of over-65-year-old farmers is 60 per cent and rising, and some 70 per cent of farming households now derive most of their income from non-agricultural employment.[9]

The World Trade Organization is moving to free farm trade, putting inescapable pressure on Japan to liberalize the farm sector. True, the farm sector still constitutes a lobbying bloc to be reckoned with, but their days are, if not immediately, numbered.

Given the political embedment of Japan's rural sector, it is easy to see why Prime Minister Koizumi was bound to experience difficulties getting enough support for his Japan Post privatization plan even from many of his own party's members, who were so entangled in the interests of farming rural areas and the construction industry. In August 2005, the Lower House of Parliament barely passed the Postal Reform Bill, and its Upper House rejected the bill. As a consequence Koizumi moved to dissolve the Lower House, called for a general election – and luckily won handsomely on 11 September 2005, securing a mandate for his privatization drive. It still remains to be seen how much support he can secure for the much-needed pension and national health care reforms.

VI   DIALECTIC OF 'PROTECTION FROM INWARD FDI AS PROMOTION'

Paradoxically enough, it is the ID sector, long shielded from inward FDI, that is now eagerly seeking foreign multinational corporations' direct participation in its stagnated businesses in order to escape from the trap of institutional obsolescence. This contradictory turn of events marks the end of 'Japan, Inc.' and the beginning of a process through which Japan's extant institutional matrix will be revamped. The outcome will be a more balanced ledger of FDI flows. As a result of setting up barriers against inward FDI in the early postwar period, Japan has long experienced an 'unfavourable' balance on the FDI account, with outward FDI far exceeding inward FDI. In 1992, for example, Japan's cumulative outflow–inflow FDI ratio was, on a stock basis, as high as 13.3, in contrast to almost 1.0 for the US and UK, 1.4 for Germany and 1.3 for France.

By 1997, Japan's ratio had declined to 5.4, reflecting a steady increase in FDI inflows, but still higher than Germany's 2.8, the UK's 1.4, France's 1.2

and the US's 0.9. This considerable decline in Japan's ratio did reflect stepped-up FDI inflows, especially in the ID sector: 'The industries that have been realigned the most by the influx of foreign capital are the telecommunications, retail, electricity-power generation, and insurance and consumer finance sectors' (JETRO, 2002: 23). In fact, inward FDI in Japan hit a record level in fiscal 2005 (the year ending 31 March, 2005), surpassing Japan's outward FDI for the first time in postwar history.

Beginning in the latter half of the 1990s, signs of fundamental changes in Japan's attitude toward inward FDI started to emerge. Foreign multinationals began to be welcomed as buyers of those Japanese companies that had gone bankrupt in the wake of the bubble burst. The most active buyers were America's so-called 'private equity funds', such as Ripplewood Holdings, Lone Start and Merrill Lynch, Goldman Sacks Group and Morgan Stanley. The first most notable case of acquisition was the takeover of Yamaichi Securities, Japan's oldest securities firm (bankrupted in 1997), by Merrill Lynch. In 1999, the Long-Term Credit Bank of Japan, which used to be one of Japan's three major quasi-public banks designed to provide long-term capital to infrastructure projects throughout Japan's high growth period, was bought by Ripplewood Holdings. It was renamed as the Shinsei Bank and soon turned into a profitable operation.

Since then, this American private equity fund has purchased a string of other Japanese companies such as auto parts makers, audio electronics firms and resorts (hotels and golf courses). Its latest acquisition is the fixed-line operations of Japan Telecom Holdings in 2003. It made news not because Japan's number three fixed-line business had already been foreign-owned by Vodafone Group of UK but because it was Japan's first and largest ($2.18 billion) leveraged buyout (LBO), involving Japan's own banks as co-lenders (Mizuho Corporate Bank, the Bank of Tokyo Mitsubishi and the Sumitomo Mitsui Banking Corporations). The rest of its financing was secured from nine non-Japanese lenders, including Citigroup and J.P. Morgan Securities Asia. The Japanese lenders finally came to grasp the potential for funding LBOs, in part because the deal entailed high fees and also because they became serious for the first time about such lending based on cash flows rather than collateral, the latter having long been the practice of Japanese banking. In other words, the deal marked an important watershed, ushering in a new age of bank-funded corporate buyouts in Japan.

The M&A Boom

Indeed, mergers and acquisitions (M&As) have recently been occurring throughout corporate Japan. Its fragmented pharmaceutical industry, for example, has been rapidly consolidated by way of M&As. Pfizer of the US bought out Banyu Pharmaceuticals, and Roche Holdings of Switzerland acquired a controlling stake in Chugai Pharmaceutical. And they are both expanding in Japan to serve its rapidly ageing population. Not outgunned, Japanese drug makers themselves are also engaged in mergers and acquisitions. In 2005, the Sankyo Company purchased Daiichi Pharmaceutical in a $7.7 billion deal to retain its no. 2 position, second only to Japan's Takeda Pharmaceutical, when the former was about to be challenged by Astellas Pharma, a new company being formed by the $8 billion merger between Japan's current number three drug maker, Yamanouchi Pharmaceutical, and Fujisawa Pharmaceutical. These Japanese drug makers' mergers are motivated by falling prices, rising development costs and worries about being targeted by foreign investors for takeover.[10]

Interestingly, the banking sector itself has been reorganized by way of many mergers and continues to be further consolidated. In August 2005, Japan's number two bank, Mitsubishi Tokyo Financial Group (MTFG), which is a merged entity itself between the Mitsubishi Bank and the Bank of Tokyo, was about to buy out the fourth-biggest, UFJ, to form the world's largest bank with assets of ¥188 trillion ($1.8 trillion). These domestic M&As are to an important extent motivated to pre-empt the potential takeovers by foreign investors. By industry sector, indeed, foreign finance and insurance companies have been most active in boosting their investment in Japan. Foreign banks, brokerage firms and insurance companies are keeping an eye on a huge pool of Japanese savings totalling 1400 trillion Yen (close to $14 billion), about half of which is lying dormant in bank deposits that pay little or no interest in Japan's near-zero interest rate economy.

We could keep enumerating many M&A deals in Japan's other industries as well, especially in retailing, real estate and manufacturing. It suffices here to note that, because of the upswing of M&A deals, the *Wall Street Journal* even captioned an article on this trend 'Japan, the New Mergers Center'.[11] In the meantime, the 'out–in' type of M&As (foreign investors buying out Japanese firms) has quickly risen, even overtaking its 'in–out' type counterparts in 2003 for the first time.

Toward the Equity Culture, American-style

The suddenly rising inward FDI in Japan is naturally boosting the presence of foreign business interests in corporate Japan. They now form an increasingly effective lobbying group that is pressuring the Japanese government to create a more business/capital-friendly hybrid matrix of institutions through deregulation and reforms, a hybrid between American-style capitalism and old Japanese-style capitalism. Inward FDI thus serves as a powerful agent of institutional change in Japan. In fact, a new culture of shareholder capitalism is in the making, and even hostile takeovers, unthinkable only a decade ago, have started to occur in Japan. In 2005, this development was dramatized by the Internet company Liverdoor's (run by its 32-year-old maverick president) attempt to buy out a big and poorly managed Nippon Broadcasting System (NBS), a subsidiary of a large slumbering Fuji TV. The attempt was financed by no other than Lehman Brothers of the US which received so-called 'death spiral' convertible bonds with the right to convert them into shares at a constant discount to the share price. This sent a shock wave throughout corporate Japan, forcing corporations to take up a defensive stance against unfriendly acquisitions and compelling corporate Japan (and the public) to debate the desirability of corporate takeovers, as well as the proper way to launch and defend against a corporate buy-out.[12]

Indeed, the landslide victory of Prime Minister Koizumi and his LDP was immediately accompanied by a strong stock-market rebound with the benchmark Nikkei Stock Average rising to 12896, its highest level in four years. The Japanese households that own approximately $14 trillion in private assets may be turning into a new group of reform-supporting constituents who gave an overwhelming majority support to Koizumi's market reform plans. The reforms will certainly strengthen the equity culture with more favourable investment opportunities for the public's assets.

VII   SUMMING UP

The Japanese experience provides a fascinating case study on the interactions between the inner matrix of domestic institutional set-ups and the outer matrix of evolving global institutions and norms. Early postwar Japan was bent on building up domestically owned (not foreign-owned and controlled) industries. And the inner matrix was specifically designed and constructed to this end. Yet the very success of such an inner matrix in enabling Japan to achieve its century-old national goal of catching up and joining the ranks of the advanced countries has made itself obsolete – and now actually deleterious to growth. It has already caused an asset bubble and its subsequent banking crisis and economic stagnation.

These days, ironically, foreign multinationals have to be eagerly welcomed by Japan to revitalize its slumping corporate business sector. They are regarded as renovators who can remodel Japan's inner set of institutions, especially those related to the ID sector, more closely in accordance with the norms of the outer matrix. In other words, Japan can no longer afford not to disregard the forces of institutional homogenization through inward FDI so as to restructure and make its inner matrix of institutions more compatible with the global economy. This change is indicative of the mandatory shift of policy orientation away from the 'nation-state-cum-mass-politics' axis and toward the 'integration-cum-nation-state' axis in the trilemma model.

The occurrence of the 'Japanese disease' (severe institutional sclerosis) should be interpreted as a necessary cathartic event for Japan to alter the course of growth. The more severe the disease, the greater the pressure on – and hence the mandate for – politicians to act in renovating Japan's old (already more than half-a-century old) matrix of institutions. Yet 'politics as usual' is a big hindrance for Japan's rebound. Reform-bent Prime Minister Koizumi's election victory on 11 September 2005 clearly mirrored the public's strong desire to remake Japan by removing the biggest market distortion, state-run Japan Post, in its financial industry. At the time of this writing (mid-September 2005), the new government appears to be becoming a tipping point to the long-obstructed process of privatization and deregulation, especially with the emergence of the new reform-demanding constituency of investors, both foreign and local. The household sector with close to $14 trillion in financial assets is finally realizing the critical importance of revamping the distorted financial markets for their own interests.

NOTES

1. Schumpeter recognized the role of securities (equity shares and bonds) in finance but he considered them as basically by-products or derivatives of the very process of development that would be brought about by bank loans in the first place (Ozawa, 1999).
2. At the then prevailing exchange rate of ¥122.52 against the US dollar, as reported in the *Wall Street Journal*, 24 April 2001).
3. 'Bank earnings soar as debt woes fade', *Nikkei Weekly*, 8 August 2005.
4. For an excellent study of Japan's postal savings system, see Cargil (2003) and Scher (2003).
5. 'Japanese finance. The state as sugar daddy', *The Economist*, 30 July 2005, pp. 68–9. Other state-backed lenders are the Japan Finance Corporation for Municipal Enterprises, the Japan Bank for International Co-operation, the National Life Finance Corporation (SMEs), Japan Finance Corporation for SMEs, the Agriculture, Forestry and Fisheries Finance Corporation, and the Okinawa Development Finance Corporation. The government-run lenders together hold ¥144 trillion of outstanding loans as of March 2005.
6. 'Big Bang: A whopping explosion', a survey of Japanese finance, *The Economist*, 28 June 1997, pp. 1–18.
7. 'Foreign shareholders boost presence, clout at meetings', *Nikkei Weekly*, 4 July 2005, p. 1.
8. The ladder of economic development Japan has so far scaled can be chronologically classified into five stages: (i) the 'Heckscher–Ohlin' stage of labour-driven industries (for example, textiles); (ii) the 'nondifferentiated Smithian' stage of scale-driven industries (for example, steel); (iii) the 'differentiated Smithian' stage of assembly-driven industries (for example, automobiles and electronics); (iv) the 'Schumpeterian' stage of R&D-based

industries (for example, computers and microchips); and (v) the 'McLuhan' stage of information technology-driven industries (for example, the Internet). See Ozawa (2005) for a stages theory of industrial upgrading.
9. 'Japan's farmers: Facing the scythe?', *The Economist*, 28 May 2005.
10. 'Japan Drug Maker to Buy a Rival for $7.7 Billion', *The New York Times* (on the Web), 26 February 2005.
11. The *Wall Street Journal*, 18 March 2005, C14.
12. For a story on the Livedoor episode, see for example, 'Hostile takeovers: Shaking up corporate Japan', *The Economist*, 26 March 2005, p. 61.

REFERENCES

Aoki, Masahiko (1994), 'Toward an economic model of the Japanese firm', in K. Imai and R. Komiya (eds), *Business Enterprise in Japan: Views of Leading Japanese Economists*, Cambridge, MA: MIT Press, pp. 39–71.
Aoki, Masahiko and Hugh Patrick (eds) (1994), *The Japanese Main Bank System: Its Relevance for Developing and Transforming Economies*, Oxford: Oxford University Press.
Arisawa, Hiromi (ed.) (1967), Nihon Sangyo Hyakunenshi (A 100-year History of Japanese Industry), vols. 1 and 2, Tokyo: Nihon Keizai.
Cargill, Thomas F. (2003), *Postal Savings and Fiscal Investment in Japan: The PSS and FILP*, New York: Oxford University Press.
Friedman, Thomas L. (1999), *The Lexus and the Olive Tree*, New York: Anchor Books.
Genay, H. (1999), 'Japanese banks and market discipline', *Chicago Federal Reserve Bank Letter*, no. 144.
Gerschenkron, Alexander (1962), *Economic Backwardness in Historical Perspective*, Cambridge, MA: Harvard University Press.
JETRO (2002), JETRO Toshi Hakusho (JETRO White Paper on Foreign Direct Investment), Tokyo: JETRO.
Kester, Carl W. (1991), *Japanese Takeovers: The Global Contest for Corporate Control*, Boston, MA: Harvard Business School Press.
Miyazaki, Yoshikazu (1980), 'Excessive competition and the formation of keiretsu', in *Kazuo Sato* (ed.), *Industry and Business in Japan*, White Plains, NY: Sharpe, pp. 53–73.
Noguchi, Yukio (1992), *Baburu no Keizaigaku: Nihon Keizai ni Naniga Okkotanoka* (Economics of the Bubble: What has Happened to the Japanese Economy?), Tokyo: Nihon Keizaisha.
North, Douglass C. (1990), *Institutions, Institutional Change and Economic Performance*, Cambridge, UK: Cambridge University Press.
North, Douglass C. (1999), *Understanding the Process of Economic Change*, London: Institute of Economic Affairs.
North, Douglass C. (2005), 'The Chinese menu (for development)', *The Wall Street Journal*, 7 April, A14.
Okazaki, Tetsuji (1997), 'The Government–firm relationship in postwar Japanese economic recovery: resolving the coordination failure by coordination in industrial rationalization', in Masahiko Aoki, Jyung-Ki Kim and Masahiro Okuno-Fujiwara (eds), *The Role of Government in East Asian Economic Development*, Oxford: Clarendon Press.

Olson, Mancur, Jr (1982), *The Rise and Decline of Nations: Economic Growth, Stagnation and Social Rigidities*, New Haven, CT: Yale University Press.

Ozawa, Terutomo (1974), *Japan's Technological Challenge to the West, 1950–1974, Motivation and Accomplishment*, Cambridge, MA: MIT Press.

Ozawa, Terutomo (1999), 'Bank loan capitalism and financial crises: Japanese and Korean experiences', in Alan Rugman and Gavin Boyd (eds), *Deepening Integration in the Pacific Economies: Corporate Alliances, Contestable Markets, and Free Trade*, Cheltenham, UK and Northampton, MA, USA: Edward Elgar, pp. 214–48.

Ozawa, Terutomo (2000), 'Japanese firms in deepening integration: evolving corporate governance', in Steve Cohen and Gavin Boyd (eds), *Corporate Governance and Globalization: Long Range Planning Issues*, Cheltenham, UK and Northampton, MA, USA: Edward Elgar, pp. 216–44.

Ozawa, Terutomo (2001), 'The 'hidden' side of the "flying-geese" catch-up model: Japan's dirigiste institutional setup and a deepening financial morass', *Journal of Asian Economics*, **12**(4), Winter, 471–91.

Ozawa, Terutomo (2005), *Institutions, Industrial Upgrading, and Economic Performance in Japan: The 'Flying-Geese' Paradigm of Catch-Up Growth*, Cheltenham, UK and Northampton, MA, USA: Edward Elgar.

Patrick, Hugh (1994a), 'Comparisons, contrasts and implications', in Hugh Patrick and Y.C. Park (eds), *The Financial Development of Japan, Korea, and Taiwan*, New York: Oxford University Press, pp. 216–44.

Patrick, Hugh (1994b), 'The relevance of Japanese finance and its main bank system', in Hugh Patrick and Y.C. Park (eds), *The Financial Development of Japan, Korea, and Taiwan*, New York: Oxford University Press, pp. 353–408.

Rodrik, Dani (2000), 'How far will international economic integration go?', *Journal of Economic Perspectives*, **14**(1), 177–87.

Scher, Mark J. (2003), 'Policy challenges and the reform of postal savings in Japan', working paper no. 211, Center on Japanese Economy and Business, Columbia Business School, June.

Schumpeter, Joseph A. (1934), *The Theory of Economic Development*, New York: Oxford University Press (trans. original work published in 1911).

Teranishi, Juro (1994), 'Japan: development and structural change of the financial system', in Hugh Patrick and Y.C. Park (eds), *The Financial Development of Japan, Korea, and Taiwan*, New York: Oxford University Press, pp. 27–80.

Tsuru, Shigeto (1993), *Japan's Capitalism: Creative Defeat and Beyond*, New York: Cambridge University Press.

Wallich, Henry C. and Mabel I. Wallich (1976), 'Banking and finance', in Hugh Patrick and Henry Rosovsky (eds), *Asia's New Giant: How the Japanese Economy Works*, Washington, DC: Brookings Institution, pp. 249–315.

Weinstein, David. E. and Y. Yafeh (1998), 'On the costs of a bank-centered financial system: evidence from the changing main bank relations in Japan', *Journal of Finance*, **LII**(2), 635–72.

7. *Kūdōka*, restructuring and possibilities for industrial policy in Japan

David Bailey and Roger Sugden[1]

I INTRODUCTION

Even as late as the mid-1990s, Japanese intellectuals and officials were promoting the merits of Japanese-style capitalism. Just a few years later, however, confidence in 'Japan Inc' was undermined by the depth and severity of the economic crisis in the wake of the bursting of the 'bubble economy' and the hollowing out of its manufacturing base. A 'reform ideology' (Dore, 2002) has instead come to dominate debate, one which advocates wholesale abandonment of government administrative guidance, deregulation of markets and supply-side 'restructuring'. Ozawa (1996, 1997), Ito (1996) and Katz (1998) inter alia have argued that, even if the Japanese system had been effective in catching up with the West in the post-war period, it had outgrown its usefulness by the 1990s. Katz (1998) blames a system that has 'turned sour' whilst Ozawa (1996, 1997) argues that Japan suffers from a 'Japanese disease' caused chiefly by excessive government involvement and a neo-mercantilist industrial policy. The prescription offered is to deregulate and become like other Western, 'free market' economies.

Whilst in our view correctly identifying some key causes of recent Japanese economic troubles in the form of government failures and barriers to entry, such 'reformist' approaches omit consideration of the role of the present-day centres of strategic decision making, Japanese transnational firms, in the hollowing-out process. The contribution of such actors to 'strategic failure' (see Chapter 4 in the present volume), whereby the decisions of elites conflict with the interests of broader communities, in the de-industrialization of Japan also needs consideration alongside the government failure approach. This chapter therefore aims to present a more complete explanation for Japan's recent economic record, one which links the government failure approach with the activities of Japanese transnational firms. In providing a synthesis of approaches, we reach a better understanding of precisely how and why government failed, for example by looking at how transnationals straddled different sectors of the economy and captured policy for their benefit rather than the broader public interest. This raises important questions over the possible consequences of deregulation in the context of transnationals' activities, and suggests that this may actually exacerbate some of Japan's current economic problems. Rather, an alternative (and we suggest more comprehensive) policy framework for structural reform is outlined, one which liberalizes imports but also aims to broaden and democratize governance structures so as to avoid problems of strategic failure. First, though, the chapter briefly reviews the evidence on Japan's *kūdōka* or hollowing out process and considers whether this has been linked with the activities of Japanese transnational firms.

II THE SCALE AND NATURE OF JAPAN'S *KŪDŌKA*

The 1990 bursting of the bubble and its economic aftermath are well documented, and Ozawa provides a fascinating account in this volume. The stock market crash in particular had a profound and lasting impact, leaving banks with bad loans and in many cases technically insolvent, leading in turn to a 'credit crunch' as they could no longer extend long-term finance. The latter had an impact especially on smaller firms and, combined with recession and the hollowing out phenomenon detailed below, led to a marked decline in the output from such firms (see JSBRI, 2002).

Beyond the 'fall-out' from the bursting of the bubble, though, there has been a more general and deep-rooted process of de-industrialization in Japan involving the relocation of manufacturing activities overseas. Whatever the precise reasons for this, the effect unquestionably has been a marked decline in domestic manufacturing employment during the 1990s, which peaked at 15.69 million in 1992 and fell to 12.22 million in 2003, a fall of almost 3.5 million (M. Ito, 2004). Meanwhile, overseas manufacturing employment in Japanese firms rose from 1.24 million in 1990 to 2.81 million in 2000 (JETRO, 2002). As overall numbers employed by Japanese manufacturing firms fell only marginally, from 16.43 to 16.02 million over this ten-year period, hollowing out would in essence appear to be a reflection of the displacement of domestic employment overseas (ibid.). This is also corroborated by evidence on relative investment and production overseas (UNCTAD, 2002; JSBRI, 2002). For example, domestic production by Japanese manufacturing affiliates overseas rose from 3 per cent of their overall output in 1985 to an estimated 14.5 per cent in 2000, while simultaneously reverse imports (as a percentage of all imports) back into Japan rose from 4.2 per cent in 1990 to 14.8 per cent in 1999 (JSBRI, 2002; METI, 2002a). Not surprisingly in this context, official Japanese unemployment rose from 2.1 per cent in 1993 to 5.3 per cent in 2002 (JSBRI, 2002) before falling back to around 4.1 per cent at the time of writing (June 2003), although many commentators suggest that this significantly underestimates the real scale of unemployment in Japan (Zhao, 2003).

Simultaneously, Japan witnessed rapid growth in outward FDI during the 1980s and 1990s, totalling over US\$595bn between 1987 and 1999 alone (MITI, 1997a, JETRO, 2005). Some of this outward FDI was tariff hopping (to Europe in the 1980s), some tariff preventing (to the US), while other investment was motivated by the search for low labour costs in South East Asia.[2] Much of the manufacturing investment has been in the form of transplant assembly operations, which may have boosted Japan's trade surplus in the short run by producing capital exports and a stream of component exports, perversely exacerbating this sector's problems back in Japan by contributing to trade surpluses and Yen appreciation.[3] Taking a longer-run perspective, however, outward FDI appears to have contributed to a de-industrialization process, with manufacturers in certain sectors producing more overseas, and importing from their overseas ventures.

Beyond this macro picture, the effects of hollowing out are not surprisingly uneven across industries and regions. Most notably, they have been especially profound in those industries that have seen most outward FDI. For example, electrical machinery lost 233000 jobs in Japan during the period 1991 to 1995 alone, with 185000 jobs simultaneously created by Japanese firms overseas (Legewie, 1999). By 1997, electronics production in Japan had halved from the mid-1980s peak, despite overall production by Japanese firms internationally being at an historic high (Cowling and Tomlinson, 2000). Indeed, Harvey et al. (2002) note that outward FDI in electronics and electrical machinery rose from \$1bn in 1986 to almost \$6bn in 1990, with a movement off-shore of large-scale consumer assembly operations setting in motion a series of 'leader-follower FDI decisions'. Similarly, domestic television output in 1995 was just 47 per cent of its 1985 level, with overseas production more than trebling during this period, whilst video production in 1995 was 45 per cent of the 1985 level, with overseas production increasing almost tenfold (EIAJ, 1997).

Where the giant firms went, smaller subcontracting firms tried to follow. However, they faced severe difficulties in doing so.[4] For example, a survey of the Ota cluster in Tokyo showed that 10 per cent of small firms had shifted production overseas during the period 1983 to 1995 (Whittaker, 1997). Remaining small firms suffered as vertical *keiretsu* relations began to fray and as large firms shifted assembly overseas or outsourced components from overseas; Kotani (2003) cites evidence that two-thirds of firms in Ota have been affected by the shift overseas by large firms. Not surprisingly, the number of firms in Ota fell by over a quarter between 1983 and 1995, employment fell by over a third, and the value of output fell by around 20 per cent in a process of decline that Fukushima (2001a) predicted to continue for some time. In this district of concentrated high-level processing technologies, small- and micro-sized firms faced severe difficulties, 'being crushed amidst the rapidly changing industrial structure . . . this concentrated area is experiencing a decline and is being penetrated by the hollowing out phenomenon' (Fukushima, 2001b). The key reason for this, Fukushima argued, was the relocation of operations overseas, with assembler–supplier linkages in Ota being weakened. Indeed, Kotani (2003) noted that, with the shift of production overseas, 'the pyramidal structure with big business standing at the top has fallen apart'. Overall, order volumes received by small and medium-sized subcontractors across Japan fell by a quarter between 1991 and 2002 (JSBRI, 2002). This is also clearly linked with outward FDI and the relocation of activities overseas; as JSBRI (ibid.) noted, the output of subcontractors whose parent companies established operations overseas fell more than that of subcontractors whose parent companies did not. Combined with the post-bubble 'credit crunch' noted above, the number of small firm bankruptcies reached record levels by 2001 (JSBRI, ibid.).

Initially this shift of manufacturing overseas was seen as favourable for the Japanese economy, as low wage assembly activity shifted to ASEAN countries, medium value-added work moved to newly-industrializing economies (NIEs) and high value-added R&D activities were retained at home, in a supposedly mutually beneficial 'flying geese formation' (Whittaker, 1997; Ozawa, 1997). Recently, though, this optimistic assessment has been questioned. While METI (2002b) noted that firms have only just begun to shift R&D activities overseas, Kitagawa (2005a) suggests that this situation could change as China's strategy to translocate ICT production and R&D into certain regions of China begins to bear fruit. An overseas shift in design and R&D activities, albeit less significant thus far than the shift in assembly operations, may in turn pose problems for Japan's service sector (see also Iwase, 1997). In this scenario, the 'flying geese formation' is in danger of becoming a full-scale and permanent migration, although it is too early to say conclusively whether higher value-added activities are shifting en masse.

In a sense every maturing economy witnesses a shift from manufacturing to services and therein a process of natural 'de-industrialization', with a fall in manufacturing's share in total employment (Rowthorn and Wells, 1987), as well as a decline in other indices such as output and trade. That manufacturing's share of total employment in Japan fell from over 24 per cent in 1994 to 20 per cent in 2000 (ILO, 2003) could perhaps reflect this natural trend. However, using Rowthorn and Wells' (1987) classification, we can differentiate between 'positive' and 'negative' variants of de-industrialization. The 'positive' type is associated with the 'normal' process of industrial dynamism in a 'developed' or mature economy, where rapid manufacturing productivity growth releases workers who are absorbed by an expanding service sector. In this positive scenario, unemployment remains low and is frictional in nature as workers search and/or retrain for new service sector employment in an expanding economy where real incomes are rising. In contrast, the 'negative' variety is a sign of economic distress; manufacturing is in severe difficulty and displaced workers are unable to take up employment in the service sector. This is associated with rising unemployment and the stagnation of real incomes. Japan appeared to be firmly in this 'negative' scenario during the 1990s at least, with annual real growth in GDP over 1991–2001 averaging just over 1 per cent, the lowest amongst all OECD countries (OECD, 2002). In addition, total factor productivity (TFP) growth declined across all industrial sectors from the late 1980s onwards, and there was a decline in the numbers of both manufacturing and service sector firms in the late 1990s (JETRO, 1997; Fukao et al., 2002; JSBSC, 1999).

Japan's productivity record is particularly interesting in this respect. Against the backdrop of an intense debate over the benefits and costs arising from globalization, an argument put forward in favour of Japan's entry into the multilateral trade system was that increased openness to trade and FDI would promote higher growth in income, investment and productivity (Ito and Rose, 2004). However, as Ito and Rose note, results from studies 'are anything but clear'. In Japan's case, work by Fukao et al. (2004) shows that the reallocation of resources across sectors – as part of the structural change taking place – reduced TFP growth in the 1990s by around 0.15 per cent per year. However, this overall decline masks marked differences across sectors (Drysdale, 2002), an issue yet to be explored in detail by researchers. Drysdale suggests that those sectors that have done relatively well in terms of TFP growth are those which have been opened up to international competition, whilst those that have not included protected service sectors (such as transport and communications). This view is consistent with characterizing Japan as having a 'dual economy' in which efficient sectors exist alongside inefficient and sheltered sectors, as detailed below.

Fukao et al. (2004) see hollowing out as reflected in a shift from high-performing manufacturing to low-performing services and thus as a cause of the slowdown in TFP growth. Yet other industrialized nations such as the United States have gone through structural change without such TFP effects. This in turn raises the question as to why TFP growth in certain service sectors is so slow, and would accord with a government failure view, with an ossification of regulatory barriers to imports in such service sectors being a significant explanatory factor. However, Fukao et al. also find that there has been a more general TFP growth slowdown across all sectors in Japan during the 1990s, including manufacturing. This would not be expected if manufacturing was becoming 'leaner and fitter' through opening up and the relocation overseas of high-cost activities. Overall, recent productivity evidence would appear to support the view that hollowing out is occurring and that, while performing well relative to protected service sectors, manufacturing has nevertheless seen a productivity slowdown. This is in contrast to experience in the UK during the 1980s, where de-industrialization was associated with rapid productivity growth as the manufacturing workforce shrank and industry became leaner (see Maynard, 1988), although it should be noted that overall manufacturing output remained static (Rowthorn and Coutts, 2004).

In summary, there appears to be strong evidence linking rising unemployment, falling domestic output and severe problems in the small firm sector with the relocation of manufacturing activities overseas by Japanese transnational firms through outward FDI. The concern is over the hollowing out of Japanese industry, which raises the question of how Japan ended up suffering such a deep-rooted malaise.

III   EXPLAINING JAPAN'S *KŪDŌKA*

The Government Failure Approach

In attempting to understand Japan's manufacturing hollowing out, various commentators such as Ozawa (1996, 1997), Ito (1996) and Katz (1998) take the view that, even if the Japanese system had been effective in catching up with the West in the post-war period, it had outgrown its usefulness by the 1970s and 1980s. Ozawa sees Japan as suffering from a 'Japanese disease' caused by excessive government involvement. This is viewed as a more complex version of the so-called 'Dutch disease', a term originally used as shorthand for theories intended to explain how a favourable boost to one export sector had a negative impact on other export sectors via the factor market (rising wages). In Japan's case, the problem is seen as caused by a long-term, sustained rise in the value of the Yen, leading to over-appreciation. This has arguably been stimulated by the export competitiveness of manufacturing sectors such as automobiles, coupled simultaneously with barriers to imports arising from government intransigence against deregulation (Ozawa, 1996, 1997; Katz, 1998). As a result, export expansion was not accompanied by import expansion, the Yen continuously over-appreciated during the 1970s and 1980s, and 'efficient' sectors ended up being penalized. Ozawa argues that an industrial policy aimed at building up manufacturing at home under protection and promotion was ultimately 'futile' as this competitiveness (here meaning export surpluses) drove up the value of the home currency and of wages, eventually making home production less attractive and forcing domestic firms to relocate production activities overseas (Ozawa, 1997).

According to this approach, an industrial dualism emerged in Japan. On the one hand there was a series of highly efficient sectors built (on the whole) with government support after World War II. These 'outer-focused' (OF) sectors were backed by the Ministry of International Trade and Industry (MITI), which addressed OF sectors such as textiles before moving through heavy and chemical industries, then on to cars and electronics and finally certain 'hi-tech' high productivity sectors, using US and other Western experience as a 'road map' of where to go in 'catching up' (see Katz, 1998; Ozawa, 1996, 1997). The approach used foreign exchange resources, low interest loans, and trade and investment protection under an infant industry or strategic trade approach (Johnson, 1982). Its objective was arguably to build dynamic comparative advantage and rapid export growth. Opening up to trade and investment was generally only allowed after the sector in question was deemed to be internationally competitive. Simultaneously, however, other ministries such as the Ministry of Finance (MoF) protected 'inner-dependent' (ID) sectors that were inefficient and sheltered, such as services, retailing, finance and telecommunications. With OF sectors backed by an infant industry approach designed to build comparative advantage and resulting in both a rising trade surplus and Yen appreciation, the outcome was ever more competitive pressure on the ID sectors (the 'Dutch Disease' type intersectoral effect). Yet cheaper imports (in Yen terms) were blocked by non-tariff barriers or prevented from reaching end consumers via barriers or inefficiencies in the distribution and retail system. In the absence of competitive pressures, government administrative guidance regulated and sheltered the ID sectors.

A 'structural gap' subsequently emerged between the two sets of sectors, a gap reflected in price discrepancies between home and foreign markets. Evidence supports this view; for example Taira (1999) showed that the Japanese domestic price level in 1993 was 50 per cent higher than the international price level, and argued that this reflected Japanese markets being extensively protected against price-equalizing international competition. To cope with the long-run appreciation of the Yen, the OF sectors had to keep raising productivity to remain export-competitive, yet, in so doing, they faced another round of Yen appreciation as the ID sector failed to absorb imports. Thus, according to Ozawa (1996, 1997), the OF sectors were trapped on a 'treadmill' of productivity improvement, rising trade surplus, Yen appreciation and the need for further cost cutting, leading eventually to rapid growth in outward FDI and production displacement overseas (see also Katz, 1998).

The implications of this analysis are that Japan needs to deregulate the ID sectors and end the rigidities of a 'neomercantilist' industrial policy. Indeed Katz (1998) argues that this need goes back to the 1970s, by which time Japan had matured and '"catch-up economics" had turned counter-productive'. He argues that, by the 1970s, there were no more infant industries needing an initial push; '"development state" policies make sense only for an economy still in the "state of development"'. Indeed, this approach has emphasized the negative long-run impact of MITI's policies and the need for deregulation, and appears to have had considerable impact, particularly on the younger generation of MITI officials, many of whom have been educated in the West (see Dore, 2002). Such views are increasingly de rigueur in both the West and Japan, and appear to have been accepted by government; by the mid-1990s MITI recognized the existence of a 'dual structure' in which low productivity in ID sectors 'acts as a drag on manufacturing . . . which feeds the hollowing out phenomenon' (MITI, 1995). MITI was in turn replaced by a new market-orientated Ministry of Economy, Trade and Industry (METI), which abandoned the use of the 'old style' industrial policy and embraced a deregulation agenda.

It should be stressed that there is a great deal in this approach that is of relevance in understanding Japan's hollowing out phenomenon, particularly in terms of government failure associated with barriers to imports, cumulative causation effects and spillovers across sectors. However, there remains the need to situate this analysis in a wider context, in particular by relating it to the activities of transnational firms, which, after all, have been the key actors in shifting operations overseas. It would seem that, as with explanations of de-industrialization elsewhere, the usual government failure approach is incomplete in that it overlooks the decision making of elites controlling transnational firms (see Cowling, 1986, on transnationals and British de-industrialization). Bringing in a 'strategic failure' dimension can situate the analysis within a wider perspective and thereby facilitate a better understanding of precisely how and why government failed.

Towards a Synthesis? Bringing in 'Strategic Failure'

In contrast to the government failure approach, Cowling and Sugden's (1998, 1999) 'strategic failure' perspective has been used by Cowling and

Tomlinson (2000, 2002) and Bailey (2003a) in emphasizing the role of Japanese transnationals in the hollowing out process in Japan. This approach is detailed in Chapter 4 of the present volume. The argument is that 'corporate strategies' are strategies for industrial development conceived by and in the interests of strategic decision makers within large transnational corporations, whereas 'industrial strategies' are those devised by and in the interests of a wider set of actors in the community. The implication is that, if strategic decision making is the preserve of only a few, there arises the potential for 'strategic failures' (including de-industrialization) where the objectives of the elite making strategic decisions conflict with wider interests in society, with the result that the economic system fails to deliver the most appropriate outcomes for the community.

The hollowing out or de-industrialization process in Japan can be viewed as an example of strategic failure precisely because policy deliberately concentrated strategic decision making in elites within giant firms (with whom senior civil servants had very close contact – see Johnson, 1982). These elites were then able to capture aspects of policy in the pursuit of their corporate strategic goals. In particular, we suggest below that they simultaneously prompted a liberalization of outward investment while leaving intact controls over imports. This allowed firms to become transnational and shift operations to lower-cost locations (leading to hollowing out), while keeping their home markets protected through import controls, with the negative consequences seen above. In this sense, whilst MITI can be viewed as having successfully built certain OF sectors, its key mistake came in fostering a 'national champions'-type approach through the promotion of giant firms which concentrated decision making. This is consistent with Piore and Sabel's earlier analysis (1984), which noted a preference in the targeting of sectors by government towards large corporate groups. These groups were then able to control suppliers and become centres of strategic decision making as vertical *keiretsu*. Indeed, Czinkota and Woronoff (1991) noted that vertical *keiretsu*, 'given their ownership and direction bring the subsidiaries (also independent suppliers and outlets) into particularly tight units or exercise controls in other ways'. Similarly, Ruigrok and Van Tulder (1995) detailed the means used by the vertical *keiretsu* to maintain control over lower tiers, such as just-in-time delivery, in a 'one way dependency' of suppliers on the large manufacturer.

Furthermore, Bailey (2003b) notes that MITI acted to increase ties and cross-shareholdings within and outside *keiretsu* during the 1960s and 1970s ahead of investment deregulation as part of a project of 'liberalization countermeasures'. To do this MITI changed the Commerce Law (Shōgyō Hō) to enable company boards to issue new shares and place them with friendly firms without the need for shareholder approval. As a result, the percentage of shares held by 'stable shareholder allies' (*antei kabunushi*) rose from 42 per cent in 1964 to 62 per cent by 1973. Whilst this had the desired effect of protecting such firms from takeover for the next 30 years or so (and is still seen as a major 'institutional' barrier to FDI through takeover), it could also be viewed as having concentrated decision making in giant groups. Indeed, even as late as the mid-1990s the 'Big Six' horizontal (*kigyo shudan*) *keiretsu* still accounted, remarkably, for a third of all Japan's corporate assets (Bailey, 2003b).

In this sense, it can be argued that industrial policy really went astray and government failure 'kicked in' when the giant firms (many of whom MITI had deliberately built up) began to capture policy in the late 1960s and early 1970s for their own benefit. By this time, MITI began deregulating, particularly in terms of inward and outward investment in the OF sectors under its remit, because of two factors: internal pressure from large Japanese firms – notably in the car sector, in which Mitsubishi led the way by breaking away from MITI control to set up a joint venture with Chrysler, followed by Isuzu with GM; and external pressure (*gaiatsu*) from the United States (Bailey et al., 1994). Initially a controlled and gradual liberalization during the 1970s, under further pressure this was extended through the 1980 Foreign Exchange and Foreign Trade Control Law that eliminated most controls on outward FDI (Bailey, 2003b). With continued protection for the ID sectors by other ministries, coupled with rising trade surpluses and Yen appreciation, this ultimately facilitated the very rapid growth in FDI outflows in the OF sectors in the late 1980s and 1990s. If this outward FDI had not been deregulated so completely, thereby handing negative freedom to Japanese transnational firms, this problem might have been avoided or at least ameliorated.[5] At the very least there is an issue over the sequencing of deregulation. The failure to deregulate the ID sector ahead of the OF sector was a critical mistake which caused many of the later problems, combined with the complete deregulation of outward investment which led to hollowing out as elite decision makers chose to move labour-intensive activities overseas.

A related issue concerns whether the 'dualism' between the 'efficient' OF sectors and the 'inefficient' ID sectors was ever really so clear-cut. Some have questioned whether the Japanese distribution system, seen as an ID sector in the government failure approach, is really inefficient. Ito and Maruyama (1998) noted that, in terms of value added, gross margins, operating expenses and labour costs, it is 'quite comparable with US performance'. Rather, in explaining price differentials with the rest of the world, they noted that *keiretsu* manufacturers cut off the Japanese market from the rest of world, enabling them to engage in 'pricing to market behaviour'. While Ozawa (1996, 1997) has stressed the existence of linkages between the OF and ID sectors, the government failure approach has generally failed to make the link with the strategic decision making of Japanese transnational firms. In straddling the OF and ID sectors (producing in the OF and selling via the ID sectors), firms producing cars, electronics and other consumer goods were able to exploit the import protection of the ID sectors and charge higher prices at home than abroad. What should be stressed, though, is that it was in the interests of Japanese transnationals to keep such restrictions and to segment their international markets, to make higher profits at home and simultaneously to shift production elsewhere to reduce costs. In this way, the persistence of 'dualism' (with simultaneous regulation and deregulation in different sectors) for so long via import restrictions, as well as the hollowing out itself, was actually prompted by the strategies of Japanese transnationals, with the maintenance of this 'dualism' part of their strategic game. Japanese transnationals increasingly free from control (that is, 'negatively free') have pursued corporate strategies that have been in their interests but not in the interests of wider communities (consumers, workers or the webs of small firms that suffered as a consequence). Such wider communities or 'public interests' as Branston et al. (2006) argue, have not been 'positively free' to contribute to strategic decision making in the Japanese economy, a case of strategic failure.

Bringing in the strategic failure approach therefore provides a different 'lens' through which to view the economy. It enables us to capture a broader range of processes at work in the Japanese economy and can complement and extend the government failure approach. In this way, the suggestion that industrial policy was 'futile' can be seen as an overly superficial response to a complex set of interrelated events which were interrelated via the activities of transnational firms. Rather, policy was ultimately misdirected and insufficiently integrated with other areas of economic policy. Moreover, it was not exactly public policy, because it became captured by private (that is, corporate) interests and used despite public interests. The misdirection occurred because it concentrated decision making in the large *keiretsu*, leading to problems of strategic failure noted above. This policy of allowing and building a concentrated governance structure was in a sense so 'successful' that the giant firms that emerged eventually challenged MITI in the 1970s and captured policy. In addition, policy was not sufficiently integrated; the straddling of sectors by powerful Japanese firms – and the resultant continued protection of some sectors while others were built up – eventually produced the trade imbalances and the 'treadmill' of cost cutting and hollowing out discussed above.

IV   TOWARDS A 'NEW' INDUSTRIAL POLICY?

Given that 'MITI is weak but has yet to find a viable new industrial strategy' (Matsuura et al., 2003), how might a viable new policy be developed to avoid problems of strategic failure? In suggesting possibilities for policy development, our analysis suggests that an objective of industrial policy should be to move towards a more decentralized and diffused economic governance structure that avoids both the concentration of strategic decision making and the capture of policies by elite groups. In addition, different aspects of policy need to be integrated so as to avoid damaging spillovers. The former requires recognizing the positive ('right to') freedom of all participants to contribute to strategic decision making, whilst the latter needs an overarching and integrated strategy that takes a holistic approach recognizing the linkages between sectors and policies. Agencies other than MITI (for example the ministries of Finance and Agriculture) were responsible for the ID sectors and opposed their deregulation; we would argue they were therefore responsible for some critical failures in government policy. If imports had been opened up earlier, the 'treadmill' of Yen appreciation and cost cutting, followed by hollowing out, might have been avoided or substantially ameliorated.

Hence, within our approach, there is not a refutation that MITI was successful in building sector-specific strength; rather, MITI actually played a central role for much of the post-war period in that trade surpluses arose via the 'success' of MITI-targeted sectors. Instead a critical failure was the lack of coordination with other agencies over opening up the ID sectors before investment liberalization of the OF sectors, a lack of coordination which ultimately suffocated the success of the latter via Yen appreciation, leading to hollowing out. The further deregulation of imports in ID sectors is indeed now necessary to avoid Yen over-appreciation leading to further outward FDI. This process has begun; for example, the retail sector is increasingly free from *keiretsu* control. However, if Japan wishes to avoid the problems of strategic failure arising from concentrated decision making, it also needs to broaden decision making amongst a more diffuse set of actors, and to stress the positive freedom of all participants in governance arrangements. In this way it can create an efficient 'free market', here meaning a market positively free for different and all stakeholders to contribute to decisions over strategic matters.

Despite MITI and other agencies having made mistakes on a large scale, industrial policy in Japan did provide some important functions. First, for many years the Japanese government placed limits on the negative freedom of elite decision makers in giant firms, thereby to some extent reducing the risks of strategic failure. For example, inward and outward FDI was closely controlled for many years so as to protect Japan's technology base from erosion by the activities of foreign transnationals (Bailey, 2003b). Second, MITI did successfully address new sectors and technologies. Third, it played an important role in consensus building, serving as the main vehicle for public–private communication (Okimoto, 1989). Recently dismantling policy without taking these successful functions into account has brought a number of problems, notably the dismantling of investment controls and the rapid growth of outward FDI. Thus deregulation alone, and therefore the handing over of negative freedom to elites of decision makers in giant firms, has been a cause of some of the current problems in Japan, with those elites having decided to relocate production overseas. Further, improperly sequenced deregulation carries the risk of reinforcing such strategic failure, by handing yet more negative freedom (freedom from control) to such elites.

Moreover, rather than a transnational-controlled pattern of internationalism, we would argue that alternative 'bottom-up' approaches are feasible. Given the hierarchically structured relationships in manufacturing 'clusters' such as Ota and Tsubame (Yamawaki, 2001), many small firms have been 'crushed' under hollowing out (Fukushima, 2001b). A key objective of policy therefore needs to be to shift the economic structure away from the vertical hierarchical relations of *keiretsu*. Specifically, we would suggest a move towards horizontal cooperation across certain sorts of clusters of small firms, with the regional scale a starting point for such development. As Matsuura et al. (2003) note, 'there is a pressing need for . . . small firms to decouple their own futures from that of large-scale manufacturing in Japan and develop the type of diversified markets and product characteristics of successful industrial districts'. Lessons in this respect might be learnt from experience elsewhere, such as from experience with the Rover Task Force in the West Midlands of Britain over the period 2000–2005. This not only succeeded in diversifying automotive suppliers away from MG Rover before it collapsed, but also encouraged a diversification strategy away from auto into new growth areas (Bailey, 2003c). The revival of the Suwa/Okaya machine manufacturing cluster in Nagano could also offer some pointers as to appropriate policies; M. Ito (2004) notes some success in shifting from a vertical pyramid-type governance structure towards a more horizontal network-based structure that has involved firms engaging in joint production in South East Asia. Such cooperation between local production systems could be promoted, so that localities can begin to overcome the (transnational imposed) inter-system competition that is weakening them, and to become more outward looking, thus reducing their reliance on the vertical *keiretsu*.

Most especially, the goal might be the creation across localities of 'webs' of small firms (Sugden, 1997; Cowling and Sugden, 1999). Webs are a certain sort of cluster. They have been explicitly identified with a set of interrelated characteristics, based partly on a response to the strategic failures of transnational corporations, and partly on economics literature discussing various network experiences. The idea is that they are large-scale production processes comprising a myriad of smaller firms in a nexus of criss-crossing relationships which span localities and international borders; in other words multi-locality (rather than transnational controlled) production processes. It is on this basis that Cowling and Sugden (1999) see the development of webs as a potential alternative to the internationalism of transnationals. The characteristics of webs also include democracy in strategic decision making; a balance of (positive and negative) freedoms across participant actors; a respect for the different experiences, histories, traditions, cultures and competencies of localities, and a drawing on those differences as a source of strength; and an economic culture where all web participants, individually and together, evolve and trust the ability of each to find successful ways of progressing.

The objective might be initially to encourage existing local production systems to look outwards to other systems, to make contact and then ultimately to build actual webs. The desirability of doing this in the Japanese case is perhaps suggested by Fukushima (2001b), who stresses, regarding Ota, the 'appeal for a widening of the development of the network from an intra-area network to an inter-area network which includes regions and overseas areas'. Moreover there have been recent and encouraging signs as to feasibility. For example, the Fukuoka Silicon Sea-belt Project has been explored by Kitagawa (2005a) as a successful example of the creation of a strategic transnational 'space for innovation' in East Asia through links between firms, research institutes, education and training institutes, and innovation support bodies. Underpinning the Project has been recognition that broader national and international alliances are required in market expansion, technology development and human resources. The Project involves Kyushu in Japan, Shinchu in Taiwan, Korea, Shanghai, Hong Kong and Singapore, and collectively has formed a 'vital centre of excellence characterized by strong partnership among industry – government – academia and industries for semiconductor design through manufacturing' (Kitagawa, 2005a). The concept of partnerships across different types of actors in multiple locations can be seen as broadly in line with the web idea, although we would also stress that partnerships which exclude – and, indeed, that are used as a means to exclude – various stakeholders from the strategic decision-making process are contrary to the web vision and might be a problem, since the exclusion might prevent outcomes that are in the wider community interests.

We would further argue that useful services to such webs could feasibly be provided by government-established bodies that monitor the activities and impacts of transnationals across a range of social and economic indicators. The aim of such a monitoring approach would be twofold: first, to provide the Japanese government with a detailed picture of the activities of transnational firms (for example, in the firms' relocation strategies), thereby enabling the government to monitor the hollowing out process, to negotiate with such firms, and to develop appropriate policy responses, building R&D cooperation across regions, and so on; second, the monitoring body could act as a clearing house, providing information on transnationals' activities and impacts to various community groups, including small firms, workers, consumers and so on. In fact, it is possible to think beyond mere webs of small firms and imagine 'community webs', particular forms of network which span all interest groups affected by production activity. This could help in building the countervailing power which would enable a wide set of actors to have an input into strategic decision making, and in beginning to build coalitions of countervailing power between such actors.

Also interesting is that, in 2001, METI (the successor to MITI) set up an 'Industrial Cluster Project' via its regional bureaus, with 19 cluster projects covering 3400 small and medium-sized enterprises and 180 universities across regional networks. These aim to improve the information flow between industry, universities and government; to foster technology commercialization; and to develop support policies to create new technologies based on local, indigenous strengths (METI, 2002c). Simultaneously, however, the Ministry of Education, Sports, Science and Technology (MEXT) has pursued a separate 'Knowledge Cluster Initiative' which has tried to build regional innovation systems based on the so-called 'triple helix' of government–university–business collaboration. This has worked through a bottom-up approach, with proposals coming from local rather than central government (Kitagawa, 2005b). Recognizing the potential lack of coordination between different ministries' cluster policies, the General Council for Science and Technology tried to combine the two approaches through its 'Regional Cluster Plan'. Whilst this has led to regional cooperation between the two ministries, policy evaluation remains separate, potentially causing coordination problems and imposing extra burdens on local actors (Kitagawa, 2005b).

In looking back at the hollowing out experience, job losses across different clusters of firms in Japan have varied widely, Greater Keihin (Tokyo) and the Central and Amagasaki/Itami Districts (Osaka) being the most badly affected, with employment falls of around 20 per cent (M. Ito,

2003). In contrast, Kitakamigawa (Iwate), West district (Shizuoka) and Otsu/South (Shiga) experienced much smaller employment falls, of 2 to 3 per cent. Interestingly, and in contrast to other nearby districts, Kitakamigawa has benefited from the creation of a local production system comprising a diversity of enterprises, with the district attracting many high-tech small firms in addition to large-firm assembly plants (ibid.). This can be seen as a more balanced form of development. It may have relevance for cluster or web development at the regional level, in the sense that a diversity of enterprise forms may be desirable in order to avoid a hierarchical governance structure.

Japan has also recently sought to actively attract FDI (see Bailey, 2003b, for details). Given the high cost base in Japan, a targeted and selective approach towards FDI is required, as lower-order assembly type operations are simply not feasible. Rather, FDI attraction needs to focus on high value-added, capital and research-intensive projects producing 'new-frontier' research such as in nano-, bio- and environmental technology (Morgan, 2002). This has only partly been recognized across regions in Japan. Morgan identifies the need for regionally based strategies linking technologies, location, people and finance, yet performance across regions is extremely uneven, with some hardly having begun to address such issues. Using carefully selected and monitored FDI as a complement to indigenous capabilities is an approach with which Japan had some success in the early 1990s, via the Tsukuba Science City programme (Bailey, 2003b).[6] However, less selective support is not likely to be successful; opening up to FDI in this sense needs to be done selectively and as part of broader regionally based industrial policies. Such a selective 'strategic' approach to FDI attraction and retention is increasingly seen as crucial in order to upgrade FDI and to foster wider spillovers successfully (see Amin and Tomaney, 1995).

The possibility that FDI can act as a channel to promote new cluster formation has become increasingly explicit in other countries such as Britain. However, FDI-generated clusters have often proved fragile, short-term and driven in a top-down manner. All too often, the transnational does not embed itself in the locality but simply relocates if economic conditions change. There tends to be little or no technology transfer and, if there are spin-offs from the transnational these tend to be to subcontractors for whom the transnational is the only buyer. De Propris and Driffield (2006) suggest that, while pre-existing clusters are attractive to inward investors, there is less evidence that inward FDI acts as a conduit to cluster formation. This raises the need for the careful use of policy to attract FDI that complements embedded cluster development, rather than attempting to build clusters in a 'top-down' way around mobile transnationals. However, as in other countries, it is not clear that in Japan there is proper coordination between policies to attract inward FDI and policies to build clusters.

Furthermore, whilst METI has abandoned the selection of sectors using 'traditional' policies, it is now trying to encourage the take-up of new technologies by service sectors so as to 'strengthen the international competitiveness of strategic industries' (Genther Yoshida, 2004). These broadly defined sectors comprise digital home appliances, robots, health and welfare, environment and energy, business support services, entertainment software and fuel cells. The combination of horizontal and vertical/sectoral measures being developed in its 'new industrial policy' has led some commentators to suggest that Japan is 'revisiting the famous government–industry collaboration that served them so well in earlier decades' (ibid.). Given the problems detailed above in terms of concentrated decision making and strategic failure, we would stress that it is imperative that policy diffuse new technologies amongst a wide set of actors in the cluster, including smaller firms, in order to promote competitive and decentralized markets.

However, a key problem in earlier attempts at linking technology and regional development via its Technopolis programme was arguably the centralized, top-down nature of the Japanese state, with regional and local tiers lacking resources and powers (Suzuki, 2001). In a similar vein M. Ito (2003) has criticized the top-down 'regional industrial promotion program' enacted in the 1980s which tried to attract mobile investments to industrial parks through a centrally led and standardized approach. Not surprisingly, the branch–plant assembly operations that were attracted soon relocated to China during the 1990s, ironically intensifying the impact of hollowing out on such districts, leading Ito to conclude that a 'stereotyped form of industrial promotion does not work'. He called instead for local governments to take a more bottom-up approach, formulating their own plans for industrial development and clustering based on regional development strategies founded on regional characteristics. This would also require the development of local capacity to implement such policies effectively. Yet Kitagawa (2005b) notes the current lack of a developed system of multi-level governance in Japan, with marked differences in the capabilities of different regions and no 'distinctive pattern of governance of regional policies at the regional level'.

Developing regional capabilities would accord with the shift to the regional level as the focus for policy design and delivery elsewhere in 'developed' economies, a shift granted an apparent legitimacy through the 'New Regionalism' (NR) perspective. The latter has emphasized the significance of the regional level as the most effective basis for post-Fordist economic management. Paradoxically, globalization has prompted a refocusing on localized agglomerations and spatial clustering (MacLeod, 2001); the regional scale to policy is increasingly seen as vital in delivering competitiveness, requiring regionally based clusters underpinned by social capital, organizational capacity and the provision of collective services. However, the assumptions underpinning this industrial policy paradigm shift have not gone without criticisms. For example, Martin and Sunley (2003) see clusters as a 'chaotic concept' which should carry a 'public policy health warning'. They note that building successful clusters can bring advantages in terms of increased innovation, growth, productivity, competitiveness, new firm formation and higher job growth. However, they also note potential downsides: the danger of technological isomorphism; inflation in the costs of labour, land and housing; widening income disparities; institutional and industrial lock-in; over-specialization; local congestion and environmental pressure.

As long as such concerns are recognized, there would still appear to be powerful arguments for conducting industrial policy at as local a level as possible in Japan. It has been argued that, 'with a greater orientation to regional specialization and with more responsibility pushed down to lower levels of government, Japan could set off a new era of entrepreneurship and cluster development' (Porter et al., 2000). We would agree with such an assessment, provided that a pluralistic and democratic approach is taken. In particular, there is a need to avoid the cluster selection process being elite-dominated; this requires the diffusion of strategic decision-making within and across clusters, in line with our arguments about webs. There is a danger that the ubiquitous, regionally-based cluster policy can be seen as a new form of localised industrial targeting, with similar inherent dangers as at the national level of picking the 'wrong' 'clusters' if the selection process is dominated by an elite group and selection processes are not democratic (Cowling and Sugden, 1999).

Democratically accountable, regional-level institutions would, however, need to work with national-level agencies and banks in developing new financial mechanisms to finance cluster or web development, given problems in the financial system. On the one hand, the banking system has suffered from a 'hangover' of bad loans going back to the bursting of the bubble, prompting a conservative lending policy amongst banks (a supply-side constraint). On the other hand, the long-term export of capital (which feeds the hollowing out process) has in turn led to a repatriation of capital back to Japan, which, along with the high savings rate (Katz, 1998), has produced an oversupply of capital for lending in a depressed economy with a lack of profitable lending opportunities (a demand-side problem). The result has been a downward spiral; conservative banks have been reluctant and unable to find appropriate investment projects while macroeconomic uncertainty has, until very recently, meant that smaller firms increasingly cut off from the security of the *keiretsu* have been unable to attract patient finance. Left unchecked, this will continue to act as a drag on growth. There are no easy answers to this profoundly challenging problem for the Japanese economy. The key point here is that the financial system needs to be adapted from a patient finance 'main bank' system that has supported *keiretsu* growth (and by implication centralized decision making) towards one that finances web-based development (with diffused decision making); for example, via regional development banks providing debt and equity finance for small firms in appropriately conceived clusters. Transplanting institutions across borders rarely works, but Japan might learn from those economies with successful regional production systems such as Italy, where regionally based banks are often part of a network of agents. The latter appear to assist banks in overcoming information asymmetries within loan contracts, thus reducing screening, monitoring and enforcement costs (Bailey and De Propris, 2001). Indeed, the success of production systems in Baden-Württemberg in Germany and in the industrial districts of Northern Italy suggests that financial systems can be effective when they are embedded within a regional institutional framework.

V   CONCLUSION

Kūdōka or hollowing out, has been a key feature of Japan's economic malaise during the 1990s and early 2000s. Much evidence links rising unemployment, falling domestic output and severe problems in the small-firm sector with the relocation of manufacturing activities overseas by Japanese transnational firms through outward FDI. In explaining this process, the 'government failure' approach identifies some key causes in terms of the long-term, sustained rise in the value of the Yen, leading to over-appreciation. This has been stimulated by the export competitiveness of OF sectors, coupled simultaneously with barriers to imports in ID sectors arising from government intransigence on deregulation. Eventually this led to outward FDI and hollowing out. However, this approach is incomplete as it ignores the central role of transnational firms, and linking it with the strategic failure perspective gives a fuller overview of the hollowing out process.

Such a synthesis suggests that MITI's industrial policy contained much that was beneficial in stimulating development in key sectors but it led to problems through the centralization of strategic decision making; the failure to coordinate suitable economic policy across sectors; the failure to sequence deregulation properly; and the capture of policy by Japanese firms that became transnational. These transnationals straddled the OF and ID sectors, and prompted deregulation of outward investment in the OF sectors before deregulation of imports in the ID sectors, a strategy which was in their own interests. This in turn exacerbated economic problems as it resulted in trade surpluses, Yen appreciation and the rapid growth of FDI in the 1980s and 1990s, which led in turn to the hollowing out phenomenon as Japanese transnationals relocated abroad. In other words, the strategy in the interest of transnationals was not in the wider community – or public – interest.

Given the failures of 'traditional' Japanese industrial policy, some may conclude that Katz (1998) is correct in arguing that 'development state' policies should be avoided. However, in a sense economies are always in a state of 'development'; for us, the key is to adapt and tailor policies holistically to that stage of development. In this regard, avoiding strategic failure requires setting in train a framework for developing in a way that reflects broader community interests. While by no means comprehensive, a policy framework has been developed in line with such an approach: democratizing strategic decision making; fostering particular forms of non-hierarchical clusters (so-called multi-locality, small firm webs); establishing transnational monitoring bodies; regionally-based and selective targeting of inward investments that complement cluster needs; and stronger regionally based institutions to build successful clusters or webs, linked with new mechanisms for their financing. These are mutually consistent and reinforcing with a common end-goal, namely, to move Japan away from the government-backed, transnationals-inspired strategic failure experienced through the hollowing out of its manufacturing base, towards an economic system characterized by a more decentralized governance structure in which the positive freedom of various participants to contribute to decision making is recognized. Such suggestions are also entirely consistent with moves to deregulate carefully the ID sectors so as to open up to imports and thus alleviate the problems of perennial trade surpluses and Yen appreciation. Taken together, we suggest that this could contribute to sustainable economic development in Japan.

NOTES

1. Institute for Economic Development Policy, Birmingham Business School, and DARE (Democratic Communities in Academic Research on Economic Development).
2. Arty and Stein (1997) examine the motives of some Japanese firms investing overseas: the main factor was access to cheap labour, followed by a desire to export products assembled overseas back to Japan.

3. Legewie (1999) sees outward FDI as having a modest but positive effect on trade and employment up to 1994 but that by 1995 the trend was clearly downwards. MITI (1997b) is more negative, and sees outward FDI having a negative impact on domestic production and employment as early as 1993. M. Ito (2003) tries to quantify this and estimates the net loss of jobs arising from outward FDI as 600 000 if one takes into account the various export-inducing, export-substituting and re-importing effects, while Matsuura et al. (2003) put the figure at around one million.
4. See Whittaker (1997) on the problems faced by small firms in moving overseas: 'many small firms either pull out or "fade out" (i.e. divest) their foreign investments'.
5. Negative freedom concerns *freedom from* and is concerned with the absence of constraints imposed by others, and ultimately concerns *choice* among alternatives or options that is unimpeded by others. Positive freedom, in contrast, concerns the *right to*, or the freedom of self-mastery of, control of one's own life, of the ability or power to act (see Berlin, 1969).
6. Although Suzuki (2001) argues that Tsukuba's success was atypical of Japan's *Technopolis* projects.

REFERENCES

Amin, A. and J. Tomaney (1995), 'The regional development potential of inward investment in the less favoured regions of the European Community', in A. Amin and J. Tomaney (eds), *Behind the Myth of the European Union*, London: Routledge.
Arty, V. and L. Stein (1997), *The Japanese Economy*, Basingstoke: Macmillan.
Bailey, D. (2003a), 'Explaining Japan's kūdōka (hollowing out): a case of government and strategic failure?', *Asia Pacific Business Review*, **10**(1), 1–20.
Bailey, D. (2003b), 'FDI in Japan: an "open door" or a legacy of "non-institutional" barriers?' *The Journal of World Investment*, **4**(2), 315–41.
Bailey, D. (2003c), 'Globalisation, regions and cluster policies: the case of the Rover task force', *Policy Studies*, **24**(2/3), 67–85.
Bailey, D. and L. De Propris (2001), 'The role for a Scottish development bank in a devolved Scotland', *Scottish Affairs*, **35**.
Bailey, D., G. Harte and R. Sugden (1994), *Transnationals and Governments*, London: Routledge.
Berlin, I. (1969), *Four Essays on Liberty*, Oxford: Oxford University Press.
Branston, J.R., K. Cowling and R. Sugden (2006), 'Corporate governance and the public interest', *International Review of Applied Economics*, **20**(2), 189–212.
Cowling, K. (1986), 'The internationalization of production and deindustrialization', in A. Amin and J. Goddard (eds), *Technological Change, Industrial Restructuring and Regional Development*, London: Allen & Unwin.
Cowling, K. and R. Sugden (1998), 'Strategic trade policy reconsidered: national rivalry vs free trade vs international cooperation', *Kyklos*, **51**(3), 339–58.
Cowling, K. and R. Sugden (1999), 'The wealth of localities, regions and nations: developing multinational economies', *New Political Economy*, **4**(3), 361–78.
Cowling, K. and P.R. Tomlinson (2000), 'The Japanese crisis – a case of strategic failure', *The Economic Journal*, **110**(464), F358–81.
Cowling, K. and P.R. Tomlinson (2002), 'Revisiting the roots of Japan's economic stagnation: the role of the Japanese corporation', *International Review of Applied Economics*, **16**(4), 373–90.
Czinkota, M. and J. Woronoff (1991), *Unlocking Japan's Markets*, Chicago, IL.: Probus.

De Propris, L. and N. Driffield (2006), 'FDI, clusters and technology sourcing', *The Cambridge Journal of Economics*, **30**(2).

Dore, R. (2002), 'Stock market capitalism and its diffusion', *New Political Economy*, 7(1), 116–17.

Drysdale, P. (2002), 'Comment on Fukao et al.', in T. Ito and A. Rose (eds), *Productivity and Growth, East Asia Seminar on Economics*, vol. 13, Chicago: The University of Chicago Press.

EIAJ (Electronic Industries' Association of Japan) (1997), *Facts and Figures 1997 Edition*, Tokyo: EIAJ.

Fukao, K., T. Inui, H. Kawai and T. Miyagawa (2004), 'Sectoral productivity and economic growth in Japan: 1970–1998', in T. Ito and A. Rose (eds), *Productivity and Growth*, NBER-EASE, vol. 13, Chicago, IL: The University of Chicago Press.

Fukushima, H. (2001a), 'Introduction', in H. Fukushima (ed.), *Changes in Agglomeration Structure of Small and Medium Sized Enterprises in the Machinery and Metal Industries*, Tokyo: Nihon University.

Fukushima, H. (2001b), 'Expectations and evaluation of medium and small-scale company policy', in H. Fukushima (ed.), *Changes in Agglomeration Structure of Small and Medium Sized Enterprises in the Machinery and Metal Industries*, Tokyo: Nihon University.

Genther Yoshida, P. (2004), 'Japan's "new" industrial policy revives old successful ways', *Research Technology Management*, **47**(6), 2–4.

Harvey, C., T. Hayward and M. Maclean, (2002), 'Good luck or fine judgement? The growth and development of the Japanese electronics industry, 1945–95', *Asia Pacific Business Review*, **8**(1), 102–26.

ILO (International Labour Organization) (2003), 'LABORSTA database on labour statistics', Geneva: ILO Bureau of Statistics (http://laborsta.ilo.org).

Ito, M. (2004), *Hollowing-out of the Japanese Manufacturing Industry and Regional Employment Development*, Tokyo: The Japan Institute for Labour Policy and Training.

Ito, T. (1996), 'Japan and the Asian economies: a miracle in transition', *Brookings Papers on Economic Activity*, 2, 205–72.

Ito, T. and M. Maruyama (1998), 'Is the Japanese distribution system really inefficient?', in P. Drysdale and L. Gower (eds), *The Japanese Economy*, London: Routledge.

Ito, T. and A. Rose (2004), 'Introduction', in T. Ito and A. Rose (eds), *Productivity and Growth*, NBER-EASE, vol. 13, Chicago, IL: The University of Chicago Press.

Iwase, T. (1997), 'Changing Japanese labour and employment system', *Journal of Japanese Trade and Industry*, 16(**4**), 20–4.

JETRO (Japan External Trade Organisation) (1997), *White Paper on International Trade*, Tokyo: JETRO.

JETRO (Japan External Trade Organisation) (2002), *White Paper on International Trade and Investment*, Tokyo: JETRO.

JETRO (Japan External Trade Organisation) (2005), *White Paper on International Trade and Foreign Direct Investment*, Tokyo: JETRO.

JSBRI (Japan Small Business Research Institute) (2002), *White Paper on Small and Medium Sized Enterprises in Japan*, Tokyo: JSBRI Publications.

JSBSC (Japan Statistics Bureau and Statistics Centre) (1999), *Establishment and Enterprise Census: Summary of the Results of the 1999 Census*, Tokyo: JSBSC.

Johnson, C. (1982), *MITI and the Japanese Miracle. The Growth of Industrial Policy 1925–75*, Stanford, CA: Stanford University Press.

Katz, R. (1998), *Japan. The System that Soured. The Rise and Fall of the Japanese Economic Miracle*, London: M.E. Sharpe.

Kitagawa, F. (2005a), 'The Fukuoka Silicon Sea-belt Project – An East Asian experiment in developing transnational networks', *European Planning Studies*, **13**(5), 793–9.

Kitagawa, F. (2005b), 'Regionalization of innovation policies: the case of Japan', *European Planning Studies*, **13**(4), 601–18

Kotani, H. (2003), 'Industry concentration in Japan: Ota's Case', in H. Fukushima and S. Kobayashi (eds), *Globalization, Regional Concentration and Clustering of Industry*, Tokyo: Nihon University.

Legewie, J. (1999), 'The impact of FDI on domestic employment', in N. Phelps and J. Alden (eds), *Foreign Direct Investment and the Global Economy*, London: The Stationery Office.

MacLeod, G. (2001), 'New regionalism reconsidered', *International Journal of Urban and Regional Research*, **25**(4), 804–29.

Martin, R. and P. Sunley (2003), 'Deconstructing clusters: chaotic concept or policy panacea?', *Journal of Economic Geography*, **3**(1), 5–35.

Matsuura, K., M. Pollitt, R. Takada and S. Tanaka (2003), 'Institutional restructuring in the Japanese economy since 1985', *Journal of Economic Issues*, **37**(4), 999–1022.

Maynard, G. (1988), *The Economy Under Mrs Thatcher*, Oxford: Blackwell.

METI (Ministry of Economy, Trade and Industry) (2002a), *Structural Reform Issues and Economic and Industrial Policy*, Tokyo: METI.

METI (Ministry of Economy, Trade and Industry) (2002b), *White Paper on International Trade*, Tokyo: METI, (available at http://www.meti.go.jp/english/report/data/gIT02maine.html).

METI (Ministry of Economy, Trade and Industry) (2002c), *Toward the Establishment of a Diversified, Creative Work System Conforming to the Trend Toward a Service Economy*, Tokyo: METI

MITI (Ministry of International Trade and Industry) (1995), *Regarding the Report of the Subcommittee for Long-Range Issues of the Industrial Structure Council*, Tokyo: MITI.

MITI (Ministry of International Trade and Industry) (1997a), *Charts and Tables Related to Japanese Direct Investment Abroad*, Tokyo: MITI.

MITI (Ministry of International Trade and Industry) (1997b), *Summary of the Twenty-Seventh Annual Survey of Overseas Business Activities of Japanese Companies*, Tokyo: MITI.

Morgan, A. (2002), 'Promoting Japan for foreign direct investment', *Journal of Japanese Trade and Industry*, **3**, May/June.

OECD (Organization for Economic Cooperation and Development) (2002), *OECD in Figures: Statistics on the Member Countries*, Paris: OECD.

Okimoto, D. (1989), *Between MITI and the Market*, Stanford, CA: Stanford University Press.

Ozawa, T. (1996), 'The new economic nationalism and the "Japanese disease": the conundrum of managed economic growth', *Journal of Economic Issues*, **30**(2), 483–91.

Ozawa, T. (1997), 'Japan', in J.D. Dunning (ed.), *Governments, Globalization, and International Business*, Oxford: Oxford University Press.

Piore, M. and C. Sabel (1984), *The Second Industrial Divide*, New York: Basic Books.

Porter, M., H. Takeuchi and M. Sakakibara (2000), *Can Japan Compete?*, Basingstoke: Macmillan.

Rowthorn, R. and K. Coutts (2004), 'De-industrialisation and the balance of payments in advanced economies', *Cambridge Journal of Economics*, **28**(5), 769–90.

Rowthorn, B. and J.R. Wells (1987), *Deindustrialisation and Foreign Trade*, Cambridge: Cambridge University Press.

Ruigrok, W. and R. Van Tulder (1995), *The Logic of International Restructuring*, London: Routledge.

Sugden, R. (1997), 'Economias multinacionales y la ley del desarrollo sin equidad,' *FACES: Revista de la Facultad de Ciencias Economicas y Sociales*, **3**, 87–109.

Suzuki, S. (2001), *Study of Hi-Tech Development Policy in Japan* (in Japanese), Kyoto: Minerva.

Taira, K. (1999), 'Japan faces the twenty-first century', in W. Halal and K. Taylor (eds), *Twenty-First Century Economics*, Basingstoke: Macmillan.

UNCTAD (United Nations Conference on Trade and Development) (2002), *World Investment Report*, New York: UNCTAD.

Whittaker, D.H. (1997), *Small Firms in the Japanese Economy*, Cambridge: Cambridge University Press.

Yamawaki, H. (2001), *The Evolution and Structure of Industrial Clusters in Japan*, Washington, DC: World Bank Institute.

Zhao, J. (2003), *Unemployment Redefined*, San Jose: US–Japan–China Comparative Policy Research Institute. (http://www.cpri.tripod.com/cpr 2003/unemployment.pdf).

8.   The national innovation system: a key to Japan's future growth

Hiroyuki Odagiri

A 'national innovation system' refers to the system of institutional and socioeconomic conditions that influence the innovation activity of a nation.[1] It has two important characteristics.

The first characteristic – the one in a, say, horizontal dimension – is its relationship with other 'systems'. In every country, the most active performers of innovation are private firms; inevitably, therefore, a nation's innovation system is closely intertwined with its business system, including the systems related to finance, corporate governance, the allocation and accumulation of human resources, and the boundary of the firm. Also innovation is dependent on scientific research. Because such research is carried out at universities and government-sponsored research laboratories, among others, a national innovation system is closely related to the country's university system and the national science system. Of course, the university system also affects the innovation system through the supply of scientists and engineers. Another is the legal system because the country's law provides a basis upon which innovation is carried out. This is particularly applicable with intellectual property laws, such as the patent law, because they influence both inventors' incentives and the speed of knowledge diffusion. Also company law and the competition law affect private investment for innovation.

The second characteristic – the one in a, say, historical dimension – is path-dependence: the way a nation's innovation system evolves cannot be free from the path it has taken until then. Because of uncertainty, bounded rationality and inertia, one's search for better alternatives is bound to be local and, hence, dependent on the historical path. In consequence, the national innovation system can never jump to the 'optimal' equilibrium but only evolves towards it, as argued by the evolutionary theory (Nelson and Winter, 1982; Nelson, 1995).

These two facts imply that a nation's innovation system co-evolves with its other systems. In this chapter, I intend to discuss how the innovation system and the business system are currently co-evolving in Japan because

I believe that the ongoing change in its scientific environment also calls for a change in the way businesses are conducted. This is something which will have important implications for the future nature of the Japanese industrial organization and economic development path.

In the next section I begin by arguing that Japan's post-WWII (World War II) development of innovation can be separated into three periods. The first period (1945–72) was the 'catch up' period where Japan relied upon technology importation, while in the second period (1973–90), the emphasis was on own firm innovation. The third period, which began in 1990, is characterized by science-based innovation, such as information technology and biotechnology, and will be discussed in detail in section II. In sections III and IV I will discuss how Japan's business system and the labour system have been changing. In section V, I will argue that an important characteristic of science-based innovation is its broad applicability; that is, innovation is carried out and the outcome is applied beyond the traditional boundary of industries. In section VI, I will discuss that, as a consequence of this changing industrial boundary, it has become imperative for firms to utilize outside capabilities and combine them with internal R&D through alliances and outsourcing. In other words, the R&D boundary of the firm also needs to change. section VII concludes the chapter.[2]

I   JAPAN'S POSTWAR INNOVATION SYSTEM

It is hardly satisfactory to discuss only the postwar history of Japan's innovation system because, as implied in the aforementioned characteristic of path-dependence, its development depended on the path it had taken in the pre-war period. Unfortunately, however, the space limitation does not allow me to discuss the prewar experience: see Odagiri and Goto (1996) for a fuller discussion of development in both the prewar and postwar periods.

The years marking the beginning and ending of each period are inaccurate because various conditions change only gradually and at different times. Period 1 started with the end of the war and covers the high-growth era of the 1950s and 1960s, ending with the oil crisis of 1973. Period 2 started when catch-up was mostly completed and many firms started emphasizing the need for their own inventions. Period 3 corresponds to the so-called 'post-bubble' depression period. As regards the innovation system, the prominent feature of this third period is the increasing linkage between science and technology. We now discuss these periods in turn.

When the war ended, Japan was technologically behind the USA and Europe owing, for instance, to its isolation during the war from the scientific and technological discovery made in the West, such as petrochemicals and penicillin. Also a large part of its production facility had been damaged by bombing. Still, the country had inherited industrial and technological bases, both tangible and intangible, from the pre-war period and, with these bases, the country resumed its efforts to catch up with the West, actively importing technologies. On a 1995-yen basis, technology import (that is, the payment for technologies licensed from abroad) increased from 26 billion yen in 1952 to 512 billion yen in 1971 at an annual growth rate of 17.0 per cent.

Domestic R&D expenditures also increased, at an annual rate of 16.9 per cent during the same period. As a consequence, its ratio to GDP increased from 0.62 per cent in 1956 to 1.85 per cent in 1971. Technology importation is never a simple process. Imported technology may be immature or unsuited to local natural and social conditions. Quite often, fierce domestic competition propelled Japanese firms to import new technologies at a still commercially untested stage. Thus they had to expend heavily on R&D to develop the technologies further in order to make them applicable to manufacturing processes and to make them commercially viable. With this technology importation supported by R&D investment, Japan gradually caught up with the state-of-the-art technologies of the world.

In Period 2, the weight of R&D shifted from improvement of imported technologies to own inventions, as evidenced by the increased patenting activity. From 1971 to 1987, the number of patent applications by the Japanese to the Japan Patent Office (JPO) increased at an annual rate of 9 per cent.[3] Technology exports also started rising, not only because of increasing inventions by Japanese firms but also because of increased licensing to Japanese subsidiaries abroad. Thus the ratio of technology exports to technology imports improved and exceeded unity in 1993.[4] Since then it has increased rapidly and, in 2002, the export of technology was 2.6 times greater than that of technology import. The ratio is particularly high in the automobile industry, reaching 75.0 in 2002, owing to the active globalization of Japanese carmakers, because 86.7 per cent of technology export by the industry is made between Japanese parents (including those partly owned by foreign firms, such as Mazda and, more recently, Nissan) and their subsidiaries abroad.

In consequence of these increased R&D efforts, Japan now has the highest R&D/GDP ratio among all countries except Sweden and Finland. This high R&D investment is led by the industries. The proportion of R&D expended by industries is around 70 per cent in Japan and in most major countries (except France, where it is 62 per cent). In 1991, the proportion of R&D funded by industries was 73 per cent in Japan, slightly exceeding the proportion expended by them, implying that the industries paid more than they expended; that is, they subsidized the R&D of other sectors. This is in a contrast to the USA where the proportion of industry funding was

57 per cent, which is lower than the proportion of industry expenditure by 15 percentage points, because the US industries received large government R&D subsidies. The same can be said of major European countries, in which the proportion of industry funding was 62 per cent (Germany), 50 per cent (UK) and 43 per cent (France). Since then, the USA and Europe have decreased the proportion of government funds, in contrast to Japan which increased it, resulting in the convergence of the proportion of industry funding among these countries, particularly among Japan, the USA and Germany.

The shift of innovation focus from catch-up with technology importation in Period 1 to own innovation in Period 2 was a response to two important changes in the global environment surrounding innovation. The first, obviously, is Japan's completion of catch-up, as most clearly illustrated by the fact that Japan's R&D/GDP ratio outweighed that of the USA for the first time in 1987 and has been higher since then. In consequence, American and European firms became more and more reluctant to license technologies to Japanese firms who, they had observed, grew to be their formidable competitors in global markets. Many of them started to ask for technologies to cross-license rather than just monetary payments in return for the technologies. Furthermore, many of them started direct investment into Japan in order fully to gain the returns to their innovations.

Second, partly in response to Japan's catch-up, the US shifted its public policy stance towards a pro-industrial one in the 1980s. Mowery and Rosenberg (1993, p. 58) assert that 'the contrast between the position of the newly elected Reagan Administration in 1981, denying any role for the federal government in the development and commercialization of new civilian technologies, and the Reagan Administration of 1987–1988, is dramatic', raising, as an example, the launching of two military-funded research programmes in civilian technology development. The USA also strengthened patent protection 'in three major ways: extending patent protection to new subject matter; giving greater power to patent holders in infringement lawsuits; and lengthening the term of patents' (Gallini, 2002, p. 133). During the 1980s, patents were extended, for instance, to genetically engineered bacteria, software and business methods. Also the creation of a special court for patent infringement cases (the Court of Appeals for the Federal Circuit, or CAFC) significantly increased the probability of patent-holders winning in such cases (Gallini, 2002).

The impact of this change shook Japanese firms through, for instance, the lawsuit brought by Corning Glass Works (a US firm) against Sumitomo Electric Industries (SEI, a Japanese firm) on the alleged infringement by SEI of Corning's patent on optical fibre. SEI maintained that its technology is different from Corning's and hence did not infringe Corning's patent;

however, CAFC interpreted the patent as covering a broad range of technologies, including SEI's, and concluded in 1989 that SEI infringed Corning's patent. In consequence, SEI was forced to pay a 25 million dollar award to Corning. This incident gave a strong lesson to Japanese firms on the need to respect others' intellectual property rights (IPRs) and also to protect their own inventions with IPRs.

With these changes, Japanese firms started to realize that it was no longer possible or desirable to depend upon technologies imported from abroad and that they had to pursue further growth with their own innovation of new products and new processes. They may still import technologies to complement and augment their own technologies. However, particularly in the case of electronics, cross-licensing has become common and, without technologies to offer, licensing bargaining became more and more difficult. It is with these changes that the emphasis on own innovation became the key aspect of Period 2.

II INCREASING IMPORTANCE OF SCIENCE-BASED INNOVATIONS

A significant change that occurred during the last two decades of the twentieth century as regards the nature of technological progress is the increased linkage of industrial innovation to science. Of course, scientific achievements always fostered innovations, from the application of chemical research findings for developing new dyes in the late nineteenth century (Murmann, 2003) to the invention of computers and transistors. However, the last couple of decades have witnessed a dramatic increase in the use of scientific discoveries in industrial R&D. Narin and his group (for example, Narin et al., 1997) have proposed measuring this linkage of industrial R&D to science by the number of citations to scientific papers per US patent. In the US, patent applicants are required to list any prior arts (mostly papers and patents) that are related to the technologies to be patented. It can be assumed that, if the application cites many scientific papers, the invention benefited greatly from scientific discoveries. Thus the per-patent number of citations to scientific papers is commonly used as an index of 'science linkage'.

This index rose from 0.31 in 1985 to 2.24 in 2003, a seven-fold increase in less than 20 years, indicating a rapid increase in science linkage.[5] Among the US patent applicants only, the index is 3.28 in 2003, higher than that among Japanese applicants, 0.51. This US–Japan difference may partly be due to a higher tendency among US applicants to cite prior arts for fear of being complained about by the patent-examiners or the authors/inventors of these prior arts, yet it should suggest more active university–industry collaboration in the USA.

Another important fact about science linkage is that, by patent code classification, several fields are known to have particularly high scores. Biology/microbiology has the highest score at 24.32 (among US applicants), followed by organic chemistry (15.83) and medicine/veterinary medicine (8.24), suggesting that biotechnology-related inventions benefited heavily from scientific discoveries.

That is, industrial innovation has become more science-based and this tendency is most evident in biotechnology. Information technology and nanotechnology are other fields in which innovation is science-based. Innovations, we note, are based on sciences in two senses. First, scientific research outcome would be applied and developed for industrialization. Second, sciences would be used to solve the bottlenecks that may arise in the course of R&D and production. Also any information discovered during R&D or production would be fed back to scientific research. Therefore the flow of information is not unidirectional from science to development/commercialization as the so-called 'linear model' of innovation implies. Information also flows from development or production to science. This bidirectional and 'chain-linked' interaction between scientific activities and industrial innovation is the essence of science-based innovation.[6]

Science-based innovation, we note, is not necessarily a discontinuous jump from more traditional engineering-based or manufacturing-based innovation. In fact, many of the industries characterized by science-based innovation are also engineering-based. The information and electronics industries probably give the best examples. The development of a next-generation mobile communication system requires both scientific knowledge and engineering know-how, and so does the development of next-generation semiconductors. In biotechnology, the development and manufacture of DNA chips, for instance, also require the engineering knowledge on hydrodynamics.

Even though science-based innovation has become common in any developed country, the USA is clearly the forerunner on many fronts and Japan has been making efforts to catch up with it. This is particularly true of information technologies. While Japanese big firms were content with their DRAM semiconductor business dominating the world in the 1980s, Intel concentrated its development efforts on microprocessors and eventually dominated the world semiconductor market.[7] Other startup firms in the USA, such as Hewlett-Packard, Apple and Microsoft, gave rise to the PC revolution. Most of them had been started by former university professors, university graduates or university dropouts.

In biotechnology, the relationship of startups with universities is even more prominent, as exemplified by the case of a pioneer biotech firm, Genentech, one of whose founders was J. Boyer, then the professor of University of California, San Francisco, whose invention of recombinant DNA method with S. Cohen is well known. Many other biotech startups were also established. Big pharmaceutical firms also introduced biotechnology into their R&D.

Being behind the USA in such development of science-based innovation, Japan started big efforts to catch up with the USA during the 1990s. Because the Japanese economy faced a post-bubble recession from 1990 and the firms were suffering from depressed demand, the introduction of science-based innovation, such as biotechnology and IT, appeared to them to open up new opportunities for growth.

The new development in the USA, as discussed above, suggest two prominent features of science-based innovations: the need for closer university–industry relationship and the role of startup firms as a significant undertaker of innovations. These features are in part dependent on the US system of universities. For instance, unlike the situation in Japan or Europe, many of the major American universities are private and financially dependent on the contributions from individuals and industries. Also many of the US state universities were established with the aim of supporting local industries.[8] With these traditions, collaboration with industries was not something to be despised by university members, even after the student movement of the 1960s. In addition, the US business system has been characterized by higher mobility of people among firms and between firms and universities, which also helped university–industry collaborations and startups. Discovering that these features of the US system fit the requirement of science-based industries, Japan also started to promote these activities in the 1990s. Thus began Period 3, as defined earlier. We therefore discuss university–industry collaboration and startups in turn.

University–Industry Collaboration

It probably goes without saying that, with the largest performer of scientific research being universities (and national laboratories), close university–industry (UI) collaboration is essential for science-based innovation. It should be emphasized, however, that, as the above-cited measurement of science linkage implies, the most common channel of information from academic research to industrial innovation is publication of papers. For instance, Branstetter's research (2003) confirms the great contribution of papers published by university faculties on industrial patenting. In other words, the greatest contribution of universities must be made through what Nelson (2004) called 'scientific commons'.

Universities can also contribute to industrial innovation in other, less public ways, because, as discussed earlier, the unidirectional flow of science to innovation is insufficient. Industrial R&D teams may face technological difficulties and, to solve them, they may seek the advice of academic scientists or propose to start joint research with such scientists. Invented technology may be transferred from universities to industries by means of the licensing of university patents. However, the development of a commercially viable product from a patented invention is not always straightforward. The licensed patent may not cover all the necessary technology and knowhow, which may be smoothly transferred only when the university inventor is actively involved. Also, as the term 'absorptive capacity' implies, a sufficient capability is needed on the licensee's side and, even with such capability, unexpected bottlenecks may arise in the course of development. Any advice by university inventors or other academics may help the industry to acquire a necessary capacity or to solve the bottlenecks.

UI collaborations may also be called for at a pre-invention stage. That is, industries often commission research to universities or propose joint research with them. Joint research is an attractive option because supposedly complementary capabilities of university scientists (who are good at, say, theorizing) and industry engineers (who are good at, say, experimenting and building prototypes) can be combined.

In Japan also, UI collaboration was by no means absent and, actually, universities did play an important role in Japan's early industrial and technological development (Odagiri, 1999). As was somewhat common with the USA, another late-developing country at the time, Japan in the mid-nineteenth century was desperate to catch up with the then state-of-the-art technologies of advanced European nations. Thus its higher education system emphasized the acquisition of practical technological knowledge and skills. Technologically knowledgeable people were scarce and mostly in universities; hence, industries actively sought information and advice from university faculties.

Unfortunately, particularly after World War II, a uniform and rigid regulation began to be imposed upon university faculties. Such regulation was strictly enforced because most of the major universities in Japan were national and their professors were civil servants.[9] Hence professors could receive industry funds only to a limited extent, as with their spending time for industries. They were not encouraged to apply for patents and could not become directors of a private company.

In the past few years, however, there has been a drastic shift towards deregulation and encouragement of UI collaborations. Professors can now join boards of directors of private companies. Policies to promote joint research with industries have been adopted. Technology licensing offices (TLOs) have been established for many universities. Furthermore, with the National University Corporation Law, every national university in Japan was incorporated into a semi-independent corporation in April 2004, giving universities more incentives to receive funds from industries and freeing the professors from the civil servant code. With these reforms, UI joint research projects have been increasing and so have the number of startups based on university-invented technologies and the number of patents by university researchers. This rise in UI collaborations and, more generally, the change in the expected role of universities has been significant in transforming the national innovation system of Japan.

Startups

The promotion of startups has been another major policy issue. The rate of entry (the number of new enterprises as a percentage of the initial number of enterprises) in Japan dropped from 5.9 per cent in 1975–78 to 3.1 per cent in 1999–2001, which is lower than the rate of exit, 4.5 per cent.[10] One may assume that the loss of market demand owing to the business stagnation of the 1990s caused this fall. Actually, however, the entry rate started to fall not after 1990 but in the early 1980s, when business conditions were still favourable.

Thus the government has adopted several policies to promote startups by, for instance, providing subsidies and debt guarantees to small and medium-sized enterprises (existing SMEs, new startups or individuals) in order to support their investment for the purpose of starting new businesses or developing and commercializing new technologies, providing tax advantages to individuals investing in startup companies and reducing the minimum amount of capital required to found a stock company.

Helped by these policies, the number of high-tech startups has been increasing. For instance, the number of biotech startups in operation increased from 60 in 1998 to 387 in 2003.[11] Three stock markets (HERCULES, JASDAQ and MOTHERS) were newly opened or reorganized from existing ones to make it easier for startups to trade their shares and, as a result, many startups have succeeded in initial public offerings (IPOs). Nonetheless, these startups have faced several difficulties because the Japanese business system has not been particularly favorable to startup activities. To understand these difficulties, let us now discuss the business system and its changes.

III JAPAN'S BUSINESS SYSTEM AND THE CHANGES

By the 1980s, that is, during what I called Periods 1 and 2, Japan's business system came to be known for its several prominent characteristics, which may be summarized as follows. A substantial share of the firm is owned by friendly shareholders, such as banks and group firms. The management is almost always appointed through internal promotion and, hence, the top executive has the experience of working with the firm for a long time, usually identifying his (and rarely 'her') interest with that of fellow employees. The internal labour system is characterized by a long-term (if not 'lifetime') company–employee relationship. In order to raise skill levels, internal training, both off-the-job and on-the-job, and rotation programmes were organized in most companies.

Such a system had significant implications for the innovation system. First, with the managers having less need to worry about hostile takeovers and knowing that the employees are mostly concerned with their future promotion opportunities, they tended to pursue long-run growth by investing in both tangible assets (that is, plants and equipment) and intangible assets (innovation and marketing). Second, owing to the long-term employment relationship with occasional intra-firm rotation, the linkage among R&D, production and sales departments was tight, fostering the manufacturing and marketing applications of innovations. Moreover, such linkages tended to extend to suppliers and other affiliated firms because the assembler–supplier relationship also tended to be long-term, which helped them to share information among them. Third, the introduction of new technologies to production lines was easier both because of the abovementioned interaction between R&D and manufacturing departments and because of the flexibility in re-arranging workshops and the broader skills of workers nurtured through internal training and rotation (for more details, see Odagiri, 1992).

Since 1990, gradual but significant changes have been taking place in this business system. Banks (excluding trust banks) reduced their share ownership of public companies from 15.7 per cent in 1988 to 5.3 per cent in 2004, while the percentage of pension funds increased from 1.0 per cent to 4.0 per cent and that of foreigners increased from 4.3 per cent to 23.7 per cent.[12] Since the latter two categories of shareholders are presumably more sensitive to returns, this change must have worked to have the management more concerned with the shareholder value. To reflect the shareholders' view better, many firms have reformed their boards of directors, often by inviting outside directors.

The sharp decrease in banks' shareholding, together with the decreased cross-shareholding among non-financial firms, also indicates that the so-called *kigyo shudan* or business group (also called horizontal *keiretsu* by some Westerners) has been losing its significance. I have indicated that the role of such a group used to be limited and it has not been more than a loose federation of independent firms (Odagiri, 1992). Now, this federation has become even more ineffectual. It is true that, for instance, Mitsui group or Sumitomo group still has its presidents' lunch meeting regularly. However, since the formation by merger of Sumitomo Mitsui Banking Corp (SMBC) in 2001, this bank participates in both presidents' meetings. Given that the bank has been considered the leader of such a group, it is hardly realistic to assume that a business group can make collective decisions of any kind (except perhaps the use of trademarks and philanthropic activities) when its member bank is also a member of a rival group. That the Japanese Fair Trade Commission stopped conducting surveys of the six largest business groups implicitly indicates their view that these groups can exert no influence on competition.

The labour system has been also changing, if gradually. One such change is the widespread adoption of a performance-based compensation scheme, in place of (or in addition to) the traditional seniority-based compensation scheme. Even if performance is correlated with seniority and hence, on average, the performance-based compensation may resemble seniority-based compensation, it has now become common for workers of the same seniority level to receive divergent pay, depending on their performance or ability. Another change is the increasing proportion of part-time, temporary or dispatched workers. The proportion of these workers among employees increased from 18.8 per cent in 1990 to 28.1 per cent in 2003, and was particularly high among the wholesale, retail and restaurant industries (45.0 per cent in 2002).[13]

Has the long-term employer–worker relationship collapsed? This is a difficult question to answer. During the recession of the 1990s, a number of companies took on a measure of voluntary retirement with extra severance pay, which, in many cases, might be regarded as de facto dismissal of workers. Bankruptcies also became more common. Hence, many workers now feel that their employment is not as secure and permanent as before. Still, according to a survey of 1066 Japanese firms in 2004, more than three-quarters of them indicated that they intend to maintain long-term employment of their regular workers.[14] In this regard, the long-term employment relationship, I would say, still remains the 'norm', if not necessarily the reality, of the Japanese employment system.

I believe that this practice is still effective in maintaining and accumulating skills within the firm. Many firms consider this maintenance of skill levels to be an acute problem, particularly because the ageing of the working population, together with the shifting of plants overseas, such as to China and Southeast Asia, have been making such maintenance urgent.

IV   THE CONSEQUENCES OF THE BUSINESS SYSTEM FOR START-UP ACTIVITIES

In 2001–02, Odagiri and Nakamura (2002) undertook interviews and a questionnaire survey of 65 Japanese biotech startups. When we asked the firms if they felt each of 13 listed probable obstacles to be a significant barrier in founding their firms, 54 per cent of them answered yes to 'the difficulty in recruiting technological staff'. This was followed by 'difficulty in financing' (49 per cent), 'difficulty in recruiting non-technological staff (e.g., finance, accounting and legal)' (23 per cent), and 'difficulty in securing wet laboratories' (23 per cent). Evidently, recruitment of technological and non-technological staff is a big hurdle for Japanese startups, together with financing.

Partly, this difficulty comes from the smaller number of specialists in Japan in comparison to the USA, such as lawyers and certified accountants. More important in our view is the lower mobility of workers in general in Japan, caused by the long-term employer–worker attachment as discussed above. Even though Japan's labour system has been gradually moving towards a more mobile one, the mobility is still lower compared to other countries, particularly the USA. The long-term attachment is most evident in big firms and these big firms tend to have talented people both because they can recruit better workers and because their workers tend to receive more in-company training and wider experience. This situation makes it difficult for startups to recruit good scientists and engineers as well as management staff, including those in accounting, finance, legal affairs, intellectual property management, and administration, as shown in our survey of Japanese biotech startups.

Nevertheless, a gradual change is occurring towards more mobile labour markets and more recruitment of talented people by startups from established companies. For instance, AnGes MG, the first university spin-off biotech company in Japan to have made an IPO, was established in 1999 with the first CEO being a person who had earlier led a startup in Silicon Valley in the USA. However, its third CEO, who led the company to IPO in 2002, was a person who had quit one of the biggest chemical companies in Japan. There are a number of similar examples; for instance, another university spin-off biotech company, established in 2002, is led by a former employee of one of the biggest securities firms. Thus movement of people from big companies to startups has been occurring and, we expect, is going to be more common in the coming years.

Japan also faces the so-called 2007 problem. In the majority of Japanese firms, 60 is the age of compulsory retirement (which, incidentally, is why I do not use the word 'lifetime' employment but merely 'long-term' employment). The largest population of postwar baby boomers will reach 60 years of age in 2007, with two consequences: one, a serious macroeconomic consequence, is the heavy burden to be placed on the national pension scheme; the other is the loss of experienced workers at many firms. On the one hand, this change makes the age composition of a typical Japanese firm healthier. This is particularly true with old firms that had been in existence before the high-growth era of the 1960s, because they hired a large number of baby boomers upon their graduation during the 1960s. Many of these firms have since then turned into the phase of maturity or even decline after the oil crisis of 1972, thus reducing their hiring significantly. The result has been a skewed age composition of their employees with a large bump around the baby boomers. Under the more or less seniority-related compensation scheme, this fact meant that the labour cost tended to increase as these baby boomers got older. Hence the retirement of these workers is expected to reduce the firms' labour costs.

On the other hand, their retirement implies that the skills and experiences accumulated and embodied within these workers will be lost from the firm. Accordingly, as discussed earlier, many firms started special efforts in the maintenance of skills, for instance, by starting new programmes in which young workers are paired with soon-to-retire workers to facilitate effective on-the-job training, or by starting to offer retiring workers opportunities to continue working with the firm on a part-time basis with lower pay.

Some of these retiring workers may also opt to establish their own startups or to work for other startups, utilizing their knowledge, experience and network, and not minding the lower and unstable pay since they are entitled to pensions and their children have grown up. Admittedly, these workers are unlikely to be suitable as researchers on frontier technology, because their scientific knowledge must be outdated, yet they may well have elaborate engineering skills with which they can help the development and manufacture of biotech devices, for instance. Also their experience in planning and negotiating in legal or management matters can prove useful. An example is a startup company that specializes in consulting biotech and pharmaceutical companies and helping them in negotiating alliance deals, which was established by a former head of the licensing department of a big pharmaceutical company.

In conclusion, the Japanese business and labour system may not have been favourable to the creation of startups. Still, it has been evolving under the changing business environment, such as the 1990s recession and the globalization of business activities, coupled with the changing age composition of workers. At this moment, I do not think we can make a precise prediction of exactly where this evolution will take us. Nevertheless, following the evolutionary theory of natural selection and path dependence, Japan, I believe, would somehow come up with a new system in which the merits of, say, a Silicon Valley-type system characterized by close university–industry interaction, active startups, and high mobility of workforce co-exist with the so-called 'Japanese system'.

V   SCIENCE-BASED INNOVATION AND THE CHANGING BOUNDARY OF INDUSTRIES: THE CASE OF BIOTECHNOLOGY

An important feature of science-based innovation is that the innovation activity is carried out, and its outcome used, across the traditional boundary of industries. For instance, computer, information and communication technologies are used in virtually all industries. Here, let us take the case of biotechnology.

Table 8.1 shows the shipment of biotech-related products by industry. The food and beverage industry has the largest shipment, accounting for more than 60 per cent of the total shipment, followed by pharmaceuticals. Still, these are not the only biotech-related industries and, as shown in the table, biotech is used in a wide range of industries from chemicals to machinery, electronics, information and environmental remediation. In addition, a wide variety of technology is used. In food and beverages, almost all the technologies are the so-called 'traditional' biotechnology ones, such as fermentation and cultivation. Although several firms in this industry also use 'new' biotechnology to diversify into pharmaceuticals, biotech services and other biotech-related fields, food and beverages including beer and other alcoholic drink are the overwhelming leaders in terms of shipment value and, as a result, nearly 100 per cent is shown to be based on traditional biotechnology.

By contrast, about half of the technologies used in the production and R&D of pharmaceuticals is the 'new' biotechnology, such as cell fusion, recombinant DNA and bio-reactors. Thus, with new biotechnology only, pharmaceuticals (including medical equipment) is the largest biotech user. In the USA also, the health care industry is known to be the dominant user of biotechnology.[15]

Thus, the range of biotech industry is not only broad but also dependent on the definition of 'biotechnology'. In consequence, a wide variety of firms, both old and new, have been conducting research, manufacturing products and providing services using various biotech-related technologies. Let me give a few examples. In agriculture, even though the public disdain

Table 8.1 Shipment of biotechnology-related products, 2003

Product field	Domestic shipment Million yen	%	Composition of shipment by the type of technologies (%)				
			Traditional fermentation, cultivation, modification, etc.	Traditional environmental remediation with organisms	Cell fusion, recombinant DNA, bioreactor, etc.	Biomaterials, and electronic and other equip. and software making use of biological knowledge	Non-response
Food and beverages	4 770 241	62.9	100.0	0.0	0.0	0.0	0.0
Misc. food	192 980	2.5	61.2	0.0	30.6	0.1	8.1
Agricultural	45 277	0.6	84.6	0.0	15.1	0.3	0.0
Livestock and fishing	33 517	0.4	48.9	14.6	22.5	8.5	5.5
Pharmaceuticals and medical equip.	1 574 072	20.7	48.1	0.0	46.2	5.4	0.3
Laboratory samples and reagents	17 870	0.2	8.3	0.0	65.9	3.8	22.0
Textile	2 711	0.0	62.5	0.0	37.5	0.0	0.0
Chemicals	445 323	5.9	40.6	0.0	59.4	0.0	0.0
Bio-electronics	32 221	0.4	0.0	0.1	0.3	99.5	0.1
Environment-related equip. and materials	196 959	2.6	1.9	87.5	0.4	10.2	0.0
Laboratory and plant equip.	44 247	0.6	27.3	0.2	13.0	41.0	18.5
Misc. manufacturing	62 102	0.8	79.4	5.2	0.0	15.4	0.0
Informatics	18 374	0.2	0.0	0.0	1.1	67.9	31.0
Services	141 103	1.9	1.5	1.2	11.7	58.8	26.8
Unclassifiable	8 964	0.1	32.4	38.6	0.2	0.1	28.7
Total	7 585 961	100.0	78.7	2.5	14.3	3.5	1.0

Source: Ministry of Education, Culture, Sports, Science and Technology et al., *Heisei 15 Nendo Baio Sangyo Souzou Kiso Chosa Houkokusho* [Report on the Basic Survey of Biotechnology Industries, 2003].

for genetically modified organisms prevented Japanese firms from developing GMO foods, Suntory, the largest whisky distiller and a beer brewer, developed genetically modified flowers, such as blue roses, which do not exist in nature. In food, Ajinomoto has been developing many products applying its technology on amino acid. In environmental remediation, plant makers and construction companies have been providing services to remedy polluted ground with microorganisms. Machinery makers have been manufacturing equipment needed for biotech research; for instance, Hitachi developed sequencers in alliance with Applied Bio-systems of the USA, and Shimadzu developed mass spectrometers, for which its inventor, Koichi Tanaka, received a Nobel Prize in 2002. Several firms have been supplying DNA chips and almost all the big electronics and communication companies have entered the bioinformatics business. Even general trading companies (*sogo shosha*) have entered the business of supplying various biotech services, using its network of suppliers of such services. There are also many small and/or new firms providing specialized services.

Put differently, the presence of diverse industrial activity is essential in the development of biotech industry, both for the efficient innovation activity and for the smooth industrialization of inventions. The presence of established firms with knowledge in traditional biotechnology, such as Suntory and Ajinomoto, and in design and manufacture of machinery, such as Hitachi and Shimadzu, has proved indispensable, and so has the entrance of new firms specializing in, for instance, supplying custom-made DNA chips or providing outsourcing services, such as specific tests and informatics. Universities can also play an important role here because, as discussed earlier, many of the innovations are science-based and benefit from the collaboration with and licensing from universities.

From the business viewpoint, this fact implies that it is now essential for firms to utilize resources and expertise of various outside players and combine them with their own R&D efforts. As a consequence, how to set a boundary between in-house R&D and external R&D has become a key factor for successful innovation. That is, the question of the *R&D boundaries of the firm* has become one of the determining factors of business success. To this topic, we now turn.

VI   R&D BOUNDARY OF THE FIRM IN BIOTECHNOLOGY

It is beyond doubt that interorganizational collaboration has become increasingly crucial in any industry today. Still, this probably applies best to science-based innovation, such as the innovation activities in biotechnology and pharmaceuticals. Research alliances are frequently and increasingly formed between firms and between firms and universities or research institutes, in Japan or elsewhere. Hagedoorn's (2002) study of the 1960–98 trend of inter-firm R&D partnerships in the world clearly indicates an increasing trend from just ten or so partnerships per year in the 1960s to more than 500 in the latter half of the 1990s. It also shows that the share of high-tech industries (pharmaceuticals, information technology, and aerospace and defence) among these partnerships has been increasing, exceeding 80 per cent in 1998.

In Japan, the ten largest pharmaceutical firms together had 65 alliances in 1989, but this number increased threefold in ten years, to 189. Also, during the 32-month period of January 1999 to August 2001, 103 cases of alliances were formed by these firms (Odagiri, 2003). Of these 103, 43 were technology acquisitions (licensing-in) and 50 were joint or commissioned R&D, with the rest being access to the database and so forth. As a partner of these alliances, new biotech firms (NBFs), particularly those in the USA, were as popular as established firms. Such an increase in the number of R&D alliances, with many of them being those with NBFs, is found among all major pharmaceutical firms across the world (see, for instance, Henderson, Orsenigo and Pisano, 1999).

In a survey conducted by Japan's National Institute of Science and Technology Policy (NISTEP), among the 146 firms who replied that they have conducted biotech-related businesses in 2000, 97 performed R&D alliances and/or technology acquisitions (Odagiri, Koga and Nakamura, 2002). Asked about the reasons why they perform R&D alliances, they gave the highest score to the 'utilization of the partner's non-patented technological knowledge and capabilities' and the next highest to 'speed', 'utilization of capital equipment' and 'cost reduction' that can be gained through alliances. This result illustrates the importance of utilizing outside assets (tangible or intangible) and capabilities, and of combining them with internal ones.

Of course, firms cannot relegate all R&D works to the outside because they have to maintain internal capabilities that are essential not only for their own development and commercialization but also to evaluate potential alliance partners, monitor them and understand and absorb the results supplied by them. In the NISTEP survey, many firms reported that they have had cases in which they could find reasonable alliance partners but nevertheless decided to perform the R&D themselves. Besides the fear for ambiguity in the ownership of the outcome, these firms raised 'utilization of internal human and other resources and capabilities' and the 'need to nurture such resources and capabilities internally' as the main reasons for this decision. That is, firms are keenly aware of the need to accumulate their internal capabilities, not just for in-house R&D but also to perform more efficient R&D alliances. This fact coincides with the discussion earlier that Japanese firms are now deeply concerned with the maintenance of skills in manufacturing.

Utilization of outside resources and capabilities also occurs in the form of outsourcing of more routine R&D-related services. In such outsourcing, the contract specifies the details of the work to be outsourced and all the output from the work is to be handed over to the outsourcer. Examples are, in the case of biotechnology and pharmaceuticals, animal tests, supply of specific samples (such as knock-out mice[16]), production of test products, software development, genome analyses and clinical tests. The amount spent for outsourcing in pharmaceutical R&D reached 36 per cent (46 per cent if clinical tests are excluded) of the R&D expenditures among pharmaceutical firms, according to the NISTEP survey.

As stated in the previous section, bio-informatics and services, as well as the provision of laboratory equipment, bio-electronics, and samples and reagents, constitute an important part of biotech-related industries. Many firms in these fields are active outsourcees, whether they are large or small and established or new. The presence of such firms is a prerequisite for innovation (and also production and marketing) in science-based industries.

In this regard, a comparison with the supply system in, say, automobile production may be useful. A close and long-term assembler–supplier relationship in the Japanese automobile industry is well known, often dubbed the vertical *keiretsu* relationship. For standardized components, arm's-length transaction is common even in Japan. However, for assembler-specific or model-specific components, the continuous close relationship is common between an assembler and the supplier. They often collaborate from the development stage to coordinate the design of a car model and the design of components necessary for the model. They also collaborate in production to achieve just-in-time delivery and to minimize inventory both at the stage of component production and at the stage of car assembly. This fact by no means implies that competition is absent. In fact, assemblers take a multi-vendor policy as much as possible, in order to maintain competition among suppliers. They also perform detailed evaluation of the suppliers leading, if necessary, to some sort of punishment (for more discussion, see Odagiri, 1992).

In comparison, the alliance relationship and the outsourcer–outsourcee relationship in biotechnology appear to be closer to an arm's-length relationship. Obviously, the main reason is that transaction-specific assets are less important here than in automobile production. Also, technologies change rapidly following the development of scientific discoveries, causing the search for new partners in constant need. As a result, entry and exit of biotech-related firms are much more frequent than those of automobile suppliers. Clearly, this fact coincides with the observation made earlier that startups play a crucial role in science-based innovation. Thus, without an active startup activity, the availability of an alliance partner or outsourcing opportunity would be limited, possibly hindering the development of biotechnology and other science-based industries. It is probably reasonable to say that, as discussed already, Japan still lags behind the USA in this regard but has been making efforts to catch up. This and other needs coming from the changing economic and technological environment have been fostering the change in Japan's business and labour system towards the one more in harmony with the new science-based innovation system. This co-evolution of the business system and the innovation system, I believe, is the most important feature of post-bubble Japan.

VII CONCLUSION

I started this chapter by separating Japan's post-war innovation activity into three periods: Period 1, which covers the 1950s and the 1960s and was the period when Japan actively imported technologies to catch up with the state of the art in the world; Period 2, which covers most of the 1970s and the 1980s and was the period when Japanese firms shifted their innovation efforts towards their own inventions; and Period 3, which started with the 1990 collapse of the bubble boom and was the period when science-based innovation became important, and once more an effort was started to catch up with the US, a nation leading in such innovation.

Taking mostly the example of biotechnology, I have argued that the salient features of science-based innovation is the need for university–industry collaboration, the prominent role played by startup firms, and the relevance of the technology beyond traditional industry boundaries. As a consequence, the boundary of the firm has been opened up to introduce more interorganizational collaborations of various kinds. To accommodate such changes, the business system has been also changing, if gradually, to allow, for instance, a more flexible inter-firm relationship and a more mobile labour movement.

Looking at the history of Japan's economic development, one notices several turning points. The Meiji Restoration of 1867, the victory in the Russo-Japanese War in 1905, the boom during World War I in 1914–18, and the defeat in World War II in 1945 are the most prominent such turning points, which resulted in not only economic fluctuation but also important changes in Japan's economic and business systems. The 1990s, I believe, will be viewed as another turning point by the observers of the future. It is noteworthy that all the previous turning points occurred as the consequences of wars (including the civil war at the time of the Meiji Restoration). By contrast, Japan since the 1990s has been trying to transform the system in (thankfully) peaceful circumstances. It is hardly surprising, therefore, that inertia and what Olson (1982) has called 'distributional coalitions' have contributed towards delaying the necessary changes. Yet, as the natural selection theory implies, only the fittest in the new environment must eventually survive in the long run. Under this force, the co-evolution of the Japanese innovation system and the business system is taking place and has to be promoted in order for Japan to accommodate itself to the new reality.

NOTES

1. For an international comparative study of national innovation systems, see Nelson (1993).
2. Some of the discussion in the following overlaps with Odagiri (2006a and b).
3. Because JPO started to accept multi-claim patent applications in 1988, the number of patent applications after 1988 is not strictly comparable to that of the earlier period.
4. The data on technology imports and exports, as well as R&D expenditures, are from the *Report on the Survey of Research and Development*, various years, Soumusho (Ministry of Internal Affairs and Telecommunications).
5. NISTEP (2004); the original data are from CHI Research, Inc.
6. See Kline and Rosenberg (1986) for the comparison between the linear model and the chain-linked model.
7. A little known fact is that a small Japanese company named Busicom, in search of a better technology for hand-held calculators, played a key role in Intel's invention of the microprocessor. See Odagiri and Goto (1996, ch. 8).
8. See Rosenberg and Nelson (1994).
9. Actually, in terms of the number of universities or of students, private universities were the overwhelming leaders, accounting for 74.9 per cent of universities and 73.5 per cent of students in 2003. However, prestigious universities (for example, Tokyo, Kyoto, Osaka, Hitotsubashi and the Tokyo Institute of Technology) were all national, with few exceptions (for example, Keio and Waseda).
10. Source: Small and Medium Enterprise Agency, *White Paper on Small and Medium Enterprises in Japan*, 2003.
11. Source: Japan Biotechnology Association, *2003-Nen Baio-Bencha Toukei Houkokusho*.
12. The average of all the firms listed in five stock exchanges in Japan (Source: Tokyo Stock Exchange, *Kabushiki Bunpu Jokyo Chousa*). Note that some of the listed firms are subsidiaries of other firms; for instance, JVC is 52 per cent owned by Matsushita Electric. Some are subsidiaries of foreign firms, for instance, Nissan is 44 per cent owned by Renault, in which case Renault's ownership is included in the share ownership by foreigners cited in the text.
13. Ministry of Health, Labour and Welfare, *Rodo Keizai Hakusho* (White Paper on the Labour Economy).
14. Ibid.
15. Source: US Department of Commerce, *A Survey of the Use of Biotechnology in US Industry*, 2003.
16. A knockout mouse is a genetic mouse, one or more of whose genes have been made inoperative through a gene knockout.

REFERENCES

Branstetter, Lee (2003), 'Is academic science driving a surge in industrial innovation? Evidence from patent citations', presented at the NISTEP Research Seminar on 'R&D Strategy and Science and Technology Policy', February 2004, Tokyo: National Institute of Science and Technology Policy.

Gallini, Nancy T. (2002), 'The economics of patents: lessons from recent US patent reform', *Journal of Economic Perspectives*, **16**, 131–54.

Hagedoorn, John (2002), 'Inter-firm R&D partnerships: an overview of major trends and patterns since 1960', *Research Policy*, **31**, 477–92.

Henderson, Rebecca, Luigi Orsenigo and Gary P. Pisano (1999), 'The pharmaceutical industry and the revolution in molecular biology: interactions among scientific, institutional, and organizational change', in David C. Mowery and Richard R. Nelson (eds), *Sources of Industrial Leadership*, Cambridge: Cambridge University Press, pp. 267–311.

Kline, Stephen J. and Nathan Rosenberg (1986), 'An overview of innovation', in Ralph Landau and Nathan Rosenberg (eds), *The Positive Sum Strategy*, Washington, DC: National Academy Press, pp. 275–305.

Mowery, David C. and Nathan Rosenberg (1993), 'The US national innovation system', in Richard R. Nelson (ed.), *National Innovation Systems*, Oxford: Oxford University Press, pp. 29–75.

Murmann, Johann Peter (2003), *Knowledge and Competitive Advantage*, Cambridge: Cambridge University Press.

Narin, Francis, Kimberly S. Hamilton and Dominic Olivastro (1997), 'The increasing linkage between US technology and public science', *Research Policy*, **26**, 317–30.

Nelson, Richard R. (ed.) (1993), *National Innovation Systems*, Oxford: Oxford University Press.

Nelson, Richard R. (1995), 'Recent evolutionary theorizing about economic change', *Journal of Economic Literature*, **33**, 48–90.

Nelson, Richard R. (2004), 'The market economy, and the scientific commons', *Research Policy*, **33**, 455–71.

Nelson, Richard R. and Sidney G. Winter (1982), *An Evolutionary Theory of Economic Change*, Cambridge, MA: Belknap Press.

NISTEP (National Institute of Science and Technology Policy) (2004), 'Kagaku Gijutsu Shihyo' [Science and technology indicators], NISTEP Report No. 73, Tokyo: National Institute of Science and Technology Policy.

Odagiri, Hiroyuki (1992), *Growth through Competition, Competition through Growth: Strategic Management and the Economy in Japan*, Oxford: Oxford University Press.

Odagiri, Hiroyuki (1999), 'University–industry collaborations in Japan: facts and interpretations', in Lewis M. Branscomb, Fumio Kodama and Richard Florida (eds), *Industrializing Knowledge: University Industry Linkages in Japan and the United States*, Cambridge, MA: The MIT Press, pp. 252–65.

Odagiri, Hiroyuki (2003), 'Transaction costs and capabilities as determinants of the R&D boundaries of the firm: a case study of the ten largest pharmaceutical firms in Japan', *Managerial and Decision Economics*, **24**, 187–211.

Odagiri, Hiroyuki (2006a), 'Advance of science-based industries and the changing innovation system of Japan', in Bengt-Åke Lundvall, Patarapong Intarakumnerd and Jan Vang (eds), *Asia's Innovation Systems in Transition*, Cheltenham, UK and Northampton, MA, USA: Edward Elgar, pp. 200–26.

Odagiri, Hiroyuki (2006b), 'National innovation system: reforms to promote science-based industries', in Tsutomu Shibata (ed.), *Japan Moving Toward a More Advanced Knowledge Economy: Volume 1, Assessment and Lessons*, Washington, DC: World Bank Institute, pp. 127–45.

Odagiri, Hiroyuki and Akira Goto (1996), *Technology and Industrial Development in Japan*, Oxford: Oxford University Press.

Odagiri, Hiroyuki and Yoshiaki Nakamura (2002), 'Nihon no Baio Bencha Kigyo: Sono Igi to Jittai' [Biotechnology-related startup firms in Japan: lessons from a survey study], NISTEP Discussion Paper No. 22, Tokyo: National Institute of Science and Technology Policy.

Odagiri, Hiroyuki, Tadahisa Koga and Kenta Nakamura (2002), 'Baio Tekunoroji Kenkyu Kaihatsu to Kigyo no Kyokai: Kenkyu Teikei, Gijutsu Dounyu, Auto Sousing, Kaigai Kenkyu ni Kansuru Chousa Houkoku' [Biotechnology R&D and the boundaries of the firm: results from a survey study on R&D alliance, technology acquisition, outsourcing, and overseas R&D], NISTEP Research Material no. 90, Tokyo: National Institute of Science and Technology Policy.

Olson, Mancur (1982), *The Rise and Decline of Nations*, New Haven: Yale University Press.

Rosenberg, Nathan and Richard R. Nelson (1994), 'American universities and technical advance in industry', *Research Policy*, **23**, 323–48.

9. The rise and fall of Japan as a model of 'progressive capitalism'

David Coates

There certainly was a time when features of the post-war Japanese economy were held up as progressive – and hence as desirable elements in a managed capitalism of a social democratic kind – by a series of academics and political commentators concerned to push back the tide of neo-liberalism. However, that time has now passed. These days, those same commentators are largely silent on this matter, or have actually retracted their initial endorsement of all things Japanese. But their Japanese moment was important even so, partly because of its impact on the emerging literature in the English-speaking world on the character and potential of the Japanese 'economic miracle', and partly because of the light their brief enthusiasm for Japanese methods of capitalist management throws on the limits of certain kinds of center–left thinking in the modern era.

As we all now know, the Japanese economy grew rapidly after the withdrawal of the American occupation forces in 1952, and did so in a manner that was both unexpected and sustained. GDP per head in the United States in 1950 was five times that in Japan: a 500 per cent gap that by 1992 had shrunk to one of just slightly over 10 per cent. Changes of that scale could not, and did not, go unnoticed. On the contrary, and for understandable reasons, the remarkable growth of the Japanese economy was matched, after a suitable time-lag, by the equally remarkable growth of an academic literature on the causes of that economic performance. The Japanese wrote about themselves and to themselves, of course; and just a few of those who did also addressed themselves to a wider audience: writers supportive of the Japanese model (including Morishima, 1982) and writers critical of it (such as Itoh, 1990). They then joined an academic debate on things Japanese that was cast entirely in English, and addressed almost exclusively to a non-Japanese audience. The central focus of the Anglo-American literature which emerged after 1970 to catalogue and explain Japanese economic performance was not exclusively Japan itself. It was a literature written about Japan but one written with a non-Japanese purpose. It was a literature written to draw lessons from the Japanese experience that might with value be applied nearer to home. In the 1970s, the hold of American-based manufacturing industry on both its domestic and export markets was being seriously undermined by Japanese competition. The many US policy makers, industrialists and academics disturbed by this outcome wanted to know why it was happening and how it could be stopped. In the 1980s, the UK economy was being seriously restructured by a Conservative Government committed to neo-liberal economics. Those UK policy makers, academics and even occasional industrialists who disliked this outcome wanted to know with what the Thatcher programme could be realistically replaced. Both groups looked to Japan, hoping to find in the Japanese growth story answers to American weakness and to Thatcherite restructuring. Each group first thought they had found that answer. Both eventually discovered that they had not.

The early texts on the Japanese growth story were mainly written from within the centre of existing economic orthodoxy. They were written by growth accountants seeking a general theory of economic growth, and by neo-classically trained economists and economist historians who thought that they already had one. Edward Denison, the father of modern growth accounting, entered the fray in 1976, jointly writing with W.K. Chung *How Japan's Economy Grew So Fast*. Their answer was as all-encompassing as it was unilluminating. Japan grew so fast between 1953 and 1971, according to Denison and Chung, because of an outstanding performance on *all* growth factors: labour supply, investment in new equipment, application of new knowledge, and redistribution of economic resources from agriculture to industry. It was the massive increase in the size of the Japanese capital stock to which Denison and Chung drew particular attention (Denison and Chung, 1976: 63); and to which they gave significantly greater weight than the less easily quantified question of culture and attitudes on which later others would put such explanatory weight – cultures and attitudes which Denison and Chung saw 'may have helped Japan' but whose precise impact they could 'not judge' (ibid.: 82–3).

The Denison and Chung position was entirely at one with the other major text available in English in the mid-1970s on the early stages of the post-war Japanese growth story: that by Patrick and Rosovsky on *Asia's New Giant*. Here too the emphasis was on what the authors termed 'ordinary economic causes', not least a highly educated work-force, 'substantial managerial, organizational, scientific and engineering skills capable of rapidly absorbing and adapting the best foreign technology', great differentials in pay and productivity between economic sectors, and a government supportive of big business. Their view was that Japanese post-war economic success was best understood as the product of a 'market-oriented private enterprise economic system' deploying high-quality factors of production; an economic success that, to be understood, did not require any additional ingredient of a specifically Japanese kind, be that 'government policy or leadership, labor-management practices and institutions, or more vaguely defined cultural attributes' (Patrick and Rosovsky, 1976: 6, 12, 43). It was true that Rosovsky had earlier been on record as aware of the importance of 'obviously non-economic factors, such as the political, social and international environment'. It was just that such things were, in his view, 'necessarily matters of speculation . . . beyond measurement, at least as that term is understood by economists' (Ohkawa and Rosovsky, 1973: 217), and as such to be discounted.

However, some of the other early participants in the growing literature on post-war Japanese economic growth were less constrained by the ruling canons of economic orthodoxy, and less convinced that causality could be attributed only to that which could be isolated and measured. Conventionally trained economists and economic historians were not the only players in the emerging literature on Japanese economic growth in the 1970s and 1980s. A string of industrial sociologists, cultural historians, industrial relations specialists and management scholars were at work there as well, arguing on the contrary that the Japanese economic renaissance quite simply could *not* be understood in these conventional terms: arguing in fact that Japanese growth would not be understood unless such explanations were supplemented by an emphasis on the qualitative differences that set Japan apart. The nature of those qualitative differences then occupied the centre-ground of the emerging Japanese analysis for nearly two decades. For some it was the uniqueness of the Japanese corporate model that was critical to the Japanese post-war growth story. For others it was the uniqueness of its labour relations systems. For yet others it was the special character of the Japanese state; and for most of them, it was also (to some indeterminate degree at least) a matter of cultural differences, a consequence of value systems unique to Japan that were providing the world with a novel (and a highly successful) model of capitalism.

It is not possible in the space available here to list all the major studies now available to us of these various aspects of Japanese uniqueness, because they came in a flood in the 1980s and early 1990s. But it is possible to point to the more influential of those studies, and to characterize the cumulative story that they told. The key scholarship on corporate Japan came from academics like Gerlach (1989, 1992) and Fruin (1992). The key scholarship on labour relations came from the likes of Dore (1973) and Ozaki (1991). The key scholarship on state practices came initially from Chalmers Johnson (1982, 1984, 1986) and then was quickly subsumed into a wider argument on the importance and effectiveness of East Asia-based developmental states in general (Wade, 1990; Weiss and Hobson, 1995).

The key cultural analyses came from Morishima (1982), Fukuyama (1995) and, as we see in more detail next, from Dore (1985, 1986, 1987, 1993, 1997). On the basis of these works, and of others, Japanese economic growth was explained as the product of a particular management system built around lifetime employment, seniority wages and enterprise union-ism. It was explained as the product of a networked capitalism that linked large export-oriented companies to loyal supplier firms and to particular (and very patient) banks; and it was explained as the product of highly sophisticated industrial policy that orchestrated carefully constrained com-petition between these networks in order to strengthen the global position of the Japanese economy as a whole. In the space of two decades, a new orthodoxy spread beyond academia into the popular press and into the policy-making processes of Japan's main economic rivals: that there was a new, and specifically Japanese, way of running capitalism: a way that was, by the standards of the time, nothing less than 'coherent, powerful, bril-liant even' (Castells, 1998: 233).

All of this literature emerged under the shadow of, and with varying degrees of congruence to, a related set of arguments about the *cultural* uniqueness of the Japanese model. The scholarship of Ronald Dore was by far the most widely cited on this in the secondary literature that emerged after 1980 in English on post-war Japan's economic success. 'What makes the Japanese different?' Dore asked. His answer: Japanese Confucianism. According to Dore, cultures infused with Confucian values were likely to leave people with 'behavioural predispositions' that were distinctly different from those prevalent in America and the UK. Behaviour in Japan and behaviour in an Anglo-Saxon world rooted in Christian Protestantism could be expected to diverge in a number of economically significant ways.

> . . . first . . . Anglo-Saxons behave in ways designed to keep their options open. Japanese are much more willing to foreclose their options by making long-term commitments. Anglo-Saxons give greater weight to their own immediate welfare or that of their family. Japanese are much more likely, by virtue of their long-term commitments, to have diffuse obligations to promote the welfare of others – the other members of firms they have joined, their partners in long-term obligated relationships, etc. Thirdly . . . there is a difference in the moral evalu-ation of different kinds of human activity. In Japan, producing goods and ser-vices that enhance the lives of others is good. Spending one's life in the speculative sale and purchase of financial claims is bad. That 'productivist' ethic is far from absent in Anglo-Saxon countries, but . . . it has become far more attenuated than in Japan. (Dore, 1993: 76–7)

These cultural differences, so the argument ran, then helped both to explain and to sustain unique features of Japanese economic practice: not least the long-term investment propensies of Japanese corporate institutions; the privileging of employee interests over shareholder concerns in economic downturns; the absence of hostile mergers and takeovers in the networked universe of Japanese corporations; even the propensity of Japanese firms to provide life-time employment guarantees and to sustain long-term working relationships between companies and their suppliers. 'Perhaps the crucial element facilitating trust in a Japanese firm,' Dore wrote, 'is the fact that the contractual nature of the employment relationship is obscured or replaced by a sense of common membership in a corporate entity which has objectives that can be shared by all its members.' In such a firm, 'the Confucian emphasis on industrious productiveness . . . both reaffirms the precedence given to employees over shareholders and provides grounds for workers to think of their skill as something to take pride in, rather than just a commodity to be sold as dearly as possible' (Dore, 1985: 212, 214).

US and UK-based CEOs were said by Dore to take a property view of their companies, and to look on all their assets – including their labour force – as in principle disposable in form. Japanese CEOs, by contrast, were said to see their companies as entities/communities and to feel bonds of obligation and trust to those they employed. This *trust-based* nature of Japanese capitalism was then said to hold the key both to why Japan had been economically so successful and to why progressive forces in the West should seek to replicate the best features of Japanese capitalism here.

These cultural explanations of Japanese uniqueness came to the fore at a very critical time in the policy debates surrounding economic performance in both America and the United Kingdom. There, the 1980s belonged, politically and academically, to the neo-liberal Right: in the United States politically to Reaganism and intellectually to the Chicago school; and in the UK to Thatcherism in politics and to a revitalized neo-classical economics in academia. Intellectuals of the centre–left needed counter-arguments to that all-encompassing orthodoxy, and examples of successful capitalisms run on non-neo-liberal lines. For a period at least, they found those arguments and that model in a particular reading of the Japanese case.

The key intellectual player on this in the United States was William Lazonick (1991, 1992, 1994, 1995), who linked a critique of neo-liberalism to an argument about capitalist developmental logics (and appropriate periodizations) that gave Japanese organizational forms a necessary competitive edge. According to Lazonick, American capitalism was out of date. Japanese capitalism was not; and one measure (and indeed cause) of American backwardness was the domination, within its intellectual and policy-making circles, of an intellectual framework, neo-liberalism, that was more appropriate to nineteenth-century conditions than to late twentieth-century ones.

In the nineteenth century, so the argument ran, small-scale (in Lazonick's terms, 'proprietary') market-coordinated capitalism did indeed hold sway; and the UK was its paradigmatic form. But during the first half of the twentieth century, 'proprietary' capitalism lost its edge to large-scale 'managerial' capitalism, as 'the most successful capitalist economies moved away from market co-ordination towards the planned coordination of their productive activities' (Lazonick, 1991: 13): and in consequence the UK was replaced in dominance by the United States. But the American moment has itself now passed because, under that same technological and organizational logic, capitalism is now moving from its 'managerial' to its 'collective' stage. 'The superior development and utilization of productive resources,' Lazonick argued, 'increasingly requires that business organizations have privileged access' to such resources. 'Inherent in such privileged access is the super-session of market coordination to some degree. The shift from market coordination to planned coordination within business organizations,' he insisted, 'has become an increasingly central characteristic of a successful capitalist economy' (ibid.: 8). It had also, according to him, been given its clearest expression in the Japanese case.

This argument was, at one and the same time, a critique of American economic practices and an advocacy of Japanese ones. In part it was a critique of American 'vulture' capitalism, and a call for longer-term financial and personal commitments to specific industrial enterprises by America's business leaders. Lazonick was particularly critical of 'top managers' in the US who 'used their positions . . . as a basis for their own individual aggrandizement rather than for the development of the organizational capabilities of their enterprises' (ibid.: 55); and he was equally dismissive of 'those who control wealth' who 'choose to live off the past rather than invest in the future' (ibid.: 57). But the Lazonick argument was also a critique of managerial attitudes to workers in US industry, and of the resulting distribution of industrial authority. 'The transition from a structure of work organization based on control,' Lazonick wrote in 1991, 'to one based on commitment that can effect the organizational integration of shop floor workers requires transformations in the traditional division of labour between managers and workers as well as in the skills and attitudes of workers themselves' (ibid.: 53).

> Through the organizational commitments inherent in permanent employment, the skills and efforts of male blue-collar workers have been made integral to the organizational capabilities of their companies, thus enabling the Japanese to take the lead in innovative production systems such as just-in-time inventory control, statistical quality control, and flexible manufacturing. Critical to the functioning of these production systems is the willingness of Japanese managers to leave skills and initiative with workers on the shop floor . . . in marked

contrast to the US managerial concern with using technology to take skills and the exercise of initiative *off* the shop floor. . . . In competition with the Japanese over the past quarter-century, the organization of work on the shop floor has been the Achilles heel of US manufacturing . . . With its managerial structures in place, American industry may have entered the second half of the twentieth century in the forefront in the development of productive resources. But its weakness lay in the utilization of productive resources – manufacturing processes in which large numbers of shop-floor workers had to interact with costly plant and equipment . . . the major industrial enterprises did not give these blue collar workers substantive training. Nor . . . did they make explicit, and hence more secure, the long-term attachment of the hourly employee to the enterprise. Without this commitment of the organization to the individual, one could not expect the commitment of the individual to the organization that might have enabled US mass producers to respond quickly and effectively to the Japanese challenge. (Lazonick, 1991: 42–3; 1994: 188)

Arguments of this kind helped to sustain a more general one, one increasingly articulated by centre–left intellectuals in the early 1990s, that success in the future required the creation of a new economic paradigm, and one that was inherently social democratic in form. Lazonick said that vulture capitalists needed controlling and workers given a bigger role in industrial decision making, Japanese style: and so did lots of others. When Bill Clinton won the Presidential race in 1992, he brought his friend Robert Reich to Washington as his first Labor Secretary; and Reich was already on record as seeing the need in the US for just such a paradigm shift (Reich, 1983: 19–20). So too was Laura D'Andrea Tyson, who would be the first head of Clinton's National Economic Advisory Council (Johnson et al., 1989). Even Michael Porter, the Harvard-based business guru, turned up at Hope in Arkansas, to the conference called by the President-elect, and argued for paradigm change (Clinton, 1993: 40–41). As the Clinton years began, modelling the US economy on Japanese lines was suddenly very popular in influential and progressive political circles.

Likewise in the UK, if slightly later, cultural change of a similar kind also swept through the British political class. Thatcherism was by then in full retreat, and the Labour Party was poised for its 'new labour' moment. That moment required its intellectual midwife, and it found it in Will Hutton. His *The State We're In* dominated the non-fiction best seller list in the UK in 1994/5 in a manner unprecedented for a work on political economy. In it, Hutton argued – among other things – that the Japanese economy had found exactly the balance of co-operation and competition vital to economic success in the last decades of the century. In Hutton's view, the general economic problem to which the Japanese had found a progressive answer was how to strike the balance between competition and co-operation. 'The perennial dilemma facing participants in a market economy,' he wrote,

. . . is that while there are genuine gains from co-operation, they can only be captured by commitment over time and the constant temptation in a truly free market is not to make such a commitment . . . there is a permanent tension in a capitalist economy between the desirability of forming committed relationships . . . and the temptation to cut and run. Trust is the cement of non-competitive market bargains . . . but trust is dependent on parties to a deal caring about their reputation as moral beings and monitoring their own conduct with integrity . . . Successful capitalism demands a fusion of co-operation and competition, and a means of grafting such a hybrid into the soil of the economic, social and political system. (Hutton, 1994: 252, 255)

Hutton was convinced that the UK had not found that balance – had not managed that grafting – and now desperately needed to do so. He was also convinced that the Japanese had. 'Here,' meaning in Japan,

. . . the attempt to capture the gains from co-operation in a competitive environment has been taken to its most extreme. East Asian and particularly Japanese capitalist structures emphasize trust, continuity, reputation and co-operation in economic relationships. Competition is ferocious, but cooperation is extensive . . . there is even a widely quoted phrase for it . . . literally 'cooperating while competing', so that out of the subsequent chaos comes harmony . . . as a result human relations and the necessity of nurturing them are centre stage: the dominant factor of production is labour, so that one Japanese analyst has been moved to call the system 'peoplism'. This is probably overstating the humanity of an economy which demands long hours and often demeaning working conditions, but it nonetheless captures the important stress on personal networks and human relationships. (Hutton, 1994: 269)

The economic future, according to Hutton, lay with *stake holding*; and Japan was on offer as a successful example of a stake-holding economy in full working order.

Unfortunately for the advocates of the Japanese model as a trust-based, stake-holding way of running a capitalist economy, two things then happened. The Japanese economy suddenly ceased to grow, entering into a decade-long recession that stood in stark contrast to the revival of a US economy that was visibly more market-based than network-driven. Evidence increasingly emerged too of the dark underside of the Japanese miracle, even in the years of its greatest competitive success, an underside of long hours, low wages, intense working routines and excessive job strain that were rarely mentioned by those keen in the 1980s to present the Japanese way of running capitalism as a progressive as well as a successful one.

After the Tokyo stock market crash of 1990, and amid the stalled growth and bank crises of the years that followed, the Japanese economy suddenly seemed neither as *trust-based* nor as *people-friendly* as it had first appeared. Where once advocates had seen trust-based networks triggering unique rates of economic growth from different units of capital, critics now saw cronyism and its consequences: high corporate debt, low corporate profits, unstable financial institutions and high levels of political corruption. And where once advocates had seen a unique system of industrial relations characterized by power sharing and mutual respect between capital and labour, critics now saw the superexploitation of vulnerable work forces behind the rhetoric of partnership.

Not that these were necessarily always the same critics. In many cases, in fact, they were not; for much of the recent academic writing on the Japanese model has split into two camps – camps that are equally critical of Japan's current economic institutions and of each other's recommendations for their reform. Many conventionally trained economists, for example, have of late been far more disturbed by the discovery of 'cronyism' and its consequences than by the evidence of the superexploitation of labour. For such economists, the key Japanese failure has been the model's recent inability to deliver sustained rates of capital accumulation for the economic institutions and social groups with whom they, as academics, characteristically identify. More radical scholars, on the other hand, whose identifications and political sympathies lie elsewhere, have been much more prone to place at the heart of their critique the adverse effects of the Japanese model on the people who actually worked inside it.

Nonetheless, though internally divided, the message of recent scholarship on Japanese economic growth has been broadly the same, and the tenor of the entire literature has now entirely changed. Once it was a literature giving us a model for the future: a model equipped with unique (and uniquely desirable) ways of coordinating capital and managing the interface between capital and labour. Now it is a literature giving us entirely the reverse: a model of capitalism that is past its sell-by date, and in need of resetting on both its capital and its labour fronts. Not surprisingly in the light of this, Japanese ways of doing things have suddenly lost their allure for those members of centre–left circles who are still seeking a route away from neo-liberalism towards a more socially equitable capitalist economic order.

The stall in post-war Japanese economic growth reinvigorated those more conventionally trained economists whose voice had been briefly drowned out, in the academic and popular literature in English on Japan, by the cultural analyses of people like Ronald Dore and the statist arguments of Chalmers Johnson and his ilk. At the very best, the economic growth explosion of the Japanese economy was now respecified by these economists as an example of successful 'catch-up', a necessarily one-off exploitation of the advantages of economic backwardness. This had long been the broad thrust of Paul Krugman's explanation of post-war Asian economic growth in general: that it 'seem[ed] to be driven by extraordinary

growth in inputs like labor and capital rather than by gains in efficiency';
and that if Japan was to some degree different in this respect, even so 'the
era of miraculous Japanese growth' was well and permanently behind us
(Krugman, 1994: 175, 178). Krugman's view had not been fashionable in
progressive circles when first developed, but it now became so. For he was
no longer alone. There was also the widely read and much admired writing
of Richard Katz' on which those disturbed by the Japanese downturn could
also draw, particularly his 1998 study of *Japan: the System That Soured*.
'The Japanese economic system,' according to Katz, 'was a marvelous
device to help a backward Japan catch up with the West. But the catch-up
system turned obsolete and counterproductive once Japan had in fact
caught up' (Katz, 2003: 15). And there were plenty of early warning signs
of that move from productive to counterproductive condition: at least there
were plenty of such early warning signs according to Michael Porter and
his colleagues: the small number of industries that were globally competitive, the low rates of corporate profits even in the years of high growth, and
the sharp decline in capital productivity in the years after 1970 (Porter,
Takeuchi and Sakakibara, 2000: 3–6). Or, as Katz had it, 'Japan was an
over-achiever in the 1950s and 1960s but a marked *under*performer in the
1970s and 1980s – the very time when it was still mistakenly considered a
growth star' (Katz, 2003: 17–18).

Porter and his colleagues painted a picture of two Japans – one internationally competitive because bank-rolled, the other inefficient because subsidized. The Katz picture was much the same. Katz called Japan 'a
deformed dual economy – a dysfunctional hybrid of super-strong exporting industries and super-weak domestic sectors' (Ibid.: 17). For both Katz
and Porter, the penetration of global export markets by leading Japanese
companies had been less a recipe for permanent economic leadership than
a necessarily one-off affair; as much the product of poor management practices and investment decisions by their competitors as of strengths in
Japanese companies themselves. In the new world created by that temporary market penetration, non-Japanese producers had now cherry-picked
what was effective in the original Japanese model; and because they had,
the model itself now needed to change if Japan was to grow rapidly once
more. It needed to change away from state management and corporate networking to a more rigorously competitive (and for Porter at least, if not for
Katz, a more Anglo-Saxon) way of doing capitalist business.

This strand of the literature had, in fact, come full circle. Seen from the
perspective of conventional economics, what had looked like a uniquely
networked form of successful capital accumulation in the heyday of the
Japanese miracle was now being relabelled as something entirely otherwise.
For Katz, the networking was really 'convoy capitalism' (ibid.: 94). For

others, it was 'crony capitalism' (Haber, 2001). But either way, it was an undesirable and competitively weak form that was uniquely prone to bank failures, political corruption and the toleration of low rates of return on capital investment. And in this manner, the very features of corporate organization that had once been used to explain Japanese success were now being reset as key elements in the Japanese malaise, a malaise solvable only through their abandonment in favour of a less corporately networked and government regulated model. Porter and his colleagues put it this way:

> . . . Japan is not a special case after all. Its industries succeed not when the government manages competition but when it allows competition to flourish. And Japanese companies succeed when they follow the accepted principles of strategy. . . . The micro-economic foundations that drive competitive performance in the rest of the world are just as decisive in Japan . . . It is time for Japan to embrace a new economic strategy: one based on a deeper understanding of the strengths and limitations of its past approaches to competition coupled with a new and more sophisticated mind-set about the role of governments and companies in the global economy. (Ibid: x, 118, 189)

So when viewed from the centre–right, by century's end the Japanese way of organizing capitalism was no longer one to emulate. If any emulation was required, it was the Japanese who now needed to do it: it was the Japanese who needed to purge their economic and social practices of the very features that had once created the impression of uniqueness and novelty. By century's end, that is, in the mainstream literature on Japan, neo-liberal orthodoxies were again on the ascendancy. There was only one way to run a successful capitalism, according to that literature, and the Japanese economy was in trouble to the degree that it was still diverging from that one correct way.

On the left of the academic spectrum, by contrast, there was no such faith in the existence of a right way to run a successful capitalism; but there was shared ground with the economic orthodoxies of the centre–right – shared ground that the way to understand Japan was simply to treat it as one specific example of capitalism in general. It might have unique features: all capitalisms did. But Japan shared with every other advanced capitalist economy the standard dilemmas and contradictions of capitalism in general. What had once seemed unique was simply the economic and social settlement created in Japan after 1945 to deal with those dilemmas; and, like equivalent settlements elsewhere in the advanced capitalist world, the Japanese way of handling class tensions within and between capitalism's producing classes had in the end been overwhelmed by the unavoidable structural contradictions between them. So at least much of the recent radical literature has claimed.

Much of that literature accepted, indeed used without serious questioning, the data on the institutional novelties of the Japanese model: its corporate networking, its special treatment of core workers, and the working relationship between the business community and the Japanese state (Tabb, 1995; Brenner, 1998). What the radical literature then added to that picture were the *wider dimensions* of the Japanese model into which those defining features were inserted: on the labour side, the pool of exploited workers within which Japan's 'protected' labour aristocracy was situated; and on the capital side, the briefly benign world of easy competition that the US state placed around a Japanese capitalist class whose 'success' it needed in the battle for global supremacy with communism. Porter's 'two Japans' was mirrored in this more radical literature by an emphasis on dual labour markets; and the capacity he noted of the Japanese export sector to flourish in American consumer markets was respecified as a dominance tolerated – for a while, and only for a while – by an American imperial state whose global interests were focused elsewhere.

The 'dark side' of Japanese labour relations was extensively documented from the mid-1980s, and used to puncture any claims (on the centre–left in both the US and the UK) that the Japanese way of managing capitalism was something that progressive forces in the West should seek to replicate.[1] It became more generally known that lifetime employment guarantees were extended to no more than one Japanese worker in four, and did not normally extend past the age of 55, at which point workers were normally deployed to smaller firms on lower wages. The subcontracting underbelly of the Japanese model so exposed was staffed, even before 1992, by a huge secondary labour pool with poorer wages and working conditions: and much of that labour was female and doubly exploited (Chalmers Johnson et al., 1989: 29; Coates, 2000: 130). Far from being a progressive way of combining employers and workers, as its advocates claimed, the Japanese model contained at its core a dual labour market dominated by a protected labour aristocracy, who were themselves obliged to work long hours in intensive fashion to protect their own position. As Burkett and Hart-Landsberg put it, in a widely cited and much reproduced article:

> Even for those who work in Japan's core corporations, the Japanese work model appears considerably less progressive, and more efficient as a framework for exploitation, once it is treated as an organic system . . . and . . . it must be emphasized that the dependence of corporate accumulation on the super-exploitation of workers in subcontracting firms (and temporary workers in core enterprises) is not an incidental or conjunctural aspect of the Japanese model. . . . The whole . . . strategy of industrial accumulation employed by Japanese capitalism . . . was predicated upon, and in turn reinforced, the subjection of Japanese workers to levels of insecurity and competitive pressures unparalleled

in the rest of the developed capitalist world. This strategy required not only secularly high rates of exploitation underpinned by long and intensive workdays, but also a high degree of inter-sectoral transferability and . . . downward flexibility of real labour costs during crisis-and-capital-restructuring periods. (Burkett and Hart-Landsberg, 1996: 72–3)

For Burkett and Hart-Landsberg, as for other radical scholars like Arrighi (1994), the origins of Japanese post-war success lay less in the uniquely networked nature of Japanese corporate organization than in the place that Japanese capitalism came to play in the Cold War world order presided over by the United States. Japan became a front-line state in that Cold War just as soon as Beijing fell to the Chinese communists. The Japanese economy was then reconstructed under American military and political leadership. Its pre-war large corporations and civilian state bureaucracy were relegitimated. Its labour movement was decisively broken; and its export sector was 'invited' into the rich club. As Arrighi has it:

> the rise of the Japanese capitalist phoenix from the ashes of Japanese imperialism after the Second World War originated in the establishment of a relationship of political exchange between the US government and the ruling groups of Japan. . . . In the interests of national security, the US government promoted Japanese exports to its domestic market and, what is more, tolerated the exclusion of US investment from Japan – an exclusion which forced US corporations seeking access to the Japanese market to license their technology to Japanese corporations. Only after the withdrawal from Vietnam and the rapprochement with China did the US government become more responsive to the complaints of US corporations about Japanese trade and investment policies. (Arrighi, 338, 306)

Japan's post-war prosperity depended on Washington's tolerance of an export-led growth strategy into open US markets (a toleration which did not survive the end of the Cold War), and it depended too on the viability of a cycle of 'scrap and build' industrial restructurings that held at bay the internal contradictions of Japanese capitalism only by exporting them into the immediate South Asian region (Burkett and Hart-Landsberg, 2000: 118–19). As class conflict intensified within Japan itself, the export of Japanese capital increasingly hollowed out the economy's manufacturing base, and corroded the capacity of even large corporations to sustain lifetime employment for its privileged core workers. External US pressure in the 1980s to revalue the Yen and to open Japanese domestic markets to US corporations, then highlighted the downside of the years of networked interaction between corporations and banks, and threw into crisis the unproductive protected sectors of the Japanese economy on which the ruling LDP depended for support: not least the agricultural sector, small retailing and construction. The result was 'the end of the Japanese post-war system' and the emergence instead, within Japan itself, of 'long periods of protracted and severe problems, which persist because the balance of political and economic forces does not permit the acceptance of an alternative regime' (Tabb, 1999: 71).[2]

The Japanese 'model' came off the rails, on this argument, not because its practices were insufficiently Anglo-Saxon or neo-liberal, but because the changing balance of class forces, both globally and at home, was shrinking the space available for a growth strategy dependent on foreign purchasing power and the limited export of capital from Japan. To quote Burkett and Hart-Landsberg again:

> The breakdown of export-led growth was hardly the outcome of 'socialist' elements in the Japanese system (state-based equity and protection of the weak rather than market-based efficiency and rewarding of the strong). It was, rather, the culminating historical dynamic of an extremely exploitative, hierarchical, undemocratic and expansionist form of capitalism. Far from socialist, Japan's export-oriented scrap-and-build accumulation was a highly competitive variant of capitalistic creative destruction. But the same scrap-and-build process, by creating more regionally and globally structured systems of production in East Asia (as well as in North America and Europe) has led to a hollowing out of the Japanese economy's growth potential and intensified competitive pressures on Japanese workers. (Burkett and Hart-Landsberg, 2000: 120–21)

By the turn of the century indeed, if Brenner is right (Brenner, 1998), the increasing interpenetration of accumulation cycles between the various poles of the global capitalist order – North America, Western Europe and South East Asia – meant that the ability of one pole to prosper depended critically on the inability of the others to do the same. Japan's growth model fell victim to the new 'zero-sum' international political economy called into existence by the deepening of globalization; and like all major capitalist economies that prospered while the communist world remained sealed away, the Japanese employing class had now to find for itself and the labour it employed a growth path compatible with the emergence of its near neighbour, China, as a fourth and very distinctive pole of growth. From a radical perspective, it is hard to see a fully market-based reconstruction of the Japanese economy meeting that need: or indeed, if one is attempted, meeting that need without simultaneously seriously corroding the already modest share that Japanese labour had won for itself during the economy's post-war rise to global eminence.

With the Japanese model of capitalism now so criticized, it is hardly surprising that its earlier advocates have been knocked backwards, forced into silence, into recantation or into wearied defence by the sheer weight and volume of the evidence and arguments coming against them. Some, like Will Hutton, for whom the Japanese post-war growth story was never more than a subordinate theme in a wider thesis, publicly regretted their brief infatuation with things Japanese: in the Hutton case seeking to separate the future he still advocates from the description of the present he once used to sustain that advocacy.[3] Others, more centrally involved in explaining Japanese success to a sceptical Western world, have conceded less ground, and with greater reluctance. 'How is it likely to pan out?' Ronald Dore asked in 2000. 'Probably – from my point of view – badly' (Dore, 2000: 220). *Badly*, because the reforms now in train 'have a tendency to increase inequality, increase the ruthlessness of competition, destroy the patterns of cooperation on which social cohesion rests, and thus promise to degrade the quality of life.' But only *probably*, because, at least when set against the equally challenged German model, 'Japan is the one which has the greater chance of resisting incorporation into American-led global capitalism and preserving its own distinctiveness' (ibid.: 220, 222). Nonetheless even this passionate a defender of the superiority of the Japanese model seems willing now to concede that, for the post-war Japanese way of running capitalism, the writing is clearly on the wall.

> The Japanese model may well not preserve its distinctiveness in the general picture of global capitalism for many more decades, but if and when change comes, it will have very little to do with the current problems of Japanese banks or with the current economic downturn, much less with the panic crises which have afflicted four Asian economies. It will result partly from the long-term pressures stemming from global financial markets, partly from the worldwide effects of American cultural hegemony, and partly from the working through of profound social structural changes stemming from Japanese society's arrival at the age of affluence. (Dore, 1998: 773)

There is a general lesson in this for all of us: the danger of establishing too close a linkage between political projects to reform capitalism and the defence of existing models of capitalism, however relatively superior those models may appear to be. For capitalism is not a system given to stasis. What works in one period is unlikely to do so in the next; and even when it 'works', its distribution of costs and benefits is never socially equal. So when deciding which tiger to ride, it is worth remembering that the choice is only between tigers; and that if a safe ride is what you want, you would do well not to ride tigers at all. For a time, a certain section of the intellectual Left forgot that, and ended up – if not with egg on their face – then at least with *sushi*.

NOTES

1. It is worth noticing that there was no total Marxist monopoly on this point. More conventionally anchored scholars also mentioned the 'dark side' of the Japanese success

story, and did so from as early as 1973 (Ohkawa and Rosovsky, 1973: 228–32): but then the dark side to which reference was made was primarily that of Japanese pre-war militarism. Even so, it was a militarism linked, in those early studies, to the superexploitation of labour – a superexploitation that Ohkawa and Rovosky implied was now long gone. This is their description of *pre-war* Japanese labour practices: 'In the modern sectors, productivity and wages rose rapidly; in the traditional sectors productivity and wages either stagnated or rose much more slowly. [There] incomes were low and frequently inadequate . . . The toilers . . . were not the large businessmen or landlords; they were not the male workers in the large zaibatsu plants; they were not the bureaucrats. Instead one found them among the small owner-cultivators and tenants in the countryside, in small-scale industry, and in many traditional and some modern services. And let us remember that these groups represented well over 50% of the gainfully employed population' (Ohkawa and Rosovsky, 1973: 229).

2. That inertia is now itself the subject of much scholarship, a lot of it mainstream in character (see, for example, Pempel, 1998; Alexander, 2002).
3. 'Here,' he has recently written, *'The State We're In* made a misjudgment I would give a lot to change. If I had made the case for stake-holding much more around Britain and America's experience – and downplayed its success in German and Japanese companies, where so much is muddled by other economic problems – the argument would have been culturally easier to accept' (Hutton, 2005).

REFERENCES

Alexander, A.J. (2002), *In the Shadow of the Miracle: The Japanese Economy since the End of High-speed Growth*, Lanham, MD: Lexington Books.

Arrighi, M. (1994), *The Long Twentieth Century: Money, Power and the Origins of Our Times*, London: Verso.

Brenner, R. (1998), 'The economics of global turbulence', *New Left Review*, **229**, May/June.

Burkett, P. and M. Hart-Landsberg (1996), 'The use and abuse of Japan as a progressive model', in L. Panitch (ed.), *Socialist Register*, London: Merlin Press, pp. 62–92.

Burkett, P. and M. Hart-Landsberg (2000), *Development, Crisis and Class Struggle: Learning from Japan and East Asia*, Houndmills, Basingstoke: Macmillan.

Castells, M. (1998), *End of Millennium*, Oxford: Blackwell.

Clinton, W.J. (1993), 'President Clinton's New Beginning: the Clinton–Gore Economic Conference', New York: Donald I Fine Inc.

Coates, D. (2000), *Models of Capitalism: Growth and Stagnation in the Modern Era*, Cambridge: Polity Press.

Denison, E.F. and W.K. Chung (1976), *How Japan's Economy Grew So Fast: The Sources of Postwar Expansion*, Washington DC: Brookings Institution.

Dore, R. (1973), *British Factory – Japanese Factory: The Origins of National Diversity in Industrial Relations*, Berkeley: University of California Press.

Dore, R. (1985), 'Authority or benevolence: the Confucian recipe for industrial success', *Government and Opposition*, **20**(2), 196–217.

Dore, R. (1986), *Flexible Rigidities: Industrial Policy and Structural Adjustment in the Japanese Economy 1970–1980*, London: Athlone Press.

Dore, R. (1987), *Taking Japan Seriously: A Confucian Perspective on Leading Economic Issues*, London: Athlone Press.

Dore, R. (1993), 'What makes the Japanese different?', in C. Crouch and
    D. Marquand (eds), *Ethics and Markets: Co-operation and Competition Within
    Capitalist Economies*, Oxford: Blackwell, pp. 66–79.
Dore, R. (1997), 'The distinctiveness of Japan', in C. Crouch and W. Streeck (eds),
    Political Economy of Modern Capitalism, London: Sage, pp. 19–32.
Dore, R. (1998), 'Asian crisis and the future of the Japanese model', *Cambridge
    Journal of Economics*, **22**, 773–87.
Dore, R. (2000), *Stock Market Capitalism: Welfare Capitalism. Japan and Germany
    versus the Anglo-Saxons*, Oxford: Oxford University Press.
Fruin, W.M. (1992), *The Japanese Enterprise System*, Oxford: Clarendon Press.
Fukuyama, F. (1995), *Trust: The Social Virtues and the Creation of Prosperity*,
    New York: Free Press.
Gerlach, M.L. (1989), 'Keiretsu organization in the Japanese economy: analysis
    and implications', in C. Johnson, L.D. Tyson and J. Zysman (eds), *Politics and
    Productivity: How Japan's Development Strategy Works*, New York: Harper
    Business, pp. 141–74.
Gerlach, M.L. (1992), *Alliance Capitalism*, Berkeley, CA: University of California
    Press.
Haber, S. (ed.) (2001), *Crony Capitalism and Economic Growth in Latin America*,
    Washington DC: Hoover Institution Press.
Hutton, W. (1994), *The State We're In*, London: Cape.
Hutton, W. (2005), 'Did I get it wrong?', *The Observer*, 9 January, p. 30.
Itoh, M. (1990), *The World Economic Crisis and Japanese Capitalism*, Houndmills,
    Basingstoke: Macmillan.
Johnson, C. (1982), *MITI and the Japanese Miracle*, Palo Alto, CA: Stanford
    University Press.
Johnson, C. (ed.) (1984), *The Industrial Policy Debate*, Berkeley, CA: University of
    California Press.
Johnson, C. (1986), 'The institutional foundations of Japan's Industrial Policy', in
    C.E. Barfield and W.A. Schambra (eds), *The Politics of Industrial Policy*,
    Washington DC: American Enterprise Institute, pp. 187–205.
Johnson, C., L.D. Tyson and J. Zysman (eds) (1989), *Politics and Productivity: How
    Japan's Development Strategy Works*, New York: Harper Business.
Katz, R. (1998), *Japan: The System That Soured; the Rise and Fall of the Japanese
    Economic Miracle*, Armonk, New York: M.E. Sharpe.
Katz, R. (2003), *Japanese Phoenix: The Long Road to Economic Revival*, Armonk,
    New York: M.E. Sharpe.
Krugman, P. (1994), 'The myth of Asia's Miracle', *Foreign Affairs*, November/
    December, 62–78; reprinted (1997) in P. Krugman, *Pop Internationalism*,
    Cambridge, MA: MIT, pp. 167–88.
Lazonick, W. (1991), *Business Organization and the Myth of the Market Economy*,
    Cambridge: Cambridge University Press.
Lazonick, W. (1992), 'Business organisation and competitive advantage: capitalist
    transformations in the twentieth century', in Giannetti R. Dosi and P.A. Toninelli
    (eds), *Technology and Enterprise in a Historical Perspective*, Oxford: Oxford
    University Press, pp. 119–63.
Lazonick, W. (1994), 'Social organization and technological leadership', in
    W. Baumol, R. Nelson and E. Wolff (eds), *Convergence of Productivity*, Oxford:
    Oxford University Press, pp. 164–96.
Lazonick, W. (1995), 'Cooperative employment relations and Japanese economic

growth', in J. Schlor and J.-I. You (eds), *Capital, the State and Labour: A Global Perspective*, Aldershot: Aldershot, UK and Brookfield, US: Edward Elgar, pp. 70–110.

Morishima, M. (1982), *Why has Japan Succeeded? Western Technology and the Japanese Ethos*, Cambridge: Cambridge University Press.

Ohkawa, K. and H. Rosovsky (1973), *Japanese Economic Growth: Trend Acceleration in the Twentieth Century*, Palo Alto, CA: Stanford University Press.

Ozaki, R. (1991), *Human Capitalism: The Japanese Enterprise System as a World Model*, Harmondsworth: Penguin.

Patrick, H. and H. Rosovsky (eds) (1976), *Asia's New Giant: How the Japanese Economy Works*, Washington DC: Brookings Institution.

Pempel, T.J. (1998), *Regime Shift: Comparative Dynamics of the Japanese Political Economy*, New York: Cornell University Press.

Porter, M., H. Takeuchi and M. Sakakibara (2000), *Can Japan Compete?*, Houndmills, Basingstoke: Macmillan.

Reich, R. (1983), *The Next American Frontier*, Harmondsworth: Penguin.

Tabb, W.K. (1995), *The Postwar Japanese System: Cultural Economy and Economic Transformation*, Oxford: Oxford University Press.

Tabb, W.K. (1999), 'The end of the Japanese postwar system', *Monthly Review*, July–August, 71–80.

Wade, R. (1990), *Governing the Market*, Princeton, NJ: Princeton University Press.

Weiss, L. and J. Hobson (1995), *States and Economic Development: A Comparative Historical Analysis*, Cambridge: Polity Press.

10.   'Can Japan compete?' reconsidered

Dan Coffey and Carole Thornley

I   INTRODUCTION

In a book intended to consider the recent travails of the Japanese economy in a way which pushes to the forefront of discussion issues that have perhaps hitherto lurked in the background of debate, it seems reasonable to consider the changing significance attaching in this regard to the question of Japan's national 'competitiveness'. The decade just prior to the recessions that beset Japan in the 1990s saw it become something of an article of faith in Western commentaries that new best practices in Japan had revolutionized the organization of manufacture in a series of consumer goods industries. Since strength in manufacture is frequently used or adopted as a benchmark indicator of the competitiveness of the mature industrial economies in the world economy, it is of some interest to ask what impact (if any) Japan's difficulties have had on the status accorded Japanese manufacturing activities – and Japanese manufacturers – in the relevant Western literatures. This is of interest not only because it affords a context within which to comment upon the ongoing debate on the topic of international competitiveness as applied to national or regional economies, but also because the light this might shed on changing attitudes in the West towards Japan has the potential to illuminate issues of relevance more generally to the study of contemporary global economic rivalries. Our principal goal in this chapter is to consider each of these issues in turn.

Some preliminary observations may be helpful. Since we by no means dispute every point made in the wider competitiveness literature pertaining to manufacture as a strategically significant part of economy activity, we commence by establishing some points of agreement before introducing what we consider a problematic topic: the historic contribution of Japanese manufacturers in the car and other industries to the organizing principles of manufacture *sui generis*. Moreover, we will also recognize as intrinsically problematic any nation-centred concept of competitiveness which ultimately reduces to a judgement on the vitality of the individual business enterprise when so many of the largest firms now operate globally, as transnational corporations. Since inward investment is often associated in policy discussions with dissemination of improved ways of making and selling, we pause in this connection to take stock of bias potentials when addressing the question of best manufacturing practices. With these preliminary observations in place, we first argue that much of what has been claimed as true regarding the substance of Japanese-style manufacture is evidently untrue, before moving on to consider – and with this point very much in mind – the changing ways in which reference is made to alleged innovations by Japanese manufacturers in the evolving West-oriented debates on problems with Japan's national competitiveness.

II THE US COMPETITIVENESS CONTROVERSY AND JAPAN

Our first point is that, notwithstanding that assumed breakthroughs in the organization of production are posited by many as underpinning the success of Japanese export drives to the West in the 1970s and 1980s, the very fact of a sustained encroachment on the market territories of Western corporations in this period might in itself be sufficient to engender the sort of febrile atmosphere which is conducive to distortion. And this would still be true even if one were to accept as relevant all of the basic issues broached in the competitiveness literature as these pertain to manufacturing industry.

There is no need to review in this connection the 'competitiveness' literature as such (which in any event would be the work of a small book rather than a book chapter) because its most relevant aspects with respect to regional strengths in manufacturing activity are readily summarized via the views of some leading commentators. That there is such a thing as national competitiveness has of course been disputed, and one could do worse here than to start with Paul Krugman's much cited strictures against the employment of the term 'competitiveness' in connection with 'national' economies:

> The idea that a country's economic fortunes are largely determined by its success on world markets is a hypothesis, not a necessary truth; and as a practical, empirical matter, that hypothesis is flatly wrong . . . it is simply not the case that the world's leading nations are to any important degree in economic competition with each other, or that any of their major economic problems can be attributed to failures to compete on world markets. The growing obsession in most advanced nations with international competitiveness should be seen, not as a well-founded concern, but as a view held in the face of overwhelming contrary evidence. (Krugman, 1994: 30)

The thrust of this criticism is that the very idea of international competitiveness as a guide to economic policy or as a diagnostic tool when considering domestic economic problems within national economies fails on what are essentially empirical grounds. The most sophisticated of the conceptualizations of international competitiveness with which Krugman takes exception is that offered by Laura D'Andrea Tyson, then Chair of America's Council of Economic Advisors who proposed (in Tyson, 1992) that the relevant concept of competitiveness hinged on a nation's 'ability to produce goods and services that meet the test of international competition while . . . citizens enjoy a standard of living that is both rising and sustainable' (see Krugman, 1994: 31–2). In considering this, Krugman does acknowledge that, where trade becomes important, an inability to sell goods abroad which leads in turn to repeated currency devaluations, and hence to deteriorating terms of trade and thus more expensive inputs, could indeed put pressure on domestic living standards. The purchasing power of a dollar, for example, could in principle decline because of the rising dollar-price of imported goods: this would be experienced in the importing country as a reduction in purchasing power relative to the income generated by its pre-devaluation output (ibid.: 32). Hence an economy forced to repeatedly devalue its currency because of competitive pressures from abroad might find that the growth in the purchasing power of its citizens fails to keep pace with the growth of its domestic output owing to a deteriorating terms of trade: it is even conceivable that the net experience is one of a declining (average) standard of living. But Krugman dismisses the relevance of this possibility for the US: he argues instead that, while the larger part of the 1970s and the 1980s came to be associated with stagnating living standards for many American citizens, the main reason was not a deteriorating terms of trade but rather a deteriorating rate of domestic productivity growth.

The main thrust of the critical response to this argument is equally familiar. A tacit assumption supporting Krugman's argument is that 'domestic' productivity growth is a variable which is determined more or less separately from factors that might give rise to or result from a weakening trade performance by domestically based producers, including loss of markets at home or abroad to foreign competition. This is an assumption which his respondents have typically found objectionable. If a loss of markets to foreign competition – whether at home or abroad – has the effect of increasing reserves of production capacity held by domestically based producers but not utilized then, for reasons which are self-evident, the productivity of resources deployed will suffer, while any attendant closure of plant or scrapping of capacity may not only generate in turn higher levels of unemployment amongst workers in those industries but

also serve to discourage the sort of innovations essential for future productivity growth.

Thus, for instance, Lester Thurow's (1994: 190) insistence that, for
strategically important categories of product, domestic innovation and
investment in production, and hence by implication the trend rate of productivity growth in these sectors, is liable to be inextricably linked to the
question of international competitiveness once trade in such goods
assumes a significant dimension. The effect of foreign competition is
potentially positive – 'competition simultaneously forces a faster pace of
economic change at home and produces opportunities to learn new technologies and new management practices that can be used to improve
domestic productivity' (ibid.) – but where foreign firms race too far ahead
and market opportunities for domestically based firms shrink to the point
where further investments cease to be attractive, the prognosis is less positive. A distinction might of course be argued between trade performance
in newly emerging industries and problems experienced in more 'mature'
sectors: for example, one response by US economists associated with the
prevailing economic policies of the earlier part of the 1980s, when
American firms operating in mature industries like cars, consumer electronics, textiles and steel were coming under considerable pressure from
foreign firms operating overseas, was to emphasize the positive value of a
reallocation of resources to other sectors (see Coates, 2000: 29–30), an
analysis with a well-established support in traditional 'comparative advantage' theories of international trade. But such an approach would be
inconsistent with Thurow's broader purview. Treating it as axiomatic that
higher living standards (on average) depend on productivity growth – itself
a function of a panoply of factors including 'domestic investments in plant
and equipment, research and development, skills and public infrastructure, and the quality of private management and public administration'
(Thurow, 1994: 189) – stress is certainly laid on the need for an economy
like the US to develop strategies by which to encourage initiatives in
leading industries like aerospace, telecommunications and computers. But
where established industries fail, the consequence is not seen as one of
resources newly released to foster and encourage growth elsewhere, but
rather stagnation. Nor should industries be divided too readily as between
'old' and 'new' products: unemployment in the rust belt is highlighted as a
problem for American workers, but at the same time opportunities for
product development exist even within mature industries like the car
industry provided they are grasped, via prospective ventures like electric
cars. And in broad terms these are sentiments with which we would certainly agree, as too with the tacit rejection in Thurow's response of the
assumption that the underlying model at a national economic level is one

of a more or less well-functioning market system in which price adjustments (as opposed to quantity adjustments) work rapidly, so that small changes on the margins of activity can always be relied upon to smooth over any imbalances that might disrupt market equilibrium in the traded goods sectors.

Now, if we take the literature on best manufacturing practices in Japan at its own face value, it is not difficult to see why this might be a topic to excite interest amongst commentators preoccupied with questions of international competitiveness. Care must of course be taken not to presume on writers when they express no view on this issue: the question is not raised, for example, by either Krugman or Thurow in their contributions above to the more general debate about concepts of national competitiveness. As we will see, however, some internationally respected commentators have certainly posited an intimate connection between Japanese manufacturing practices and Japan's national competitiveness, and in ways which it is partly our purpose to reconsider. And while we are certainly in broad agreement with economists (like Thurow) who emphasize the inter-connectedness of innovation and investment on the one hand and trading relations on the other, and the importance of state intervention and support, it does not follow that automatic credence should be given to now popular views on this topic.

There is no need by way of preliminaries to separate out each of the distinctive strands of opinion which have subsequently congealed in an enormous body of writing which claims that a radically new type of manufacturing system emerged in post-World War II Japan, said to have developed first in the production of cars but consisting of a set of related principles and methods which quickly spread to other consumer goods industries to form the basis more generally of the Japanese challenge to the American model of industrial supremacy. The 'American model' in turn is usually described in this literature as being based on systems of mass production of a kind first set down on a massive scale in the Highland Park factories of Henry Ford – the 'Fordist' system. It is sufficient here merely to take as an example the following representative comment from a well known American commentator on contemporary production trends:

> The mass-production system spread [in the US] from the auto industry to other industries and became the unchallenged standard around the world . . . While the 'American method' was enjoying an unqualified success in world markets in the 1950s, a Japanese auto company, struggling to recover from World War II, began experimenting with a new approach to production – one whose operating assumptions were as different from those of mass production as the latter was from the earlier craft methods of production. The company was Toyota, and its new managerial process was called *lean production*. (Rifkin, 1995: 96)

As this summary comment makes clear, in much the same way that Ford motors is sometimes said to have created the template for the dominant industrial model which held sway more generally in the 'golden age' of American capitalism in the 1950s and beyond, the Japanese car industry leader Toyota is credited with a series of innovations in manufacturing method which has in turn engendered a new and improved way of making complex manufactured goods, encapsulated here in the words 'lean production'. The shock occasioned by this new system is generally described as being all the greater because it overturned American industry where it had hitherto been strongest:

> The most spectacular example of the redesign and reorganization of a production process and the associated network of subcontractors was of course the 'lean production system' of the Japanese automobile industry. The worldwide export of cars and consumer electronics were probably the most vivid evidence of Japanese technological strength for large numbers of people all over the world. In the United States especially the reversal of their prolonged dominance in the archetypal mass production industry was bound to make a very deep impression. (Freeman and Soete, 1999: 151)

The definitive emergence of this new manufacturing system is typically dated to the earlier part of the 1970s, appearing on the world stage more or less coincidentally with the definitive ending of the long period of continuous post-war growth in the US, marking the end of an era in a twofold sense: and it remains a commonplace to see it asserted, as with the second of the two passages cited above, that the growing US deficits in trade with Japan in the 1970s and 1980s are best explained in this way.

If this were all true then in one obvious sense the contribution on these points to the debate on international competitiveness would be cut and dried. The case would show how a loss of competitive edge for one country (America) brought about by developments in manufacturing know-how in another (Japan) can threaten economic stability by increasing the threat of dislocations arising from a growing trade deficit while inducing lay-offs and plant closures in the less competitive region: if the negative impact on domestic productivity growth of a sharply deteriorating trading position is accepted, then the basis for a worrying decline in hitherto staple industries is evident. The case, moreover, is one which could be cited to illustrate the benefits of managed trade: for example, the imposition of 'voluntary export restraints' in 1981 on the export of cars from Japan to the US could be interpreted not only as a logical consequence of criticism heaped on Japan for expanding its economy in the 1970s on the back of manufacturing exports while keeping its own domestic markets closed to effective competition, but also as the sort of measure which would allow the US to close down a competitiveness gap which had opened up in the meantime between its own manufacturers and Japanese firms at the level of manufacturing know-how (see, for example, the discussion of these points in Robert Gilpin's recent and careful review of international relations in the global economy: see, in particular, Gilpin, 2001:82, 232). But by the same token the very fact that Japanese manufacturers were enabled in the 1970s to export to the West from a relatively protected base might in itself be expected to engender some degree of panic amongst affected constituencies both in the US and else-where, of a type which would not in itself demonstrate the existence of this kind of competitiveness gap: the conditions in which major 'domestic' industries are threatened by new players on the world stage are also condi-tions in which exaggerations and embellishments are liable to thrive.

III   SOME ISSUES OF FORMULATION

Our second point concerns some of the difficulties posed by a literature that is concerned with a concept of competitiveness which is defined at the level of a national economy but which at the same time also lends some primacy to competitive performance at the level of the individual firm in determin-ing national performance on the world stage. Some obvious complications arise from the fact that large firms today often operate as transnational pro-ducers: in particular, a redistribution of manufacturing capacity as between countries or regions by large firms may certainly affect 'competitive' per-formance at a national level, as this concept is employed by Tyson and others. But this is not the same thing as the identification of an improved performance at a plant or company level as regards either the desirability of the products produced or the effectiveness with which operations are managed – this is a separate issue. But while the distinction is clear it is one which is perhaps insufficiently appreciated in much of the competitiveness literature, even in undoubtedly sophisticated formulations.

For example, Candace Howes and Ajit Singh (2000), editors of a recent and lively collection with a self-explanatory title, *Competitiveness Matters*, which contends that some at least of the economic ills experienced by workers and citizens in the US economy in the last quarter of the twentieth century have indeed reflected the erosion of its industrial base under the pressures of foreign competition in traded goods industries, set out an analysis in which the following three propositions figure heavily:

1.   manufactured goods account for by far the largest part of US trade;
2.   manufactured goods industries at national level are dominated by large firms aware of their mutual dependencies, so that non-price forms of

competition are paramount and competitiveness as between industrial nations is principally reflected in the size of their income elasticities of demand for each other's manufactured products;

3. the income elasticity of demand in the US for all foreign goods is high compared to the income elasticity of demand in foreign countries for all US goods, from which can be inferred the existence of a competitiveness gap in the US for manufactures.

Of these only the first proposition is wholly empirical (for supporting statistics on the significance of manufactured goods for US trade, see Howes, 2000: 191–2). The second also frames an analytic judgement. Observing that product markets for the quantitatively important manufacturing sectors in developed economies are typically characterized by oligopolistic structures so that non-price forms of competition are basic to initiatives by firms to increase or maintain market shares, Howes and Singh (2000: 4–5) make a direct connection between this and changes in trading patterns as between the national economies which house production. On this they follow the views of the famous Cambridge economist Nicholas Kaldor – Howes and Singh cite Kaldor (1978, 1981: 603) – who inferred from this that in a growing world economy export growth was to be principally explained by reference to the income elasticities of demand in each of the importing countries for the exporting country's products. The judgement here is that changes in international balances of trade as between developed economies largely reflect the attractiveness to prospective customers abroad and at home of the products made and sold by the private firms operating in each economy: if the firms in the US (say) make uncompetitive or unattractive products, demand for those goods in foreign countries will be that much less responsive to rising national incomes. Given this, the inference set out in the third proposition follows from the observation that the income elasticity of demand in the US for foreign-made goods is higher than the income elasticity of demand in foreign countries for US-made goods (see Howes, 2000: 182).

While an approach that is commendable for taking note of product market structures in trade, and while entirely cogent on its own terms, this formulation nonetheless highlights the problem immediately encountered when attempting to make a direct connection between national economic performance and corporate performance in a context where many of the large firms in question now operate as transnational firms. In the case, for example, of the world car industry, about which so much has been written, American transnationals Ford and General Motors operate both in the US and in Europe, and accordingly do not export to Europe the finished cars which they make there: a comparison of the income elasticities of demand in the US and Europe for cars manufactured respectively in Europe and the US need not reflect the attractiveness of Ford or GM products, but will certainly reflect their positioning as transnationals. The macroeconomic implications for US trade (say) might still be significant, but the reasons for a trade imbalance in cars between the US and Europe are not those at the centre of the Howes–Singh and Kaldor framework: '[product] quality, marketing, design, reliability and service' (see Howes and Singh, 2000: 4). A consideration of how comparative income elasticities of demand for imports change over time as between trading countries will undoubtedly always be of considerable interest, but the assumption that national performance in trade necessarily reflects in an obvious way the innovativeness of firms is necessarily qualified by transnational organization. It would be wrong to suggest that in this instance this is not understood: for example, the improved US trade balance with Japan in auto products is identified with the decision of Japanese manufacturers to establish production facilities in the US (see Howes, 2000: 192), rather than any change in the performance of operations or sales at existing sites. But in the car industry, as with others, such qualifications are now major considerations. Moreover, so far as trading relations are concerned, geo-politics clearly play a role: a low income elasticity in Japan for imports from the US as a result of protectionist measures, for example, again invokes a different set of issues; and the increasingly assertive stance shown by the US in its relations with Japan throughout the 1980s and into the 1990s as regards market access encouraged Japanese firms to invest directly in the US.

It is crucial to bear such points in mind when the issues under discussion involve both the contribution of Japanese firms to worldwide manufacturing industry and the changing balance of perceptions as regards the strengths and weaknesses of Japan's national economy, not least in its dealings with, and in relation, to the US. The qualifications carefully made by Howes and Singh when delivering examples of the relationships between performance at the level of a private firm and at the level of a national economy are sometimes altogether missing in these debates. The view that Japan's post-war export drives in the sale of manufactured goods to the richer industrialized countries of the West were predicated on superior manufacturing methods frequently comes in tow with a predisposition to see in the establishment of Japanese manufacturing facilities in the US and elsewhere nothing less than the worldwide spread of these methods via the medium of foreign direct investment. The revitalization of plant-level operations in countries outside of Japan is taken as granted, the 'hollowing out' of the Japanese domestic industrial base attributed by some to this process – see, for example, Cowling and Tomlinson (2003), and Chapter 4, this volume – is ignored.

IMAGINING THE REVOLUTION

In this respect our position must be one of a measured but thoroughgoing scepticism. What evidence will actually admit to hardly measures up to the substance of the more extravagant claims advanced on behalf of (and indeed by) Japanese corporations with respect to their historic contribution to the design and execution of manufacturing activities in the car and other industries. For brevity's sake let us consider two examples, each of which has a direct bearing on the notion of 'lean production', the phrase which is now used so widely, and, as already instanced above, by commentators seeking a summary description for what they believe to have been a series of innovative contributions to best manufacturing practice originating in Japan.[1]

The notion of a distinctively 'lean' form of production was in fact first introduced to the managerial lexicon via the findings of a worldwide survey of workforce productivity differentials in car assembly plants carried out in the latter part of the 1980s under the auspices of the International Motor Vehicle Programme (IMVP) centred at MIT: the main findings of this and related studies are reported in Womack et al. (1990). In this survey Japanese plants were found to be typically highly automated while reporting low scores on the hours of labour employed to perform a designated set of assembly tasks: while this naturally raised the possibility that Japanese factories were productive from the viewpoint of the workforce because of typically large investments in capital equipment, the received interpretation then and since has been that what was in fact uncovered by the survey was that Japanese car assemblers managed to produce with fewer workers for reasons which were first and foremost organizational. Following Coffey and Thornley (2006a) (for a further discussion see also Coffey, 2006; Coffey and Thornley, 2006b) we might visualize the logic of this position *vis-à-vis* the basic shape of the data reported in this survey by recourse to the stylized representation in Figure 10.1(a). We can think of a region like W as containing the scatter of the observations obtained for labour hours employed per car built against the survey index of factory automation for the world sample as a whole, with Japanese observations clustering in a region like J, reporting *en bloc* both an apparently high labour productivity and an unusually high automation. The only statistical analysis reported in Womack et al. (1990: 94) is an exercise in simple regression undertaken for the body of data as a whole, which concluded that automation could account for only about one-third of the variation in labour productivity. On this basis, the conclusion duly advanced, and a conclusion which has carried the day since, was that superior organization rather than more automation was the secret of high Japanese manufacturing labour productivity at the point of production.

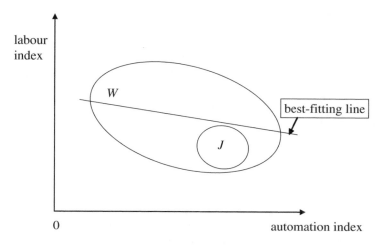

Source: Coffey and Thornley (2006a).

Figure 10.1(a)   A stylized representation of IMVP survey data

But other interpretations of these data could have been considered, even allowing that the statistical analysis of the data went no further than simple regression and taking the survey measures of labour productivity and automation at face value. For example, if the scatter as a whole had been divided so that factories based in Europe (including those factories managed by non-European firms operating as overseas transplants) were treated separately from factories operating in the rest of the world (**ROW**) then the situation would have looked rather different. A 'best-fitting' line for observations on factories located outside of Europe – in Japan, North America, Australia and the Newly Industrializing Countries (NICs) – would have passed through rather than (largely) above the cluster of Japanese car plants in Japan. The difference in the exercise can again be visualized by reference to the stylized Figure 10.1(b), compared with Figure 10.1(a). A movement along a regression line can be interpreted as capturing the expected effects of one sample variable (automation, say) on another (labour productivity). On the basis of assessing whether Japanese plants in Japan sat above or below the regression line more or less typically than plants elsewhere – for example in the US – an exercise conducted along the lines represented in Figure 10.1(b) would have vitiated any easy conclusion. Some Japanese car plants would have looked more productive than expected and some less; but the same would also have been true of plants in the US and elsewhere. With no clear patterns other than differences in automation as between non-European regions, the case for distinguishing Japan on

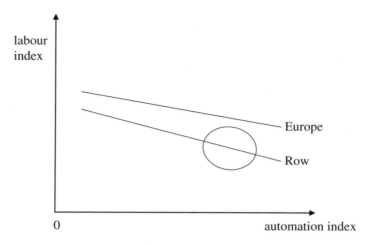

Source: Coffey and Thornley (2006a).

Figure 10.1(b)   A stylized re-assessment of IMVP survey data

other grounds would have appeared far weaker. The question of Europe as a particular case would remain, and Japanese plants would be noted for their high automation, but this is not the premise of 'lean production'.

In this connection consider now Luria (2000). Luria's is a later study which deals in part with changing employment practices in the US small manu-facturing firm sector, which argues that the big story with regard to the previous 30 or so years has been not so much a massive process of de-industrialization as a re-distribution of manufacturing activity from large plants to small plants, accompanied by a substantially deteriorating terms of employment (ibid.: 166–8): at the same time, this shift is also associated with a move into sites with much lower labour productivity.[2] In quantitative terms the loss of manufacturing jobs in the US over the 1980s (a difficult decade) paled beside the disappearance of unionized positions for American workers; while US manufacturing employment fell by 6 per cent, unionized employment fell by 38 per cent, with non-union job holders in manufacture registering an absolute increase. Some disdain is expressed in this connection for the accompanying 'clatter' about partnership, long-term contracting and 'emerging American *keiretsus*': Luria judges that the relocation of jobs from large to small plants has been less about the growth of a specialist small firm sector than as a shift to smaller sites with substantially lower wages and low overheads which exist solely as workshops to service the 'build to blueprint' requirements of the giant corporations. What is of particular interest for present purposes is accompanying evidence presented from the database held at the Ann Arbor (Michigan) Industrial Technology Institute (containing data annually updated since 1992 on more than 1000 small US manufacturers). This shows that different firms employ 'radically different production recipes' even in the manufacture of similar products. Using a wide range of (more than 100) performance measures – the series of variables employed for this purpose include for example value-added per employee, employee training, on-time deliveries to customers, turnover of working capital, and so forth – the compilers of this database distinguish between 'low-road' and 'high-road' producers (ibid.: 170–71). The low-road producer is distinguished by a 'sweating' approach to labour, and characterized both by the low wages paid and a poor record of investment in both product and process technologies and in workers' skills and training: these firms are also judged to be typically weaker performers in other areas, offering their services on a build-to-blueprint basis and unable to command premium prices for so doing. The high-road producers, which eschew simple sweating, include shops involved in engineering specialist products like special tools, dies, jigs and fixtures and as such concerned to invest; but as Luria also notes, some firms engaged in more routine production also share this characteristic owing to other factors, as for example where unions have retained an effective shop presence.[3]

What is then of considerable interest is that Luria (ibid.: 170–73) identifies what he and his colleagues label a 'hybrid' class of 'lean commodity' manufacturing firms. These are described as being on the one hand 'self-conscious and improvement-oriented', and given to the deployment of what are perceived to be 'Japanese-style methods'. As such, they score well on the criterion of being systematic in their approach to organization. At the same time, in other respects they sit 'substantially' towards the 'low-end' of the spectrum, with the Ann Arbor database finding that these firms not only score badly on employment variables like wages and training but also on 'modernity': they are most typically poor investors in hardware and software for business scheduling and quality functions, and poor investors in product development and shop-floor automation. And they score badly on indicators like value-added per worker generated by sales.

Our examples therefore comprise the following observations. First, one of the appeals of the original MIT-based study which gave birth to the words 'lean production' has undoubtedly been the claim that significant productivity gains are possible for firms without further investment either in plant or in plant equipment: our criticism here is that this inference was always based on a tendentious reading of the data.[4] Second, the small manufacturing firms included in the Ann Arbor panel which take lean production seriously do indeed shy away from investment expenditures of this kind: but the net result here appears largely akin to that characterizing the less systematic sweatshops operating in the US small manufacturing firm sector: there is no evidence that 'lean-commodity' producers have been able to realize productivity gains despite low investment. In both cases the serious evidence which might support claims of an industrial renaissance based on a revolution in manufacturing practices at firm (indeed plant) level is missing.

V 'CAN JAPAN COMPETE' RECONSIDERED

We might summarize points so far as follows. In the evolving competitive-ness debate we sympathize with writers like Lester Thurow and others who see an important place for state policy in structuring industrial develop-ment, and similarly with regard to the interconnectedness between factors determining productivity growth on a national plane and developments in the international sphere. We also take a similar position on the views set out by Candace Howes, Ajit Singh and others on the desirability of policies to promote investment in key areas of economic activity and the undesirabil-ity of policies which facilitate or even encourage a squeeze on the living standards and conditions of employment of workers as basis for interna-tional competition. But we recognize as important too the possibility, implied by Krugman, that any debate on national competitiveness might become prey to distortions induced by the encroachments of producers operating from one country on markets previously dominated by produc-ers operating from another. We accept too, albeit for quite different reasons, that there are difficulties in defining competitiveness at a national level in ways that seek to connect directly with the performance of firms in key sectors. Private firms are a locus of strategic investment and employment decisions, but the comparative economic performance of nations clearly need not coincide with the international standing of firms once these firms cease to conduct operations from a solely national base. Moreover, in such cases there are pitfalls to be avoided when seeking to draw conclusions about the comparative abilities of firms either to design or to manufacture marketable products. When considering, for example, foreign direct invest-ment by Japanese transnational producers in the car and other industries in (say) the US, notwithstanding any immediate gains in employment or capacity it does not follow as a sensible maxim to conclude that inward investment is thereby proved an effective vehicle for dissemination of improved manufacturing know-how; there is no alternative here but to engage in proper study of the relevant dimensions of manufacturing activ-ity, and what in this same example may be necessary or beneficial for the Japanese firms may inflict costs on Japan as a 'nation'.

When broaching the particular question of the organization of manufacturing activities as this pertains to Japanese firms we observed that in some quarters at least 'lean production systems' – the most popular titular summation for the assumed package of organizational principles and techniques – are invoked in a way which is almost synonymous with an enhanced manufacturing performance at a firm or a plant level. We have suggested, and *à propos* the qualifications above to our stance in the competitiveness debate, that the evidence here stands somewhere between the nugatory and the perverse.

But this in turn suggests that there might be value in broaching the assumptions made by adherents to the idea of a Japan-inspired revolution in manufacture from another direction, by asking what light imagined transformations in production potentials might shed on responses to the fact of Japan's emergence on the world stage. And in this connection it is of interest to take note of the ways in which writers that adhere to the notion that lean production gave Japanese manufacturing corporations a competitive edge in the 1970s and 1980s over firms in the US and elsewhere have adjusted their precepts to accommodate the subsequent travails of Japan's national economy.

Consider for example the following comment by Professor Gilpin, a leading authority on international economic relations, who, in a review of literature post-dating the onset of recessions which beset Japan in the first half of the 1990s concludes:

> Various techniques associated with lean production . . . became central to the production process in Japan; these highly efficient techniques, pioneered at Toyota and associated with the technological and organizational revolution, diffused rapidly throughout Japanese industry . . . Japanese superiority in manufacturing rather than in product innovation has been the key to Japan's outstanding export success . . . however, as the Japanese system of lean production diffused to other countries, the overwhelming Japanese advantage decreased . . . during the 1990s, American corporations, through downsizing, heavy investments in computers, and development of new enterprises regained much of the competitiveness they had lost in the mid-1980s. (Gilpin, 2001: 136–7)

In other words, while lean production methods are held to have delivered a competitive edge to Japanese producers over US firms in the 1970s and 1980s, this lead is held to have gradually dissipated with subsequent dissemination of these methods.

Consider likewise Porter et al.'s (2000) study, *Can Japan Compete?*, which attributes Japan's post-World War II successes in key manufacturing industries like cars and consumer electronics to lean production: 'The lean production system played a central role in the Japanese corporate model . . . [it] achieves high levels of quality, productivity, timely delivery and flexibility' (ibid.: 70). While associating the genesis of this new system with the car manufacturer Toyota, Porter et al. make this the basis more generally for Japanese manufacturing success: 'In the 1970s and 1980s, the Japanese set the world standard for operational effectiveness – that is, for improving quality and lowering cost in ways that were widely applicable to many fields' (ibid.: 78). And like so many other writers in recent years they emphasize dissemination of these new standards beyond Japan: 'Japanese companies taught the world an array of approaches . . . that improve productivity in nearly every company in every industry' (ibid.). But at the same time, they also see in this one reason for the blight since besetting Japan's economic self-esteem: as a consequence of the international dissemination of lean production, through a process of 'competitive convergence', Japanese firms are alleged to have seen their lead over Western competitors at the level of operational effectiveness dissipate, exposing in turn their vulnerabilities on a quite different front. 'Because Japanese companies think of competition *only* in terms of operational effectiveness – improving quality and cost simultaneously – they have made it almost impossible to be enduringly successful . . . slower growth and competitive convergence have become a painful combination . . . By competing on *organizational effectiveness alone*, then, many Japanese companies have been caught in a trap of their own making' (ibid.: 81–2) (emphasis added). In other words, Porter et al. charge Japan's corporate leaders with a systemic failure to develop strategies to create a more distinctive market profile, relying instead on the short-term global lead gleaned from the lean manufacture of unimaginative products.

Perhaps the first thing which springs to mind in both examples is the very significant explanatory weight attaching in each to lean production as means of accounting both for the strength of Japan on the world stage and its subsequent travails: and in both cases the viewpoints in question (reviewed in Gilpin, advocated in Porter et al.) are concerned not to investigate the substance or otherwise of the lean revolution, but rather to use this as the pivot around which Japan's fortunes have been turned. And in the case of the thesis advanced by Porter et al. the case is put in no uncertain terms: lean production methods, hitherto the sole province of Japanese corporations, are now deemed to be part and parcel of the artillery brought to bear not only by comparably equipped US corporations, but by US corporations bringing other pressures to bear. Clearly this is a thesis which, if taken as a whole, necessarily fails if the lean revolution is denied;[5] and in this regard we would certainly argue that an explanation for the sustained economic downturn experienced by Japan in the 1990s must look elsewhere, with due account taken of changes in the wider political economy.

But there are other observations worth making. After noting, for example, the elevated status given to the private corporation in these analyses we might then wonder at the abiding nationalism which continues to identify Japanese corporations with Japan's success or failure, notwithstanding their transnational organization. And it is possible to see, in outline at least, and in commentaries still devoted at one level to praise of the historic contributions of Japanese manufacturers (notably Toyota) the re-emergence of an old abuse, namely that Western producers 'think', while Asiatic rivals 'make'.

VI CONCLUSION

In this chapter we have considered the issue of changing perceptions about Japan and Japanese corporations as economic challengers in the world economy from the viewpoint of the developing nuances of the international 'competitiveness' debate. Observing that strength in manufacture is frequently adopted as one benchmark of the relative competitiveness of industrialized economies, we set out the case for considering how the economic difficulties which beset Japan in the 1990s are reflected in the treatment accorded its leading firms in the best manufacturing practices literature. The phrase 'lean production' is often used today as a summary term by which to encapsulate a series of contributions to best manufacturing practice believed to originate in Japan. Drawing a careful distinction between the interests of private firms and the economic success of nations, and following a critical review of some exemplary contributions to the US competitiveness debate, the chapter considers both the reception given in the US to the idea of lean production, and the subsequent use of this notion in criticisms both of Japan's competitiveness as a nation and of Japan's corporations as strategists. In a provocative twist, we argue that, while the evidence to support the idea of lean production as a positively effective and novel set of manufacturing practices has always been nugatory, viewed as a fiction it is a construct which has the potential to shed much light on aspects of the changing course of global economic rivalries.

NOTES

1. A more extended investigation is set out in Coffey (2006) which concludes that the lean and flexible production model associated with Japan's car makers is a myth founded on a series of historical and empirical counterfactuals, but one which by construction and impact offers material of a type which potentially reveals much about the attendant stresses of globalization.
2. A potentially appropriate framework by which to consider some aspects of the linkages established in Luria's (2000) paper between poor terms and conditions of employment on the one hand and low labour productivity combined with diminished factory overheads

on the other, and in an express context of subcontracting, is set out in Coffey and Tomlinson (2006).

3. Concerns about 'low-road' as opposed to 'high-road' trajectories within national or regional economies are of course by no means confined to the US. Coffey and Thornley (2003) presents a set of contributions on a series of related themes for the UK, including for example, Oughton (2003) on industrial policy and Kitson et al. (2003) for investment and competition, while Thornley (2003) surveys changing employment patterns. So far as best manufacturing practices and UK industrial policy are concerned, also of relevance to this chapter, see Coffey (2003).

4. We might note here that Luria presents data for the manufacturing sectors in both the US and Japan for larger and smaller firms, which show quite clearly the very high investments made by Japanese firms compared to US firms in a range of pertinent areas (Luria, 2000: 168). It is all the more remarkable then that Japanese-style production should have become so closely associated in sections of the Western business press with a motto of 'organization over investment'.

5. On which see also Coffey and Tomlinson (2003, esp. ibid.: 135–41).

REFERENCES

Coates, D. (2000), *Models of Capitalism: Growth and Stagnation in the Modern Era*, Oxford and Malden, MA: Polity Press.

Coffey, D. (2003), 'Best practice manufacture as industrial policy: lean production, competitiveness and monopoly capitalism', in D. Coffey and C. Thornley (eds), *Industrial and Labour Market Policy and Performance: Issues and Perspectives*, London and New York: Routledge, pp. 45–61.

Coffey, D. (2006), *The Myth of Japanese Efficiency: the World Car Industry in a Globalizing Age*, Cheltenham, UK and Northampton, MA, USA: Edward Elgar.

Coffey, D. and C. Thornley (eds) (2003), *Industrial and Labour Market Policy and Performance: Issues and Perspectives*, London and New York: Routledge.

Coffey, D. and C. Thornley (2006a), 'Automotive assembly: automation, motivation and lean production reconsidered', *Assembly Automation: The International Journal of Assembly Technology and Management*, **26**(2), 98–103.

Coffey, D. and C. Thornley (2006b), 'On Galbraithian conventional wisdom and the power of ideas: towards an alternative study of the manufacturing revolution', mimeo.

Coffey, D. and P.R. Tomlinson (2003), 'Globalization, vertical relations and the J-mode firm', *Journal of Post Keynesian Economics*, **26**(1), 117–44.

Coffey, D. and P.R. Tomlinson (2006), 'Multiple facilities, strategic splitting and vertical structures: stability, growth and distribution reconsidered', *The Manchester School*, **74**(5), 558–76.

Cowling, K. and P. Tomlinson (2003), 'Industrial policy, transnational corporations and the problem of "hollowing out" in Japan', in D. Coffey and C. Thornley (eds), *Industrial and Labour Market Policy and Performance: Issues and Perspectives*, London and New York: Routledge, pp. 62–82.

Freeman, C. and L. Soete (1999), *The Economics of Industrial Innovation*, 3rd edn, Reprint Issue London and Washington, DC: Pinter.

Gilpin, R. (2001), *Global Political Economy: Understanding the International Economic Order*, Princeton, NJ and Oxford: Princeton University Press.

Howes, C. (2000), 'US competitiveness and economic growth', in C. Howes and A. Singh (eds), *Competitiveness Matters: Industry and Economic Performance in the U.S.*, Ann Arbor: The University of Michigan Press, pp. 180–205.

Howes, C. and A. Singh (2000), 'Competitiveness matters' in C. Howes and A. Singh (eds), *Competitiveness Matters: Industry and Economic Performance in the U.S.*, Ann Arbor, MI: The University of Michigan Press, pp. 1–28.

Kaldor, N. (1978), 'The effects of devaluation on trade in manufactures', in N. Kaldor, *Further Essays on Applied Economics*, London: Duckworth.

Kaldor, N. (1981), 'The role of increasing returns, technical progress and cumulative causation in the theory of international trade and economic growth', *Economie Appliquée*, **34**(4), 593–617.

Kitson, M., J. Michie and M. Sheehan (2003), 'Markets, competition, co-operation and innovation', in D. Coffey and C. Thornley (eds), *Industrial and Labour Market Policy and Performance: Issues and Perspectives*, London and New York: Routledge, pp. 29–44.

Krugman, P. (1994), 'Competitiveness: a dangerous obsession', *Foreign Affairs*, March/April, 28–44.

Luria, D. (2000), 'A high road policy for US manufacturing', in C. Howes and A. Singh (eds), *Competitiveness Matters: Industry and Economic Performance in the US*, Ann Arbor, MI: The University of Michigan Press, pp. 165–79.

Oughton, C. (2003), 'Industrial policy and economic development', in D. Coffey and C. Thornley (eds), *Industrial and Labour Market Policy and Performance: Issues and Perspectives*, London and New York: Routledge, pp. 9–28.

Porter, M.E., H. Takeuchi and M. Sakakibara (2000), *Can Japan Compete?*, Basingstoke and London: Macmillan Press.

Rifkin, J. (1995), *The End of Work: The Decline of the Global Labor Force and the Dawn of the Post-Market Era*, New York: G.P. Putnam's Sons.

Thornley, C. (2003), 'Labour market policy and inequality in the UK', in D. Coffey and C. Thornley (eds), *Industrial and Labour Market Policy and Performance: Issues and Perspectives*, London and New York: Routledge, pp. 83–108.

Thurow, L.C. (1994), 'Microchips, not potato chips', *Foreign Affairs*, July/August, pp. 189–92.

Tyson, L. (1992), *Who's Bashing Whom? Trade Conflict in High-Technology Industries*, Washington, DC: Institute for International Economics.

Womack, J., D.T. Jones and D. Roos (1990), *The Machine That Changed the World*, New York: Harper Collins.

Index